CW00820407

COMBAT LAND ROVERS
LRM Portfolio No.1

by Bob Morrison

ISBN 1 85520 6048

BROOKLANDS BOOKS LTD.
P.O. BOX 146, COBHAM,
SURREY, KT11 1LG. UK
sales@brooklands-books.com

A-LRCP

Printed in China

ACKNOWLEDGEMENTS

It is now twenty years since I first turned my camera on the military Land Rover. At the time my hobby was constructing prize-winning models of military vehicles, but many of my friends were more interested in making models of aircraft. During the summer season we would attend Open Days at many of the large RAF and USAFE air bases, and I would be the subject of their sympathy as I turned my back on the flight line to photograph Land Rovers, while their motor drives chewed up roll after roll of film in their quest to take the perfect picture of the latest piece of aviation hardware on display.

In 1987, Richard Thomas and John Cornwall spotted that Land Rover owners had a particularly strong allegiance to their vehicles, and so they decided to create a monthly magazine on the subject. Few in the publishing industry thought they had much chance of success, but the lads were soon to prove them wrong. I picked up the second issue of their magazine and, once I had summoned enough courage, I telephoned them to offer an article on the military Land Rover. From that germ of an idea it was decided that a short series might be more appropriate as there were far too many military Land Rover variants to cover in a single article. The rest, as they say, is now history and I am half way through my fifteenth year of writing monthly military Land Rover features.

Back in these early days when I was taking my first military Land Rover pictures, it was still taken pretty much for granted that the Solihull-built vehicle would equip Britain's armed forces purely because it was British. However, times were changing faster than they had since the Second World War, and the defence procurement chain would soon be forced to also consider vehicles produced by our European partners. Fortunately, the modernised coil-sprung and diesel-powered version of the Land Rover, what has now evolved into the Defender, was at the pre-production stage, and the foreign challengers were thwarted.

The coil-sprung, diesel-powered military Land Rovers of the eighties were a quantum leap forward when compared to their Series II/III predecessors which, let's face it, were essentially a mid-fifties design. However, the introduction of computer design technology in the nineties, with the then New Range Rover being the first domestic vehicle to be completely designed by the new medium, led to another major advance in the military Land Rover. With the last of the leaf-sprung fleet fast approaching demob, and the massive mid-eighties batch of Ninety and One-Ten models already in mid-life, military buyers issued detailed specifications for an even more modern and much tougher light and medium utility fleet, more suited to the changing post-Cold War world where rapid response and mobility were to the fore. The humble Land Rover, which almost since its inception in 1948 had bimbled around with the largely static British Army of the Rhine, now had to evolve into a frontline, first-into-action transport, liaison and command vehicle, with the capability to be transformed into a gunship. It was also decided that active service life for this new beast would be a minimum of fifteen years and it would become a combat asset rather than just another garrison hack. The Wolf, or Defender XD in company terms, was born.

As the Wolf was evolving, so was the specialist Land Rover magazine world. The original LRO Magazine was now one of the major magazine success stories of the decade, and had attracted the interest of the major publishers, with one of them buying it outright in the mid-Nineties. The new owners retained me as military correspondent for a time, but eventually they decided to bring all editorial in-house. Fortunately, Richard Thomas was now contractually free to start up another magazine by this time, and had founded Land Rover Monthly. He invited me to continue my regular monthly military features in LRM, and the circle was complete. My brief from Richard is exactly the same as it was in the early years of his first magazine, "cover what you see fit and try to meet the deadline, please!" Thanks Richard.

The contents of this Brooklands compendium are basically my military features and side columns from issues of LRM between March 1999 and July 2001, to which I have added a number of colour plates which complement the subjects covered. As the latest Wolf model features quite heavily, now seems like the right time to change from the term 'military' to 'combat' in the title, to echo the Land Rover's official elevation from a second echelon utility vehicle to a frontline battlefield asset.

Bob Morrison : Military Editor, LRM,

Websites: Land Rover Monthly - www.lrm.co.uk   Bob Morrison - www.military-scene.com
www.brooklands-books.com

CONTENTS

DISTRIBUTED BY

Brooklands Books Ltd., PO Box 146, Cobham, Surrey, KT11 1LG, England
Phone: 01932 865051 Fax: 01932 868803
e-mail: sales@brooklands-books.com   web site: www.brooklands-books.com
Brooklands Books Ltd, 1/81 Darley St., PO Box 199, Mona Vale, NSW 2103, Australia
Phone: 2 9997 8428 Fax: 2 9979 5799
CarTech, 39966 Grand Avenue, North Branch, MN 55056, USA
Phone 800 551 4754 & 651 277 1200 Fax: 651 277 1203

sentry duty

it takes all sorts to help keep the early warning radar planes in the air from their lincolnshire base

Words and pictures by Bob Morrison

Above: Squadron Leader Kim Martin at the wheel of her Soft Top Defender 90

The British Army is by far the biggest fleet user of Land Rovers, with no less than twenty-one types and around 250 individual variants being deployed recently at the height of the IFOR operations in Bosnia. However, the Royal Air Force, typified by RAF Waddington in Lincolnshire, also uses many different variations of the Defender and its 110 Series predecessor.

For more than six years, the early warning aircraft of the Royal Air Force have policed the skies over Bosnia to prevent the former warring factions using air power against each other or helpless civilians on the ground. Based at Waddington, but operating in turns from a base on Italian soil, these distinctive aircraft with their mushroom-like radar scanners have been the United Nations' and NATO's eye in the sky.

Helping to keep this small fleet of Boeing 707-derived aircraft in the skies is a much larger fleet of Land Rovers, of many different variants.

Unless you come across the RAF police on road traffic or security duties, the first Land Rover you are likely to see at RAF Waddington is the duty ambulance parked outside the medical centre. In addition to being a round-the-clock, 365-days-a-year workplace, the base is also home to more than 3,000 personnel and dependants, so its medical facilities are on a par with those of a small town.

To cope with any potential industrial or domestic medical emergencies, one of the fleet of airfield crash rescue ambulances is permanently garaged alongside the medical centre. From there it can reach any part of the vast complex in just a few minutes.

During daylight hours, the duty ambulance driver is usually a civilian, and the paramedic is a member of the medically qualified serving personnel. At night, ambulance crew cover is provided by serving personnel.

The ambulance itself (10KJ82) is one of the 1989 batch, built on the 127 inch wheelbase chassis. Originally badged One-Two-Seven by Land Rover, but later designated 127 before becoming the Defender 130 in late 1990, this stretched wheelbase was found to be ideal for ambulance conversions and at least three major batches were ordered by the Ministry of Defence.

Initially the type was only procured for airfield crash rescue duties (both RAF and Royal Navy). But as Britain's peacekeeping commitment in the former Yugoslavia grew the type was also issued to the British Army as a unit ambulance to replace the FC101.

Powered by the 3.5 litre V8 petrol engine, the 127 ambulance is fast enough to cope with crash rescue duties, and it can reach even the most remote parts of airfields. Normally it is configured for two stretcher

cases, though it can carry three, or for one stretcher case and up to four seated patients, but eight seated can be carried if all stretchers are stowed.

The medic would normally travel in the cab, but should he need to administer care to a patient, there is a drop-down seat fitted to the bulkhead. Unlike its Series IIA/III predecessor, the 127 ambulance is tall enough for the medic to stand upright. A full range of medical and resuscitation equipment to cater for both domestic and crash rescue casualties is carried.

fire and police

The Royal Air Force also has its own on-site police and fire service cover. In addition to their massive airfield fire tenders, the firefighters have a pair of dedicated rapid response Range Rover 6x4 crash rescue tenders, but they do not normally use utility Land Rovers.

The RAF Police, on the other hand, have their own individually marked fleet of 90 and 110 models. These are used both for the normal day-to-day policing activities on the station, including traffic management, and for airfield security duties.

With one of the longest runways in Britain, RAF Waddington has a massive perimeter fence, which must be constantly checked for security breaches. With high visibility red stripes, roof mounted blue lights and white RAF police markings, these 110 FFRs are a familiar sight as they constantly patrol the perimeter track and delve into every remote corner of the airfield.

We spent some time with Corporal Bob Stewart as he carried out routine security and traffic check duties around the station. A Cornishman, Bob spent six years with 42 Commando Royal Marines before joining the RAF Police nine years ago.

In the old Cold War days, RAF Waddington was a V-bomber base and formed part of Britain's nuclear deterrent. As a consequence it had massive armament storage areas to safely house its weapons. Today only a small 'explosives safety area' remains in use as the sentries carry out their duties unarmed, but airfield defence missiles and other items of explosive ordnance still have to be housed in bomb-proof bunkers for safety. Special 90s, with screened electrical systems, are the only Land Rovers allowed inside the high security compound.

Designated Truck Utility Light – Aircraft Armament Support, these windowed hard top

Top: RAF police Defender 110 FFR, viewed under the nose of a decommissioned Phantom. Above left: Corporal Graham Shawcross, a medical administrator at RAF Waddington, sits on the drop-down attendant's seat in the casualty compartment of the duty ambulance. Above right: An Aircraft Armament Support 90 at work inside the tightly regulated Explosive Storage Area

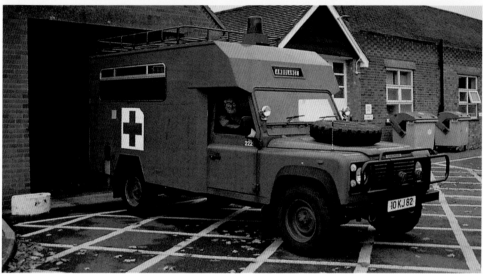

90s date from around 1987. Despite seldom having left the airfield in more than a decade, 61KF60 has clocked up nearly 48,000 kilometres or 30,000 miles. On our visit to the 'bomb dump' SAC Mike Taylor was hitching a special air-transportable trailer to the AAS 90 for weapons transportation, though lighter cargo is usually carried in the rear. In addition to being used as a prime mover, the vehicle is also equipped with removable inward facing bench seating for four in the rear.

and the rest

The majority of the other Land Rovers to be found operating in the aircraft handling areas are hard top 110 FFR (Fitted For Radio) models. Little different from their British Army equivalents, and indeed often coming from the same manufacturing batches, these are the workhorses of the base.

As minibuses are usually used for aircrew transfers these days, the Land Rovers are primarily used in the cargo role, both on the aircraft handling areas and around the various outlying workplaces. It is only after you have spent a few hours driving around a base like Waddington that the true scale of an RAF Station and

the variety of support tasks undertaken become apparent.

One minor variant of the 110 which could easily be overlooked is the GS cargo windowed hard top. For most of the year, this specialist variant trundles around undertaking routine tasks like its more conventional 110 FFR brothers but, as the first frosts of winter arrive, it is fitted with special bracketry at the front. From this state, in next to no time, it can be converted into an all-wheel drive snowplough to clear the base's roads and perimeter tracks, while the larger snowploughs keep the main runways clear. When the snowplough blade is fitted, large concrete counter-balance weights are carried on the rear load bed.

In addition to the military 110 fleet, the transport pool also has a small fleet of virtually civilian specification Defender 110 Tdi hard tops which it uses as pool vehicles and for inter-establishment cargo transporta-tion. Although these vehicles carry Land Rover Special Vehicles plates under the bonnet, other than a front mounted spare wheel and NATO towing jaws, they are virtually identical to the 110s found on any construction site or farm yard. Even their paint scheme is to civilian standards.

In front of the control tower are usually to be found a pair of Defender 90 GS cargo soft tops. One of these is the 'company car' of the Senior Air Traffic Controller (SATCO), Squadron Leader Kim Martin, who has operational responsibility for the Control Tower and all landings and take-offs, plus military air traffic movements within a forty mile (64 km) radius. She is also in charge of all airfield surfaces and navigation aids, the Fire Section and the Bird Control Unit. Sqn Ldr Martin, who rose from the ranks and has spent 20 years in the service, is one of the most familiar faces airside at Waddington as she monitors the operational readiness of the airfield.

Defence of the airfield from air attack is the job of the RAF's own army, the RAF Regiment. Just back from a long posting to Germany, 26 Squadron RAF Regt has now taken over the airfield defence role. The squadron is the first unit on the base to be re-equipped with the new Defender XD or 'Wolf' model. Actually designated Truck Utility Medium HS by the military (the HS stands for high specification), these Land Rovers are powered by the 300 Tdi engine, modified for military use. The vehicles also have computer designed chassis which

are more like the Range Rover than earlier Defenders, uprated suspension, internal roll-over protection and a host of other upgrades.

RAF Waddington is also home to 2503 Squadron of the Royal Auxiliary Air Force Regiment. The air force equivalent of the Territorial Army, they have their own fleet of military Defenders, including V8-powered 127 Rapier Tractors which they use in the cargo role.

As **LRM** goes to press, the British Army has just been deployed to Macedonia to provide an extraction force for the unarmed Verification Mission which is attempting to monitor the cease-fire in Kosovo. Should the Army be required to rescue the monitors in the event of renewed hostilities, they can rest assured that the ever-present airborne sentries will be watching over them, while back at RAF Waddington the Land Rover fleet will be quietly getting on with the support tasks.

■ We would like to express out thanks to Dale Donovan at Strike Command, CRO Jacqui Wheeler, Squadron Leader Kim Martin, WO Jeff Meadow, and all the officers and personnel at RAF Waddington who **LRM** assisted in the preparation of this feature.

Clockwise from top left: RAF police 110 has a typical military FFR cab, with the only minor addition being the Philips two-radio set; Snowplough attachment intended to keep access routes clear; Police duties include checking the emergency access routes onto the airfield and the security status of the perimeter fences; SAC Michael Maclean had driven this RAF Regiment 110 HS back from Germany a few minutes before this picture was taken. Inset: Truck Utility Medium HS identity plate from a 110 HS

*Words
and
pictures
by
Bob
Morrison*

Despite

the British Army garrisons on the Mediterranean island being at times just a stone's throw from armed protagonists on the Cypriot 'Green Line', they have not always benefited from the most modern equipment. Indeed Cyprus is usually the last place that a particular type of vehicle or weapon will see service, as the majority of the Land Rover fleets will bear testimony to. Series IIA ambulances, Series III 109s and Lightweights are now almost as rare as rocking horse manure on most British bases, but Cyprus still has more than its fair share in daily use.

However, things are slowly changing, and the first of the new Defender XD models have now arrived on the island. Code-named Wolf by the Land Rover design team, and called the XD (eXtra Duty) model by Government and Military Operations at Solihull, these new vehicles are designated Defender HS (High Specification) by the Ministry of Defence, to differentiate them from the rest of the vast military Defender fleet. Nearly 9,000 of the new vehicle, in 90, 110 and

stretched, 130, wheelbase versions have been ordered, the latter being a battlefield ambulance variant.

Externally, in soft-top configuration the new 90XD and 110XD Land Rovers (classified Truck Utility Light HS and Truck Utility Medium HS by the MoD) appear little different from the earlier Defender 90 and 110 models. However, closer inspection reveals louvred air intake boxes on the wings ahead of the A-pillars and, in the unloaded state, the rear body sits much higher than on earlier models. The keen-eyed will also spot that the canopy is slightly higher, because of the enhanced roll-over protection offered by the redesigned canopy frame.

well-covered

On hard top versions, the new plastic upper body is also taller than before, as it is designed to drop over the roof cage cum canopy frame. There are also other minor external differences such as the side-mounted spare wheel and the jerrycan compartments behind the front doors on the 110XD, but it is underneath the familiar body panels that the greatest changes are to be

island driving lessons

as winter temperatures plunged in **britain, bob morrison** headed off **to the** winter sunshine **of cyprus, to cover the** long awaited introduction **of the wolf to the** british bases

found.

The chassis of the XD or HS models are actually a derivative of that found on the new Range Rover, and although they still bear a passing resemblance to that of earlier models, they are allegedly much stronger and more capable. On top of this new, computer-designed, chassis sits a sub-frame which supports the rear load tray. Behind the rear body panels, additional strengthening plates have been added to give enhanced roll-over protection, and the inward facing rear bench seats have safety belts fitted. The cab seats are also of a much more ergonomic design and, for the first time, the MoD has actually specified head restraints.

Under the bonnet lurks a version of the 300Tdi engine, slightly modified for military use. Even the radiator is of a new design and can now be much more simply removed.

In due course, about 200 of the new Land Rovers will be deployed to the Sovereign Base Area garrisons in Cyprus. When **LRM** visited in late January, the first 20 had already been received, and driver familiarisation training was under way. I joined the army's Master Driver on the dedicated training area at Dhekelia, as he supervised corporals from the Second Battalion of the Royal Anglian Regiment (The Poachers) practising their skills.

As his title suggests, Warrant Officer Rick Shepherd is the British Army's senior driving instructor on the island. One of his jobs is to oversee the successful introduction of new vehicle types and ensure that soldiers detailed to drive them are adequately trained. The Wolf might look like just another Defender, but with its 2.5 litre turbo direct injected engine delivering 83 Kw (111 bhp) of power at 4000 rpm and 265 Nm of torque at 1800 rpm, it is no slouch.

Compared to the naturally-aspirated

Above: Andrew Piper instructing fellow corporal Eddie Hunter on one of the new hard top 110s. Inset: The additional power and rear-end height of the newly-introduced vehicles mean that driving training is essential

Top left: Wolf Hardtop 110 clearly showing the side-mounted spare wheel and higher than 'normal' roof line. Above left and right: Off-road conditions on the instruction course are not extreme but reflect likely terrain around the island

Defenders that most army drivers are used to or, more importantly, the tired-out 15 year old Series III 109s still found in the garrisons, the Wolf has almost rally car qualities. The additional load carrying capabilities and the improved suspension – the 110XD, has double coil springs at the rear – both give the new vehicles different handling capabilities and drivers must be trained to deal with these, both on tarmac and off-road.

When the Wolf was first introduced to service in Britain, there was a dramatic jump in the accident rate. This was mainly attributed to drivers not allowing for the increased power under their right boot, plus perceived familiarity leading to contempt. As the 90XD is fast on-road, and incredibly sprightly off-road, it is little wonder that boy racers had the odd prang or two.

Of course this phenomenon is not new – when the V8 powered Defender CAV (Composite Armour Vehicle) was introduced to Ulster a few years back, one was rolled on a motorway within days – but today's more efficient and safety conscious Army works to reduce such incidents through pertinent training.

share and share alike

The British Army, which prides itself on the high standards of its non-commissioned officers (NCOs), has found that the best way of teaching young soldiers is through leading by example. This is achieved by sending NCO representatives on training courses and, when they get back to their unit, they pass their skills onto their fellow soldiers. In some cases, this will mean

that a sergeant or corporal will take a basic course and then pass his acquired expertise onto the other corporals or lance corporals in the unit, who in turn pass their skill down to the ordinary soldiers.

When I joined The Poachers for the morning, Corporal Andrew Piper was instructing fellow corporal Eddie Hunter on one of the new hard top 110s. As the unit's Driving and Maintenance Instructor (DMI) and a member of 2 Royal Anglians MT (Motorised Transport) Platoon , Andrew has been trained to operate and maintain every vehicle in service, and also to pass on these skills to the other soldiers in the battalion. Incidentally, the post of DMI is being allowed to lapse and the latest instructors now qualify only as Defence Driving Instructors (DDI), as it is felt that separate instruction is now needed on driving and maintenance skills due to the increasing complexity of vehicle mechanics and electronics.

The Poachers were actually first issued with the Wolf when they served as the Demonstration Battalion in England, so most of their men only needed a refresher course. Most of the Light Infantry, based at Episcopi, however, will need to undertake full conversion courses as, in the main, they have only used Series III and 90 or 110 Land Rovers to date.

Under current regulations, Army personnel who have to drive Land Rovers "as part of their established duties", must hold a relevant full driving licence and must complete six separate sets of performance criteria, under assessment by a DMI or DDI. These

British Forces Cyprus

When Britain granted Independence to Cyprus in 1960, full sovereignty and jurisdiction were maintained over two areas, measuring about 100 square miles in total, to allow Britain to keep a military presence in this key region. At the extreme eastern end of the Mediterranean, the island was an ideal stepping stone for long haul flights to the remoter parts of the British Commonwealth, and its garrison troops could be mobilised quicker than those at home if a military or humanitarian assistance situation arose in the Middle East.

Back in the '60s, British Forces were still garrisoned throughout the Commonwealth and Cyprus was just another one of those exotic postings seen in recruiting adverts. Today it represents the last major out-of-area regular posting that most regiments are likely to undertake. However, although the Cyprus garrisons are sometimes seen as the last bastion of the British Empire, troops posted there actually perform a crucial task.

Less than four years after Independence, in response to intercommunal violence between the Greek and Turkish factions on the island, the United Nations instituted a peace-keeping force (UNFICYP). British troops played a major part in this force, and still do to this day. UNFICYP managed to maintain a fragile peace for another decade, but after a Greek Cypriot military coup in 1974, Turkish troops invaded the north of the island, to guarantee what they saw as the constitutional rights of the minority Turkish population. The Turks conquered about one third of the country, including half of the capital Nicosia and the Famagusta Bay holiday area, but they stopped on the boundary of the easternmost British Sovereign Base Areas and UNFICYP troops occupied the vital international airport just outside of Nicosia, to prevent either faction using it.

After brief but bloody fighting, a cease-fire was arranged, and a British officer marked out the demarcation line on a map with a green chinagraph pencil. To this day, a quarter of a century on, the two armies are still facing each other with loaded weapons and the boundary between them is still referred to as the green line.

include : Knowledge of the vehicle's specification, licensing requirements and speed limits; identifying controls, instrumentation, fuse boxes, and so on; undertaking routine maintenance duties – safely and correctly; driving the vehicle with or without trailer on public roads, by day or night, over a route of at least 40 kilometres and including close manoeuvring; driving the vehicle with or without trailer, by day or night, over a cross country course of at least two miles after formal training and knowledge of the principles of safely loading the vehicle.

the bumpier, the better!

Before driving the off-road course in the presence of an instructor, the trainee has to complete a minimum of four hours of formal cross-country driver training. The route itself has to include soft ground, ruts, ridges, ditches, V-shaped gullies, steep ascents and descents, plus, if possible, a suitable wading area. Suitable use of transfer gears and differential locks must be demonstrated to pass this part of the course.

The formal off-road course at Dhekelia is laid out in a pleasant valley which offers a mixture of rough tracks, soft sand, loose scree and scrubland. In summer, like most of the island, it is dry and relatively barren but,

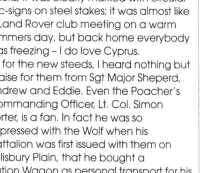

when I visited, the winter rains had turned it into a pleasantly green amphitheatre, with washed out tracks and even the odd pool of standing water.

As with all military training areas, wildlife abounds here as intensive farming and pesticides are banned, and the Cypriot hares just have to be seen to be believed. Today's Army is actually very conservation minded, so where the route deviated from the main tracks, it was clearly marked with circular tac-signs on steel stakes; it was almost like a Land Rover club meeting on a warm summers day, but back home everybody was freezing – I do love Cyprus.

As for the new steeds, I heard nothing but praise for them from Sgt Major Sheperd, Andrew and Eddie. Even the Poacher's Commanding Officer, Lt. Col. Simon Porter, is a fan. In fact he was so impressed with the Wolf when his battalion was first issued with them on Salisbury Plain, that he bought a Defender Tdi Station Wagon as personal transport for his family when he came to Cyprus.

Indeed the last thing I saw as I left the Poacher's headquarters was one of the new Land Rovers, in Fitted For Radio role, parked outside the Ops Room – it proudly carried the Poacher's cap badge insignia and the Commanding Officers CO abbreviation on its bumper.

LRM

Top: Many of the Cyprus-based vehicles, such as this Series III, are getting very long in the tooth. Above: Rick Shepherd is the British Army's senior driving instructor on Cyprus

bob MORRISON
military scene

resurrected

only too
pleased
to come
back
into the
fold

It was back in January 1988 that Editor Richard Howell-Thomas first allowed me to write a 'Military Scene' article for a magazine catering exclusively for Land Rover enthusiasts. What had been conceived as a one-off feature then became a short series, and soon developed into a regular monthly column. For the next six years and 80 issues of the magazine my Military Scene column expanded even faster than my waistline.

Photographing military Land Rovers had already been my passion for several years, but it was the opportunity to write this regular column that allowed me to develop my 'hobby' to its fullest extent. One of the greatest advantages of now being an accredited photojournalist specialising in military Land Rovers for a mainstream publication was the opportunity it gave me to travel far and wide to record Solihull's finest at work.

By late 1990 the Military Scene column was widely read, and by the military as well as the general public and when British troops deployed to the Persian Gulf, my phone line was red hot with information on the developing crisis. In the final build up to the Gulf War, both Land Rover Ltd and the Saudi Defence Attache in London went to extreme lengths to ensure that I could record Land Rover's forthcoming part in the operation to liberate Kuwait and I still have my official Saudi Ministry of Information Press Pass to this day.

During those first six years, I visited many European countries photographing military and public service Land Rovers at work, as well as covering countless military exercises and developments at home in the UK. When redundancy finally struck at my 'proper' job, I even turned writing about Land Rovers and other military matters into a second career.

All good things must come to an end of course, and when a large publishing house bought out the magazine, the Military Scene column lasted only one issue. I continued to contribute though, writing on a variety of other subjects, military matters having been relegated to second echelon. While not denying that I enjoyed writing most of these later articles, I made many new friends in the various Land Rover circles, I always held a yearning to get back to the 'old' way of doing things.

When Richard first approached me to write for **LRM**, I was unable to accept the offer due to other commitments, but when just before Christmas I became a free agent, I was only too pleased to come back into the fold. Now, after sounding out our military enthusiast readers and our specialist advertisers, we have decided to resurrect my Military Scene column and hopefully keep everyone abreast of the contemporary and historic world of those special Land Rover variants used by armed forces around the world.

We hope you will enjoy it and if there is a good tale to be told or a part of the military Land Rover story jigsaw to be slipped into place, I will do it with your help.

You can write to me care of the LRM office, or better still, e-mail me.

LRM

You can contact Bob Morrison by email on bob@lrm.co.uk

A couple of months before writing my first Military Scene column in late 1987, I changed from using negative film to transparency, as reproduction from this type of film is much better. The downside is the photographer has much less leeway and correct exposure is essential. I had previously experimented with transparency film and so I do have some earlier photos of Land Rovers on slide, but the first 'official' numbered slide (A1/1) in my now vast collection is of a Dutch military 110.

This soft top 110 was one of the first batch of vehicles procured by the Royal Netherlands Marine Corps and it was photographed during a training exercise on Dartmoor. In addition to lighting modifications to meet Dutch military specifications, it is fitted with a snorkel air intake for amphibious operations. The front winch, tow bar and roof-mounted light bar (under covers) on this Land Rover were only fitted to Forward Repair Team vehicles operated by the Dutch Marine equivalent of Britain's REME.

This was the first time that the Dutch Marines, who work closely with the Royal Marines, had taken their new vehicles on exercise. The Dutch Army later rejected the Land Rover in favour of the Mercedes Benz G-wagen, which is actually built by Steyr Puch in Austria, but the Marines have stayed loyal to the Land Rover. Later Dutch Marine Land Rover batches were built to Defender Tdi specification.

In the late 80s and early 90s, the G-wagen stole much of Land Rover's traditional military market share in Europe, but over the last few years Solihull has started to claw its way back.

The break-up of the former Republic of Yugoslavia at

better exposure

since **Bob Morrison** changed to using **slide film** in 1987, lots **has happened** in the world **of** military **Land Rovers**

the beginning of this decade saw civil war return to Europe, and by the mid 90s military Land Rovers had taken on a new peacekeeping role in the region. The Defender CAV, a Land Rover with a plastic armour body which had been procured in numbers to patrol the streets of Ulster, was dispatched to Bosnia under UN colours as an armoured liaison vehicle. When NATO took over responsibility for monitoring the cease-fire, Defender CAVs mothballed in response to the first IRA ceasefire were shipped to the region to give protection to IFOR troops.

turkish & italian

Throughout the Balkans crises, news teams and aid agencies made widespread use of armoured Land Rovers, and it seemed that hardly a day would pass without one of Solihull's products appearing in newsreel footage. Other armies working alongside the British in the Balkans also started to field Defenders, and even some of those built in Istanbul were deployed in IFOR markings by Turkish Army peacekeepers.

Late last year, as the Balkans crisis spread to Kosovo, the British Army CAVs were painted bright orange and deployed into areas where the Yugoslav Army and Kosovo Liberation Army (KLA) had been fighting, to give protection to the unarmed verification monitors. When the follow-up Rambouillet Conference collapsed without agreement and NATO subsequently attacked Yugoslavia to stop 'ethnic cleansing' of Kosovo

Albanians, several European countries committed military forces to the region, and once again the Land Rover was to the fore.

As was to be expected, Britain deployed large numbers of the Defender HS (Wolf) model, and its battlefield ambulance 'Pulse' variant, to the region. But it was the deployment of Italian Defenders which surprised most observers. The initial procurement of some 300 Tdi Defenders by the Italian Army, mainly for peacekeeping duties in Bosnia, had been discreetly announced by Solihull but had passed almost unnoticed. For decades the Italian motor industry has provided its own armed forces with highly regarded light utility off-roaders, but such is the military Defender's reputation for endurance and reliability that it was the natural choice to replace part of the aging Fiat Campagnola fleet. We now understand that a second order has been placed by the Italians, and by the end of this year about a thousand 90 Tdi Defenders will be in service.

Despite the forthcoming introduction of the 'new' Defender there is clearly still a market for the traditional military light and medium Land Rover. Even if, as some commentators insist, Solihull ceases production of the current body style, I am convinced that production will continue elsewhere. But even if it does not, the traditional Land Rover should battle on in military guise until at least the end of the first decade of the new millennium. **LRM**

Story Bob Morrison, pics by Bob Morrison and Yves Debay

Main pic: V8 powered Defender CAV shown during the early days of NATO deployment in Bosnia. Above left: Author Bob's first slide of a military Land Rover, ref No (A1/1), it shows a Dutch Marines Defender 110. Above right: Italian Army 90 Tdi Defenders photographed in Macedonia. Inset left: Turkish Army Defender Station Wagon, built by Otokar in Istanbul, on IFOR duties

death warrant

what role for the Land Rover in the army now?

Tom Sheppard's article on the way ahead in last month's issue of **LRM** set me thinking. When the replacement Defender arrives, could it sign the death warrant for the military Land Rover as we know it?

Times are changing. All around the world the, mainly Japanese, 4x4 pick-up truck has eaten deeply into the traditional military utility market, mainly on cost grounds, but also due to the comfort factor. Civilian-Specification off-roaders are nibbling away at the liaison vehicle sector, too.

No matter how good the Defender is at its job, the bean counters who make the final decision on procurement will always try to substitute a cheap, off-the-shelf pickup truck on the basis that in peacetime it can do most of the jobs required of it. If the new Defender is priced competitively - presumably it will not be built using the man-hour consuming bolt and rivet construction of the traditional Land Rover - it should be much cheaper, I suspect that it will fulfil the accountants' wishes on cost and the rear echelon soldiers' desires on comfort.

For second line liaison duties, the Discovery already fits the bill and is competitively priced as well. There will still be a need among specialist units for the traditional Land Rover, in the shape of the Defender XD or Wolf model, but will the quantities be enough to keep the model in production?

During this decade, peacekeeping operations have come to the fore, mainly as a result of the break-up of the Soviet Union and the demise of the Warsaw Pact. The massive Cold War standing armies in Europe, with their vast fleets of light utility vehicles, are a thing of the past and are slowly being replaced by small, professional, crisis reaction forces.

These troops, operating where there is no front line and where it is difficult to know exactly who is the enemy, tend to travel in armoured light vehicles which use Land Rover-style mechanical components, but have mine-proof monocoque construction hulls rather than pressed metal bodies. The British Army still uses Land Rover-derived vehicles for the armoured liaison/utility role when it is desirable for internal security vehicles to appear as 'normal' as possible, but the French VBL and the similar Land Rover-derived Scorpion from Otokar, Turkey are in some ways more suited to the task, though several times the price.

The large British Army fleet of leaf-sprung Land Rovers has now been totally replaced. With the Wolf in widespread service with active units and set to last until around 2010, plus the numerous older Defenders available to second line units still having plenty of life left in them, it may be some time before the government orders anything other than small quantities of top-up or specialist role vehicles.

Few other armies have plans to buy massive quantities of Land Rover-type vehicles so, if no major military orders are forthcoming and the new Defender meets the needs of all but the most specialist off-road worker and adventurer, will there be sufficient market for the traditional Land Rover in the 21st Century?

You can contact Bob Morrison by email on bob@lrm.co.uk

LRM

Some of the Army's best treated and maintained Land Rovers must have been those used ceremonially by the Honourable Artillery Company, Britain's oldest regiment. Housed in a purpose-designed, centrally heated building on London's City Road, these immaculately turned-out vehicles were used primarily as gun tractors on State occasions, when they took part in gun salutes at the Tower of London.

In April 1990 I was allowed the privilege of photographing these five Lightweights, recently demobbed, as they took part in a 41-gun salute at the Tower to honour a visiting Head of State. At the time, these vehicles had been in service with the HAC for eighteen months, though a simple check of their registrations showed that they were much older than they appeared.

all is revealed

Having finally ended their service careers, we are able to reveal a little more of their history. Five Lightweights were assigned to ceremonial duties with the Gun Troop of the HAC, but they were not built specifically for these duties, being reworked from issued stock by 44 District

the shining

for sale, five immaculate lightweights, one owner from new, Bob Morrison reports

Workshop REME in September 1988. From chassis numbers, makers plates and registration, we know that two are from the 1978/9 batch and two from a similar contract from the following fiscal year, with the fifth coming from a batch issued in 1983.

At present we have no firm record of their service before 1988, but their mileage would suggest that they led a reasonably active life prior to refurbishment. In one case either a new speedometer has been recently fitted, as I suspect, or else the Lightweight has covered 100,039 miles. The others are showing more reasonable figures of between roughly 26,000 and 58,000 miles. Though not high mileage for twenty year old Land Rovers, it must be borne in mind that for the last decade they have only ventured a handful of miles from home on a few occasions each year.

On these comparatively rare occasions four of them towed equally immaculate 25 pounder field guns, each weighing just under two tonnes. In addition to driver and gun commander, the latter standing on the front passenger seat and holding a grab rail on the top edge of the windscreen, two or three troopers were carried in the rear, along with a box of blank ammunition for the gun. (Before anybody writes in to point out that artillery soldiers are called gunners, not troopers,

the mixed infantry and artillery roles of the HAC have resulted in the cavalry designation for private soldiers being adopted by them instead). The fifth vehicle in this small fleet, usually 84KB49, served as the commander's vehicle, although in the event of a breakdown it would have been used to tow the errant vehicle's gun.

pinzgauer welcome

For more than two decades the HAC used Series IIA 88 inch wheelbase Land Rovers to tow their guns, which themselves are Second World War veterans, from 1966 until their replacement by the Lightweights in 1988. Back in 1990, the reason that I was given for Defenders not being used to replace the 88s was the turn radius required to manoeuvre the guns and tractors in one sweep into line opposite the firing platforms, was too tight for the newer vehicles, which had a wider track. However, I cannot say that I am convinced by this argument as, on paper, the reduced track of the Lightweight ➤

These lightweights are now retired, there's something not right about Austrian-built vehicles welcoming visiting heads of state to the UK

actually gave it a wider turning circle than the
Defender 90, as less lock could be achieved. I wonder if
those responsible for procurement tried it out with an
actual vehicle?

It has been said the Lightweights were retired
because they did not conform to latest Health and
Safety Regulations for towing guns, but in reality it was
the decision to phase out all leaf-sprung petrol Land
Rovers in late 1997 that sealed their redundancy
papers. However, the introduction of the latest road
traffic regulations and the resultant implications of the
maximum train weight of 3500kg possibly made
replacement by Defender or Wolf 90 models problem-
atic. Currently, Austrian Pinzgauer gun tractors are used
to welcome foreign Heads of State to Britain and for
those Royal Salutes conducted at the Tower.
Interestingly, the Pinzgauer, which is roughly six inches
(150mm) shorter than the 110, has a vastly greater turn
radius than either standard wheelbase Land Rover
models.

chrome and gloss

When REME refurbished the Lightweights for their
ceremonial role in 1988, most of the work was purely
cosmetic. Naturally, the Land Rovers have a highly
polished deep green paint finish instead of the usual
drab infra red reflective NATO green/black seen on
those likely to be used in a combat environment, and

their chassis are finished in a semi-gloss black.

To complement this, front and rear bumpers have
been given a chrome finish, as has the radiator grille.
Wiper arms and even the screen washer jet nozzles are
also chromed, plus windscreen frame and all
galvanised trim is buffed up to the highest finish. All
seats, front and rear, have been re-covered in white
leather and there is a matching cover for the bonnet-
mounted spare wheel. On the earlier vehicles, indicators, sidelights and rear lights have been replaced with
late production types.

The HAC Lightweights were high profile ceremonial
vehicles and to allow the crews to be constantly on
view the soft top and door tops were not fitted. Also, to
allow the gun crew sharp exit from and access to the
rear of the vehicles, tailgates were not fitted.

In late 1995, all five Land Rovers were temporarily
withdrawn from service for a second refurbishment at
Ashford, which now falls under the Army Base Repair
Organisation (ABRO) designation. Presumably at that
time it was assumed they would continue in service with
the HAC for a good many years more.

This refurb, plus the conditions in which they have
since been stored and the care lavished on them by
the HAC, has meant that today all are in remarkably
good condition. During the photo shoot, I had the
chance to drive two of them and found them to be
excellent runners which, after all, is only to be expected

of ceremonial vehicles. However, one of the others decided to become temperamental on the day, so we left it behind to sulk. As this is the only incomplete vehicle - it lacks front bumper and some seat cushions, I was not too worried about leaving it behind.

dirty tyres - shock, horror

On reflection, the **LRM** photo-call was probably the first time these Land Rovers had been off-road since their first refurbishment in 1988.

With due deference to their status, we did not hammer them, but low box and diff lock still had to be engaged to get at least one of them over roughish terrain to reach one of the locations. Somehow I think this might be the last time they get their tyres dirty if the Ministry of Defence asking price is paid for them.

Should you be interested in purchasing one or all of the five HAC Lightweights, they are being sold off through MVS of Lichfield, the Government's agents for the direct sale of Series Land Rovers. The price put on them is a hefty £12,500, but I suspect it is rather unlikely the MoD will be able to realise this figure.

Unlike their Series IIA predecessors, which had incredibly low mileages, had always been roled for ceremonial duties and were of a type that had been out of production for nearly two decades, the Lightweights had been used for normal duties for up to nine years before taking on their new role, have high mileages, and are of a base type which has flooded the market over the last couple of years.

At least one person is making a serious bid for these vehicles as this article goes to press, though I doubt if he will be offering anything like the price suggested by the Ministry of Defence. I understand that he would like to keep all vehicles together, but this might not be practical, especially if the price is too high. Possibly though, because of their links with the Tower of London and the monarchy, an American buyer or buyers might be interested in these unique vehicles. It would be a pity to think that another little piece of British and Land Rover history may be disappearing overseas, but at least a good home or homes could be assured, albeit in private hands.

■ MVS can be contacted on 01543 417733.   **LRM**

Clockwise from top left: Even the interior remains spotless; Late style lamp glasses are fitted to all five vehicles; Seats and spare wheel cover are trimmed in white leather; One careful owner, full service history. Yours for just £12,500 - ouch; One advantage of something like this is the total lack of restoration required. Inset: Who needs a log book?

rewrite

LRM

the ever changing situation in Kosovo keeps our Bob on his toes

This last month has been one of these infuriating ones when, no matter what I write, the situation changes just before I put the work in the post. In addition to my articles for **LRM**, I also edit a mainstream military magazine, and the ever-changing situation in Kosovo has really kept me on my toes. Kosovo has also had a knock-on effect on this column, and this is actually the fourth rewrite.

The first British Army Land Rovers to go into Kosovo were the bright orange Defender Composite Armour Vehicles (CAV), of the type designed for duties in Ulster but which quickly gained popularity as light transport and liaison vehicles in Bosnia. The CAVs originally deployed to Bosnia were used by the Kosovo Verification Mission Monitors (KVMM) before the breakdown of the Rambouillet Talks, but they were withdrawn prior to the commencement of bombing on 24th March.

Just before Christmas, a quantity of the new Defender 90XD and 110XD (Wolf), plus 130XD battlefield ambulance (Pulse), were deployed with the British Army to Macedonia as part of KFOR (Kosovo FORce). The original mission of this mixed group was to assist in the withdrawal of the KVMM if necessary, but when NATO commenced military action against the Former Republic of Yugoslavia, they became the nucleus for the proposed Kosovo peace implementation force. On 28th May another 12,000 British military personnel were assigned for KFOR, duties and further large quantities of all three Defender XD models were readied for rapid deployment. When KFOR eventually moved into Kosovo early on Saturday 12th June, many of the vehicles transported forward under RAF helicopters were Land Rovers of The Parachute Regiment and The Royal Gurkha Rifles.

Another of the units at the forefront of the British KFOR deployment is the specialist 23 Parachute Field Ambulance, who were among the first to re-equip with the Pulse ambulance variant on the Defender 130XD chassis. British Army Pulse ambulances have appeared numerous times on newsreel footage from the front line, but these are not the only ones in-theatre. The Royal Netherlands Marine Corps has also bought a batch of these vehicles, with minor detail differences to suit national requirements and specifications. Close inspection of a Belgian Defence Information Service photograph of their logistic base at Durres in Albania reveals two of the latest new 130XD ambulances in shot, and minor differences suggest that these are probably Dutch vehicles.

Away from Kosovo, I have been picking up tips that Germany's border guards are about to reequip with Land Rovers. Back in the fifties the Bundesgrenzschutz ran a fleet of Tempo Land Rovers, assembled in Germany with some locally produced components, for border patrol duties. For the last few decades though, they have bought German or Austrian manufactured vehicles for this task. Solihull's Government and Military Operations department does not seem to be involved with this contract, which it is thought is being handled by Land Rover's German dealer network. It is good to see Land Rover reclaiming another of its lost markets. I wonder which will be next?

You can contact Bob Morrison by email on bob@lrm.co.uk

crash and smash

military helicopter crashes are mercifully rare, **but when** tragedy strikes **this specialist team** is called in

Royal Navy Warrant Officer Keith Laycock was out practising with his team on the off-road driver training area on the edge of Salisbury Plain, when the call to action came in; Army helicopter down; casualties; rural Leicestershire. The tri-service Rotary Wing Aircraft Transport and Salvage Team was in business.

Part of the Mobile Aircraft Support Unit (MASU), which comes under the Royal Naval Support Command, Keith's team are tasked with picking up the pieces whenever and wherever a British military helicopter, irrespective of its arm of service, is involved in an accident. A similar RAF team, also nicknamed Crash & Smash, performs the same function for all fixed wing RAF and Royal Navy aircraft.

In addition to their military duties, because of their vast experience of recovering helicopters from often near inaccessible sites, the MASU team are also frequently invited by the Air Accident Investigation Board, the civil organisation which provides the answers to precisely why an aircraft crashed, to recover crashed civilian helicopters as well.

Military helicopter crashes are a relatively rare occurrence in Britain, as are civilian ones, though, as with all air crashes, when one does go down it attracts national media coverage. However, like all forms of mechanised transport, helicopters also routinely just break down from time to time and in these situations the pilot has to set the aircraft down in the nearest available open space, as you or I would park an ailing vehicle by the

side of the road or on the verge.

Helicopter components are built for high speed, long life running, but because of system complexity, a minor fault in say a gearbox or drive shaft can put unacceptable loadings on other components, or even the airframe, so in peacetime it is not just a case of taking a spanner to the fault and then setting off again. The aircraft nearly always has to be loaded onto a flatbed trailer and then towed back to the workshops for fault rectification and detailed examination for any potential knock-on mechanical problems. Hence the reason for the Wide Load light bar on top of the MASU Defender.

Keith's call-out on Tuesday May 18th was the one he and his team hate most. A British Army Lynx helicopter with four soldiers on board had developed a serious mechanical fault during a routine flight between its base at Dishforth in Yorkshire and the Army Air Corps establishment at Middle Wallop in Hampshire, and had crashed heavily on landing. Three of the four crew died as the aircraft impacted, the fourth was thrown clear and survived, though with serious injuries.

As the helicopter crashed, close to the village of Tilton-on-the-Hill, locals contacted the emergency services and raced to the scene to try to help. Fire crews from nearby Oakham were the first to arrive, but one of the distinctive red and yellow 'battenberg' fire service Defenders from Loughborough was also dispatched as the crash site was in fields, a couple of hundred yards from the nearest road. Naturally, police and ambulance services were alerted too, and the former quickly threw a secure cordon around the area,

but as the crashed helicopter was a military aircraft, the Royal Air Force Police were also called out.

The crash site was within the area of responsibility of the RAF police detachment at RAF Cottesmore, so a four man team under Squadron Leader Paul Robins was dispatched to set up an incident control point and protect the aircraft. The vehicle that this team used was a standard naturally aspirated, soft top, Defender 90, of the type used at virtually every RAF establishment. Painted in standard NATO Green, with black overspray as a disruptive camouflage, the 90 also sported the distinctive high visibility red side bands used by RAF police units on peacetime duties. Incidentally, the black edging to these day-glo stripes is not just for neatness, it is highly reflective under infrared light and stands out equally as well in the dark as red does in the day when night vision devices are used.

Towed behind the 90 was a military trailer containing a 12 x 12 tent for use as an operations base, communications and admin gear, equipment for marking off and lighting the crash scene plus all the personal kit for the team. From a distance this trailer looked like one of the 'fish fryer' type used by some specialist units, closer inspection revealed that the upper bodywork was actually homemade from plywood.

The MASU Defender, in complete contrast, is basically a civilian specification Defender 110 Station Wagon with bumper mounted drum winch. One of a special purchase batch, it is powered by the 200 Tdi engine instead of the usual naturally aspirated military engine, but it carries a military registration plate

Report and pictures: Bob Morrison

Incident Control Point at the site of the fatal Lynx crash. This role calls for little more than a bog standard Defender 90

19

Brooklands Military Titles

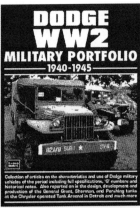

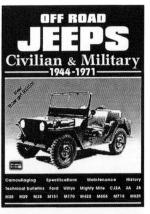
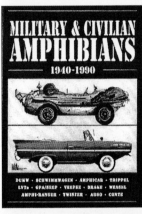

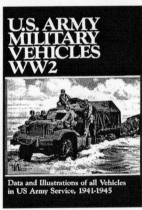

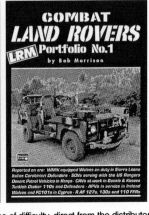
From specialist booksellers or, in case of difficulty, direct from the distributors:
Brooklands Books Ltd., P.O. Box 146, Cobham, Surrey, KT11 1LG, England Phone: 01932 865051
Brooklands Books Ltd., 1/81 Darley St., P.O. Box 199, Mona Vale, NSW 2103, Australia Phone: 2 9997 8428
CarTech, 39966 Grand Avenue, North Branch, MN 55056, USA Phone: 800 551 4754 & 651 277 1200
E-mail us at info@brooklands-books.com or visit our website www.brooklands-books.com

Top left: Off to the Gulf in support of Royal Navy Sea King helicopters. Top right: Suitably adorned this 'Rum Rats' Defender 110 awaits shipment to the Gulf. Above left: Basically civilian spec Defender highlighted as a Royal Navy vehicle by the RN letters in the military registration plate. Above right: Defender is regularly used for escort duties, hence the flashing lights and 'abnormal load' sign

and is classed as green fleet, not white fleet. In other words it is a combat vehicle and not a rear echelon fleet car.

This vehicle's main function is to transport the MASU Crash & Smash team rapidly to the site of an incident, but it also doubles as a convoy escort vehicle to lead the invariably large lorries that are required for recovery of aircraft.

This Tdi Station Wagon spends much of its time on the road as it also accompanies routine aircraft road movements, but it also has to transport men and materials to remote crash sites over rough terrain, hence the reason for the winch. The winch also comes in useful for recovering airframes and larger pieces of wreckage, and when I remarked to Keith that his one looked to be well used, he told how he even used it to recover the fuselage of the aircraft in which businessman Matthew Harding died, from inside a wood.

The Lynx crash site in contrast, though on a sloping hillside, was actually comparatively easy to gain access to, but this tends to be the exception rather than the rule. It is more usual for a crash site to be halfway up a mountain, in woodland, or on remote farm land, as most military helicopter activity takes place well away from populated areas.

In addition to transport and salvage duties the 141 strong staff of MASU, of which 30 percent are civilians,

also handle tri-service aircraft damage categorisation and repairs, plus they carry out service modifications to the fixed and rotary wing aircraft of the Fleet Air Arm. They also design and issue specialist tool kits to allow naval aircraft to be modified and repaired in the field.

During the 1991 Gulf War, MASU deployed from its base near Gosport in Hampshire to Saudi Arabia, with a small fleet of 110 hard top Defenders towing 'fish fryer' tool trailers to ensure that the Commando Sea King helicopters had full back-up for their prime task in the war, and to be on hand for the recovery, salvage and repair of any crashed or damaged naval aircraft. Britain's 4th and 7th Armoured Brigades were known as the Desert Rats, so MASU nicknamed themselves the Rum Rats, marking their vehicles accordingly to ensure that everybody knew that the Royal Navy was ashore.

LRM

This combined service operation to guard and recover the crashed Army helicopter went off without a hitch, but on this occasion the job was marred by the sad loss of three military personnel in the accident. **LRM** wishes to express its sympathy to the relatives and colleagues of Warrant Officer Andrej Prenczec, Staff Sergeant Stuart Donnan and REME Staff Sergeant Peter Clyne, and to wish Major Murray Whiteside a speedy and full recovery.

I wonder...

who reads
a column
like this?
wonders
Bob
Morrison
here's the
answer

I often wonder if anybody actually ever reads my ramblings in an editorial column like this, or if you all just dive straight on into the main feature. With this in mind, it's good to know that at least one member of senior management at Solihull does read the column and, not only that, has taken me to task on a couple of comments as well.

In the July issue, I pondered if there was actually a market these days for the utility Land Rover, or if the forthcoming new Defender would sign the death warrant for the basic specification workhorse that many of us have that unique love/hate relationship with. Well, I was told in no uncertain terms by the big man that the light and medium utility military Land Rover will definitely be around through the first decade of the next millennium. According to him, the contractual obligations that Land Rover has with the British and other governments for the life span of currently ordered vehicles ensures that construction must continue for some time yet, though he did not say where, and there are several other major military orders in the offing that will underscore this commitment. Good to know, isn't it.

As if to highlight that the need for the traditional utility Land Rover still exists, many of the aid and relief agencies plus the non-governmental organisations (NGOs) that are flooding into Kosovo seem to have opted for Defenders to get them around the rough roads of the battered province. After brief forays with Japanese vehicles in Croatia and Bosnia earlier in the decade, it appears that many are now returning to the fold. Could it be that the comfort factor of the all-singing, all-dancing, electronically-dominated 'super off-roaders' is losing out to the practicalities of the dedicated off-roader?

While on the subject of relief agencies in Kosovo, I noticed that one of the Defenders provided by Land Rover to the Department of International Development (see page 14), was a former Camel Trophy support vehicle. Land Rover's PR supremo Bill Baker confirmed that both of the Defender 110 Station Wagons, dispatched for Pristina on board a giant Russian Ilyushin cargo jet, were actually refurbished Camel Trophy vehicles. Five Discoverys, originally used on an adventure programme in Jordan, were also flown out to provide much needed mobility for relief agencies working with the DoID. The Defenders will be used by the World Health Organisation. Incidentally, Land Rover tried to deliver these vehicles overland to Albania a couple of months ago, but problems with Albanian frontier guards prevented their use for humanitarian aid to Albanian Kosovars (see **LRM** July 1999 page 15).

Lastly, thanks for all the emails about me engaging the diff lock on an HAC Lightweight. I know full well that your average Series III has no such thing. What I meant to say was that I engaged low box and four wheel drive. A case of typing without first putting my brain in gear.

contact Bob
Morrison by email:
bob@lrm.co.uk

LRM

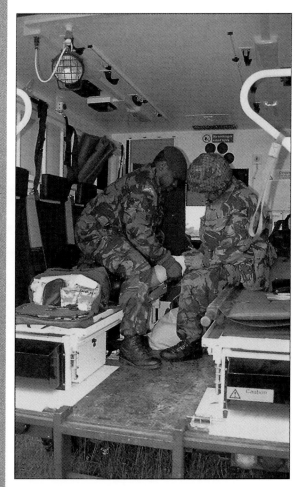

During

the last two weeks of June hardly an evening passed without newsreel footage being shown of British troops inside Kosovo as part of KFOR. To us Land Rover enthusiasts, one of the most noticeable things was the presence of large numbers of the latest Defender XD models, known to the Ministry of Defence as the Defender HS, but more commonly referred to by the troops as the Wolf.

Of the 8000 or so Defender XD models originally ordered by the Ministry of Defence about four years ago, virtually all of which are now believed to be in service, approximately ten percent are of the Battlefield Ambulance variant. Code-named Pulse by Land Rover during the design and trials phase, this version is based on the stretched 130 chassis, but from the back of the cab forward it is virtually identical to the 90 and 110 Truck Utility Light (TUL) and Truck Utility Medium (TUM) versions. The rear body is manufactured by Marshall of Cambridge, who mass-produced ambulance bodies on Land Rover chassis for at least 35 years.

As we plan to take a detailed closer look at the design of the ambulance body in the near future, I do not propose to cover this in any great detail, but instead will concentrate on the operational use of the vehicle. Configured to carry up to six seated patients, though in practice nine could be accommodated in relative comfort, or four stretcher cases, the new ambulance is now in widespread service, and it is well liked by every driver and medic that I have talked to.

the truth is out there

By now all of the old Series IIA/III 109 ambulances, which were the mainstay of British Army forward medical services since the mid-sixties, and the large batch of Forward Control 101 ambulances which saw widespread service from the early eighties, should have

para's pulse

real bullets flying on exercise **with the latest Land Rover** battlefield ambulance

Words and pictures Bob Morrison

been pensioned off and replaced by Pulse. However, at some remote garrison somewhere, there is bound to be the odd survivor still soldiering on.

The ambulances photographed for this feature belong to the London-based 10th Battalion of the Parachute Regiment. This battalion, which under the Government's Strategic Defence Review has now been reduced to company strength, is part of the Territorial Army and is manned by volunteers.

Although its members are only part-timers, they are still fully trained paratroopers and, with their colleagues in 4 Para, are regarded as the cream of Britain's TA soldiers.

To ensure that they are fully prepared for their prime role as battlefield casualty replacements for the regular Parachute Regiment battalions, every man in 10 Para makes several low level static line parachute drops each year and spends many weekends on live-fire training exercises. I recently joined these TA Paras on one such exercise on Salisbury Plain.

The exercise scenario, which incidentally took place exactly a week before 1 Para advanced into Kosovo as lead element of KFOR, called for a company-sized formation to parachute behind 'enemy' lines and make a surprise assault on an enemy position. The assault would be supported by mortars and heavy machine guns, with live ammunition being used by all participants.

Medical cover on the drop zone, to cater for an expected casualty rate of up to ten percent, was provided by the unit's own parachute qualified medics, and two of the new Pulse ambulances were pre-positioned close by for rapid response. Two Gazelle helicopters were also on call to transport anybody with serious injuries direct to hospital, but primary care would be down to the medic and driver in each ambulance, plus a small number of medics who also parachuted in as part of the assault force.

In the event, there were only three casualties, all minor, despite the ground being rock hard after several days of hot, dry weather. A couple of paras were blown slightly off course by the gusting wind and ended up in the trees at the edge of the drop zone, but even they escaped injury. Once the three Hercules transport aircraft had cleared the drop zone and all the paras had landed, the ambulances cruised across more than a kilometre of rough ground searching for possible casualties in the long grass, but the worst that they found was a badly strained knee and a case of minor concussion. As parachute drops go, this had been one of the safest, with a casualty rate of only about three percent.

bringing up the rear

With everyone safely accounted for, the Paras then turned their attention on the assault on the enemy positions which were a few kilometres distant. With mortars and machine guns laying down covering fire and sustained machine gun fire passing overhead, the possibility of accidental injury was high, so one of the ambulances followed behind the last man, just in case. The other covered the mortar line but as the British Army makes safety its number one priority, there were no casualties for the paramedics to treat this time.

Within 24 hours of having left their jobs on a Friday afternoon, the part-time soldiers of 10 Para had rigged themselves and their kit for airborne operations, had parachuted into mock battle after two hours of low level flight and taken out an enemy strong point. Behind them, and almost unnoticed, a couple of Land Rover ambulances provided safety cover.

Meanwhile, the men of 5 Airborne Brigade were preparing to do the business for real in the liberation of Pristina, safe in the knowledge that Pulse ambulances would be backing them up too, if required. Thankfully, they were not. **LRM**

Left: The worst casualty following an extremely successful jump was this badly strained leg. Top right: Pulse is based on a stretched 130 inch chassis. Above right: A live-fire exercise, an ambulance follows up behind the last advancing soldier, just in case of an accident

Kosovo Rovers

Wolf-equipped for speed and flexibility, British forces were at the forefront as KFOR troops flooded into Kosovo

by Bob Morrison

Top left: Soft and hard top Wolves parked outside 1 PARA's HQ in Pristina - nearest vehicle is a piggy-back 90. Top right (and lower picture opposite page): A Gurkha Wolf 110 with forward firing machine gun patrols in Kosovo. Inset: Parachute regiment Wolf, with canopy partially removed exposing roll cage, moves forward into Kosovo Opposite page top: A company commander from 1 Para on patrol, behind one of his men covers him from a Wolf 110. All pictures copyright Defence Picture Library

During

the second week in June, as Yugoslav commanders prepared to sign the Military Technical Agreement which would lead to their withdrawal from Kosovo and the end of the NATO bombing campaign, Britain's 5th Airborne Brigade readied itself for the role of spearhead formation in the liberation of Kosovo.

In front of the world's television cameras, the Brigade's Paras and Gurkhas, plus their support arms, practiced for the forthcoming heliborne operation. Underneath the RAF Chinook transport helicopters, dangled the Land Rovers that would play such a crucial part in the advance on the Kosovar capital Pristina.

After a false start on Friday 11th, allegedly because President Clinton wanted to put American troops in with the first wave but they were not yet ready, the order was given to advance up through the Kacanik Pass on the following morning. In a series of bounds, the men of 5 Airborne Brigade secured the main route north from Macedonia to Pristina, and by Saturday evening British General Mike Jackson was holding his promised press conference in the liberated capital.

As the Paras and Gurkhas advanced, Land Rovers were very much in the vanguard, and it was noticeable that the majority of these were the new Defender XD (Wolf) models.

united forces

A key component of Britain's rapid reaction forces, until recently 5 Airborne Brigade consisted primarily of two

parachute battalions, two airborne infantry battalions and all necessary support arms such as engineers, logistics, signals, and artillery, with many of the latter being parachute qualified as well. However, as of September 1st, the Brigade will be stood down and amalgamated into the new 16 Air Assault Brigade, which is essentially just a fusion of our airborne and airmobile forces into one cost-cutting brigade.

The good news though is that the Paras have at last been almost completely re-equipped with Wolf model Land Rovers to replace the large number of Series III 109s and Lightweights which they were rapidly running into the ground.

In addition to their old fleet of leaf sprung Land Rovers, the paras also had a number of Defenders, including some petrol 110s plus a small quantity of 90s specially modified for parachute drops. Nicknamed piggy-back 90s, the latter had removable rear upper body panels which allowed two Land Rovers to be stacked nose up on the same medium stressed platform for parachute insertion by Hercules.

A similar batch of Tdi-powered piggy-back Wolf 90s has now also entered service, and some of these vehicles have been deployed into Kosovo. The identification feature of these vehicles, in addition to the standard Wolf features of front wing baffle boxes, side-mounted spare wheel and higher canopy line, is the horizontal cut line in the bodywork, just above the rear wheel cheeks.

Although the majority of the Wolves deployed by 5 Airborne on KFOR duties are soft tops, in both 90 and 110 wheelbase, they

fast attack vehicle

Land Rover recently responded to a United States Marine Corps (USMC) requirement advertised on June 4th for an Interim Fast Attack Vehicle (IFAV). The IFAV is required as the short term replacement solution for the current USMC Fast Attack Vehicle, a variant of the M - 151 Jeep, pending the 2004 fielding of the all new ITV/LSV (Internally Transportable Vehicle/Light Strike Vehicle.

The 62 IFAVs were required to be delivered to the US Marines by the end of 1999 at the latest. It was therefore deemed essential they be of proven commercial design. Among other more detailed requirements, which included performance and mobility criteria, the IFAV was also required to be internally transportable by all current USMC helicopters, and capable of deploying armament up to heavy machine gun calibre.

Interestingly in these days of defence expenditure cuts, official USMC documentation stated that: the following factors listed in descending order of importance shall be used to evaluate offers: (1) Operational effectiveness, (2) Supportability, and (3) Past performance. Price would be evaluated but the contract was to be awarded using what was referred to as 'best value' criteria.

The vehicle offered by Land Rover (in two versions differing only in level of specification) was very close to the WMIK (Weapon Mount Installation Kit) version of the proven Defender XD (Wolf). Designed jointly by Land Rover and Ricardo Special Vehicles, WMIK is shortly to be issued to troops of the Army's newly formed Air Assault Brigade (see *LRM* upfront April).

Land Rover have also supplied the US Rangers with the Defender SOV (Special Operations Vehicle).

In what by British defence procurement standards is exceptionally quick time, the USMC awarded the IFAV contract on July 15th. Regrettably not to Land Rover. From the five eventual contenders, the production contract was awarded to Advanced Vehicle Systems of Washington DC, USA. Valued at $6,571,244 (and 14 cents), cost of the most highly specified of the two XD WMIK offerings made by Land Rover was believed to have been some 25 percent lower than this figure.

While naturally disappointed at not securing this particularly prestigious contract, Land Rover report that the USMC had actively considered their offer. The company have accepted an offer from the USMC for a formal contract debrief on July 22nd.

Information collated from this debrief, together with the exercise as a whole, will enable Land Rover to build on the lessons learned for their future tenders for such contracts worldwide.

It is also a point worthy of mention and praise, that to answer a detailed military tender such as this in around 28 days, is no small task in itself.

Land Rover pitch for US Marine Corp vehicles but **the contract stays** at home

WMIK Wolf of the type proposed by Land Rover for the US Marine Corps

have also taken a number of hardtop 110s and several 130 Pulse ambulances. The hardtop vehicles are used primarily for communications duties and are fitted for radio (FFR).

If necessary, the one-piece moulded plastic hardtops can be removed to reduce profile, as the full canopy frame which doubles as roll-over protection is fitted underneath the hardtop. During the initial phase of the deployment, both the Paras and the Gurkhas stripped off their canopies, or at least rolled them clear of the rear compartment, to allow troops in the rear to rapidly jump out if they had to go into action.

coming soon...

It is noticeable that some of the Gurkhas' Wolf Land Rovers were fitted with forward firing general purpose machine guns (GPMGs) as a temporary expedient. A full Weapons Mount Installation Kit (WMIK) for the Wolf has been designed and trialed, but it has not yet been procured, though we understand that a decision on the eventual contractor should be made soon.

Once again, it appears that the trials and procurement chain is lagging well behind the operational requirements of the British Army, but has it not always been so?

By the time you read this, 5 Airborne Brigade should be packing up to return home at the end of a successful mission. As lightly-equipped rapid reaction troops, their job is to pave the way for the rest of the army and then retire to prepare themselves for the next potential crisis. Their job in the Balkans may be over, at least for now, but informed commentators reckon that KFOR will be a ten year commitment. If so, we can expect to see a lot more Wolves in action out there with the rest of the British Army, and with some of our allies as well.

LRM

where to go?

I know this will sound corny, but one of the best things about writing on the subject of Land Rovers just has to be the opportunity that it provides to meet genuinely nice people. Most Land Rover enthusiasts seem to be incredibly easy to get on with and, as a bonus, their hospitality is second to none.

This summer the Billing and Beltring shows fell on separate weekends for once, and I managed to make it to both events. So too did the beer loving, bacon buttie munching, private army that masquerades as the Ex-Military Land Rover Association (EMLRA), plus many of the more genteel members of the Forward Control and Lightweight Land Rover Clubs.

At the end of visits to both shows, I was nearly hoarse from talking to so many interesting owners, but I would not have missed the opportunities for all the 6X in Wiltshire. Well, maybe that's a bit of an exaggeration, but I'm sure you know what I mean.

As was to be expected, there were plenty of former military Land Rovers present at both shows. Many had been seen before, but the odd newcomer still turned up to keep everybody interested.

True to form, Billing was interesting, but this year it was the War and Peace Show at Beltring which I had been really looking forward to the most.

Over the last eight years – contrary to what the editorial in the programme said, Billing's tenth birthday is not until 2001 – I had to man a magazine stand and could not make it to Beltring as well, so I didn't realise just how much the event at the Hop Farm has grown.

Next year the shows will clash again, but I know which one I'll be at - Beltring.

Of course, Land Rovers are only a small part of the overall picture at Beltring but, unlike the first shows run by the Invicta Military Preservation Society in the early eighties when only the odd Solihull vehicle could be found, military Land Rovers must be the largest single marque in attendance these days. I reckon that the last time so many Series IIA Pink Panthers appeared in the one place must have been during SAS operations in the Middle East or Africa.

However, despite the attention that the Pinkies always grab, the most welcome visitor to both shows must have been Darren Parson's rare Luxembourg FC101 ambulance – watch Military Scene for more details.

■ Although many present and past Solihull employees provide information for my column, and the other regular **LRM** contributors also chip in whenever they can, I still need your help to provide missing parts of the jigsaw.

While visiting one of the specialist ex-military vehicle dealers recently, I came across a rather unusual Defender 130 which was being prepared for private sale.

This unique truck cab variant has a trooper body, suitable for carrying ten soldiers, and was formerly rigged with a canvas canopy over the rear. I know that it visited at least one African country on a sales tour and possibly also travelled to the Far East.

Can anybody provide any further information? **LRM**

> ## it's Beltring not Billing for me next year

In August's **LRM**, when reporting on the Royal Navy's specialist helicopter accident recovery team (the Mobile Aircraft Support Unit) I mentioned that the Royal Air Force was responsible for all fixed wing aircraft recovery. The regrettable recent crash of an RAF Harrier has provided the opportunity for a sequel on the RAF's accident recovery team far earlier than I had anticipated.

Fortunately on this occasion the circumstances were much less tragic than that earlier helicopter crash, and the Harrier pilot was able to eject just seconds before his aircraft impacted in a grain field. Despite possibly being as low as 150ft, his only injuries were spinal compressions caused by the explosive charges which launched his ejector seat.

At their RAF St Athan base, just next door to Cardiff Airport, Flight Lieutenant Jon Warren and Warrant Officer Mike Phillips, the Duty Team for the RAF Aircraft Recovery and Transportation Flight, were on one hour's notice to move in the event of an incident which might lead to the overland recovery of an RAF aircraft. No matter where in the world an RAF aircraft crashes or becomes terminally grounded, the St. Athan team has to respond, and that could even mean a flight inside an RAF Hercules for one or both of the team's white Discoverys.

The latest crash site was 270 miles from the St Athan base, in rural Lincolnshire and, despite the typical Friday afternoon traffic and the fact that the team's Discoverys do not warrant blue lights, Jon and Mike

harrier
down

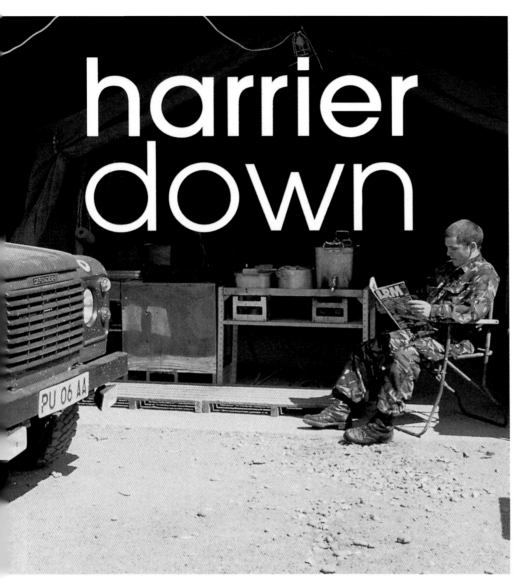

Land Rovers were heavily involved in the clean-up operation following an RAF Harrier crash

were on-site within six hours of the crash.

The spot where the Harrier crashed was not the usual near inaccessible mountainside, but a field of tall grain by the side of a busy A-road, so it was relatively easy for the emergency services to get to it. However, as fields in Lincolnshire are pretty big, the nearest access track was still several hundred yards short of the site and a circuitous route avoiding deep irrigation and drainage ditches meant that it was actually more like a couple of kilometres from tarmac to crash scene. Fortunately the ground was baked hard after a prolonged spell of good weather and the full off-road capability of the Discovery was not really needed this time – but most crash sites are less forgiving.

shell-seekers

The primary role of the RAF Aircraft Recovery and Transportation Flight (like their RN counterparts nicknamed Crash and Smash) is to recover the damaged or wrecked aircraft, for either repair or accident investigation dependent on severity, and to collect all parts and evidence from a crash scene. The first duty of the initial response team, however, is to protect personnel, incident site, and the environment from hazards.

In addition to aviation fuel, hydraulic fluids, lubricants and the other potentially hazardous liquids routinely carried on aircraft, the site also has to be cleared of any ammunition that might be present. Breathable particles of burnt carbon fibre can also pose a hazard to health, so the area must be cordoned off until these are

removed by a back-up team wearing protective suits and respirators.

By the time Jon and Mike had arrived on the scene, the pilot had long been removed by the emergency services, the fire had been extinguished and the local police had secured the site. An incident team had also been dispatched from one of the nearest RAF bases.

The Discovery Jon and Mike drove up to Lincolnshire was a five year old white Tdi with 113,000 miles on the clock, running on Michelin XM+S 244 tyres. Despite the unusual nature of its job, the vehicle is completely standard and, as it runs on civilian registration plates, there is nothing to differentiate it from any other Discovery on the road. But that, according to Jon and Mike, is the vehicle's greatest advantage. The off-the-shelf Discovery performs all the tasks required of it as a matter of routine, and they know that no matter where they take it at home or abroad, maintenance backup is readily available when required.

Though the team had no gripes about their vehicle, I did make one worrying observation. Although this Discovery had not yet reached its sixth birthday, there was an alarming amount of rust evident on the steel window columns and closer inspection showed that other areas were beginning to suffer as well. I appreciate that RAF St Athan is but a stone's throw upwind from the salty air of the Bristol Channel, but Land Rover did not build its reputation for longevity on poor coating finishes like this.

Of course a job like this takes more than just ➡

Report and pictures Bob Morrison

Main picture: To while away the periods when his services as chef were not in demand, Discovery owner Barrie Jenkinson takes in the latest issue of LRM

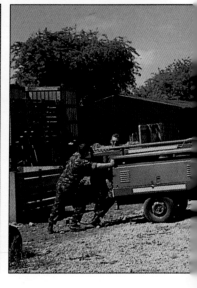

Clockwise from top left: The site where the Harrier crashed was relatively easy to get to; The AR&TF team's Discovery is just the same as any other civilian Discovery. It's covered 113,000 miles but at under six years old, is already showing signs of rust; The RAF 'White Fleet' Defenders, many of which can be spotted by their civilian paint finish and white roofs, are essentially to civilian specification; Breathable particles of burnt carbon fibre can pose a hazard to health, so the area must be cleared by a back-up team wearing protective suits and respirators

Jon and Mike and working with them are a vast team of unsung workers needed to ensure that the clear up and recovery is undertaken as quickly and skillfully as possible. At the Harrier crash site, the AR&TF team numbered about fifteen operatives, and nearby RAF Coningsby provided a similar number of bodies to man the Incident Control Post and to undertake routine support duties.

Dependent on the severity of the accident, it can take from several days up to a few weeks to clear a crash site and return it to its original condition. During this period the site has to be guarded around the clock, both to prevent the public straying into possibly hazardous areas and also to ensure that that nobody removes parts of the wreckage as 'souvenirs'.

This particular site was relatively compact for this type of incident, and most of the aircraft remained in one piece. This, and the fact that nearly all of the wreckage ended up in the one large field, made the job of picking up the bits relatively easy, though the waist-high crops outside the area of the ensuing fire did cause some problems in locating minor pieces of wreckage.

privately financed

To transport the salvage team to and from the site and to help in the general administration of the incident, a small fleet of Tdi 90 and 110 Defenders was brought in from RAF Coningsby. These vehicles, which are to near standard commercial specification, are known as White Fleet, as opposed to those dedicated to combat roles and known as Green Fleet.

White Fleet vehicles run by the MoD include saloon cars, light trucks and pickups, Transit class vans, and minibuses, plus some 4x4 utility vehicles which are

unlikely to see much service outside the immediate vicinity of military bases and establishments. In the past such vehicles were mainly bought by the MoD, but the current trend is to lease them under what is known as the Private Finance Initiative or PFI.

In this way, the Government saves on the capital outlay and can theoretically then divert public funds to more deserving areas. Just as most companies now lease staff cars rather than buying them, this concept seems to make good financial sense in theory, though whether it will be equally beneficial when applied to long service utility vehicles such as Land Rovers remains to be seen. Most of the presently fielded Land Rover White Fleet does not appear to have been procured under PFI, but it is likely that future vehicles will be sourced this way.

The current RAF White Fleet Defenders, many of which can be spotted by their civilian paint finish, plus their white roofs which are so coloured to make them more visible on airfields, are essentially to civilian specification. However, as they have to tow military equipment as part of their everyday duties they are fitted with NATO tow hitches. All carry standard military registration plates, though some assigned to specialist duties have civilian registrations as well.

The typical type found on most RAF bases, whether in short or long wheelbase variant, is van bodied and has provision for its spare wheel on the bonnet, though these are usually removed when on the airfield to give short drivers better forward visibility. Defender Station Wagon variants are also sometimes used, mainly for crew transportation duties.

The Defenders sent by RAF Coningsby to the Harrier crash site were a mix of 90 and 110 models, varying in age from about one year old to about three. Their main

Italian Defenders

Though by no means completely peaceful, the situation in Kosovo has now stabilised somewhat and an air of near normality is returning. This is mainly due to the presence of large numbers of soldiers and policemen from the NATO nations and Russia, who are patrolling the streets of the war-ravaged country.

At present the country has been divided into five military Areas of Responsibility, with Britain mainly controlling the capital Pristina and its surrounds. Germany administers the southwest sector, America and Greece control the southeast, France looks after the north and Italy holds the northwest sector.

Like Britain, the Italians use Defenders as their prime light utility and liaison vehicle. It was the Carabinieri, a paramilitary police force established in 1814, who were the first Italians to order Defenders.

The initial batch were blue hard top 90s powered by the petrol Mpi engine, but later batches used the Tdi and one of their elite sub-units also ordered military green Tdi soft tops. Today the Italian Army has also procured soft top 90s and the Italian Air Force uses hard top 110s, both with the 300 Tdi engine. **LRM**

duties were to transport the clearance teams and their equipment, including mobile generators and floodlight trailers, from the Incident Control Point and administration area out to the crash site. With an average of 30 personnel at the scene at any one time and constant traffic between the two locations, the Defenders easily proved their worth in the round-the-clock operation.

To keep the team nourished during the onerous clearance task, Coningsby also dispatched a field kitchen behind one of the Land Rovers. For about a week, Senior Aircraftman, and Discovery Tdi owner, Barrie Jenkinson provided three square meals a day for the team, from a tented kitchen set up in an open-fronted farmyard barn.

To while away the periods when his services as chef were not in demand, Barrie made sure that he picked up the latest copy of **LRM** from his newsagent before setting out on his assignment – it's amazing the places this magazine gets read. By coincidence, this was the very issue that covered the Royal Navy Crash and Smash team at work.

Little more than a week after the Harrier crashed, virtually all evidence of the incident had been removed, the top soil and crops from the contaminated area had been taken away for safe disposal, the farmer had his field back and the pilot was almost recovered from his comparatively minor injuries. The White Fleet Defenders were back at their base, and the Crash and Smash Discovery was back on standby. **LRM**

THANKS TO Squadron Leader Jim Christie from Ops Wing RAF Coningsby, who was the Incident Commander, to Jon and Mike from Crash and Smash, and to Community Relations Officers Katie, Caroline and Andy at the three RAF Bases involved in the incident.

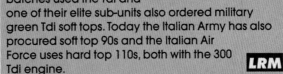

Top: A typical Italian Army specification 90 Tdi in Kosovo. Above Left: A brace of Carabinieri Defender 90s with drop-down windscreen shields. Left: Note the side-hinged tailgate, similar in design to that originally proposed for British Army Wolves, plus the spare wheel carrier

natural beauty

rang

Being a Land Rover enthusiast, and not just one of those staff journalists who happens to be writing about Britain's favourite 4x4s just because it pays the bills, I read **LRM** from cover to cover as soon as it drops through my letterbox. Last month both Les Roberts and Ross Floyd set me thinking as I read their columns.

Les, having been brought up on the farm, and having started fixing Land Rovers while still in short trousers, waxed supreme on the subject of olfactory Land Rover experiences.

To him "the sharp sulphurous smell of hot oil leaking from the gearbox and the smell of new mown grass" are nasal nectar.

To me it's the smell of fast revving engines mixed with the dusty pollen of the military training area and the acrid tang of cordite that sets my pulse racing. I wouldn't exactly say that "I love the smell of napalm in the morning" to quote from *Apocalypse Now*, but stick me behind the wheel of a Lightweight on a sunny day, on a military training area as the pyrotechnics and blanks go off, and I'm in my element.

But military exercises are not all big explosions and fast moving advances. For most of the time that a soldier is in the field, he or she is usually sitting in a trench or lying in long grass, watching the world go by.

Three of the most pleasant places that I have ever passed time on a sunny summer afternoon, excluding Illetas beach on Formentera which wins hands down every time, are the Dartmoor, Otterburn and Salisbury Plain military training areas.

Lying there in the long grass in complete silence, miles from the nearest road, surrounded by natural vegetation that has not been ravaged by over-prescription of pesticides or over-grazing by dairy cattle, one cannot fail to be impressed by the flora and fauna.

In this under-farmed state, hares grow to the size of small greyhounds, bolting just as fast when disturbed, and the biggest of dragonflies hover from shell crater to crater with wings sounding like Lynx helicopters in the still air.

Salisbury Plain a wasteland? I think not Ross.

Through my job as a military journalist, plus the village 'commoners rights' that I used to have on a part of Dartmoor, I have been privileged to drive over most of Britain's training areas. Contrary to public, and sometimes political, misconceptions, they are in the main not barren moonscapes littered with military detritus. They are actually virtually unspoiled tracts of natural beauty.

Sometimes, I even wonder if it would not be in the national interest to cordon these areas off and preserve them solely for military use, to preserve these last vestiges of natural Britain, though I admit that am too selfish to seriously suggest this.

Often now, when the range flags are down, instead of driving the length of an off-road track just because it is there and because I have the right to, I park up my vehicle and casually ramble off into a natural paradise for an hour or two.

But don't you dare insult me by calling me a Rambler!

> Morrison takes a walk on the wild side and finds there's life on the plain

LRM

During the 1991 Gulf War campaign to liberate Kuwait from Iraqi occupation, elements of the 75th Ranger Regiment, America's premier light infantry unit, worked alongside Britain's Special Forces. Usually the copious military equipment that the Americans have is both bigger and better than ours, but one particular piece of British kit caught their attention for once. It was the Land Rover 110 Desert Patrol Vehicle as used by the SAS.

The US Rangers, a unit that can be traced back to the 1670s, maintain a constant high level of readiness. Each of their three battalions is theoretically able to deploy to any part of the globe at just eleven hours notice, by land, sea or air, to conduct specialised light infantry operations, to recover trapped American nationals or military personnel, or to conduct direct action. To maintain their readiness status, Rangers regularly train for arctic, jungle, desert, mountain and amphibious operations.

To enable the Rangers to deploy so rapidly, their equipment must all be transportable by aircraft or helicopter. They must also be able to carry just about everything they need for their initial deployment on their backs, and are only allocated a small number of vehicles to assist them with land mobility. When they saw how the

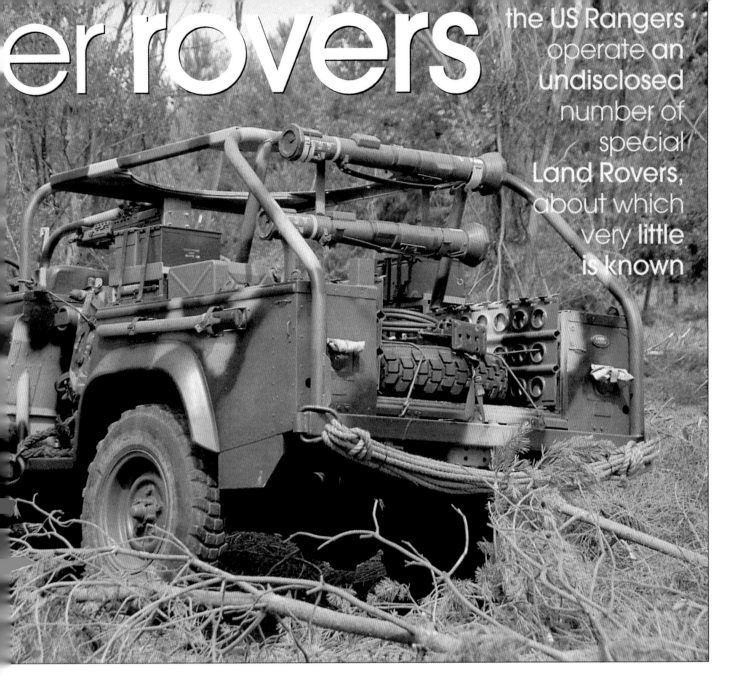

British SAS were able to mount long range patrols deep inside Iraq, with Land Rovers that could be transported inside Chinook helicopters without prior modification, they resolved to procure a fleet for themselves.

Land Rover Ltd is very coy when it comes to talking about military sales in general, and sales to foreign clients in particular, so they were not exactly forthcoming with information when I first questioned them about the Rangers contract in 1992. By this time, the guys at Fort Benning had procured at least one stock Defender for themselves, and modified it in their own workshops to meet their very specific requirements. They had then presented the finished article to Solihull and asked them to build an undisclosed number. The new vehicle would be called the Rangers Special Operations Vehicle, or R-SOV in military speak.

very hush hush

Some of my British Army contacts, especially a couple of Parachute Regiment NCOs, kept me abreast of the military gossip about the new Land Rover, and after badgering Government and Military Ops at Lode Lane, they eventually allowed me access to photograph what I believe was the prototype. They would not, however, confirm the client, the specification, or even the engine type, and I had to make my own assumptions about the

vehicle's role.

In its original form, this plain sand-coloured vehicle appeared to be based on a left-hand-drive 110 Station Wagon, minus doors and upper body, with a stout tubular frame to carry a pulpit weapons mount. Little clues like the mph speedometer and the wiring of the rear lights to act as turn indicators, hinted that Uncle Sam was indeed the end user.

On June 22, 1992, the Land Rover Special Operations Vehicle made its public debut at the Eurosatory defence exhibition in Paris, and the company press embargo on the vehicle was lifted. A couple of months before though, it had been demonstrated at Eastnor to the Defence Minister and senior officers of a potential Far East customer. Land Rover allowed me to attend this event to photograph the vehicle with all of its weapons, on condition that I did not publish them before the show. It would now appear that the vehicle present on this occasion was the company demonstration vehicle, and not the prototype that I had seen at Solihull the previous month.

This was a seriously armed vehicle of which even Mad Max would have been proud. Body colour was now two-tone sand and brown, hinting at an intended desert role. Built to carry just six men, with little concession to crew comfort, the SOV was clearly designed as

Report and pictures Bob Morrison

Sporting a distinctive three colour paint scheme the vehicle is shown here at BAEE '93

a short range rapid intervention vehicle. It did not have the extended range fuel capacity of the British, or for that matter the Australian, SAS vehicles as its main purpose was to go in with a bang, and then get out as fast as possible.

serious protection

The ten tie-down shackles around the chassis were a clear indication that the vehicle was designed for dramatic low level insertion by transport aircraft or helicopter, and the fitting of a Southdown Engineering underside protection kit showed that its users had firm plans to take it seriously off-road, or maybe down rubble-strewn streets. A front-mounted Warn winch was also fitted for self-recovery.

Other than the roll cage weapons mount, the front brush guard frame and the various equipment stowage bracketry, the SOV was essentially an off-the-shelf Defender 110 with slightly modified upper body panels. Company literature stated that both the 3.5 litre V8 petrol and the 2.5 litre 200Tdi engines could be specified, but my sources say that only the diesel engine was fitted to production vehicles.

If the Rangers did specify diesel, they were way ahead of the rest of the US Army, which has only relatively recently introduced the diesel Humvee. Incidentally, one major reason for the Rangers choosing the Land Rover is that its compact dimensions and high load capability

are completely opposite to that of the Humvee, which cannot be transported inside Chinook helicopters. Some say that the Rangers use the R-SOV acronym to describe their vehicles because that is just what they do - beat the R-SOV a Humvee.

For their first couple of years in service, the R-SOVs kept a particularly low profile, as befits vehicles designed for the special operations role, and the few who observed them confirmed that they were painted either black or a very, very dark green. Rumours abounded at the time that they had been pre-positioned around Spain to counter a perceived terrorist threat to the Barcelona Olympics, but this was never confirmed.

One trusted source has said that he witnessed two R-SOVs exiting from a taxiing Hercules during a Ranger demonstration in front of a military audience, which would account for the bumper side tie-downs, which seem excess to requirements for Chinook transportation. Another contact, a British NCO, also reported that at least one pair was used on a joint Anglo/American Airborne and Special Forces exercise in Scotland in the early mid-nineties. But other than this, sightings have been quite rare until recently.

At the end of August of this year, one of the American contributors to *Combat and Survival* magazine, which I edit, was fortunate to be allowed to work with the Rangers for a few days. He was able to photograph their Land Rovers, and I am waiting with baited breath

Clockwise from top left: The prototype vehicle in its original overall sand finish; Company demonstration vehicle on its first outing; As it is today. After being pensioned off last year and in the hands of a specialist ex-military dealer

to see the results. Some of the initial batch, which numbered somewhere between 60 and 80 units, are known to have been of a different design and had hard tops. I have been aware of the communications variant, known as the Shark, for several years now, but I was surprised to hear that there is also an ambulance version. Watch this space for more details.

in retirement

As for the company demonstrator, after appearing at many international defence shows around the globe, it was finally pensioned off last year. For most of this time it sported the catchy three-colour 'multi-theatre' camouflage scheme dreamed up by Land Rover's Mike Gould for an earlier vehicle. Still in these colours, it is now owned by a specialist ex-military vehicle dealer, who is refurbishing it with British weapons of the type carried on its late sales tours and when evaluated by units in 5 Airborne Brigade. The vehicle is currently not for sale, but is stored in a dry, warm hangar where it is protected from the ravages of time and the elements.

One little footnote, there is also a second Special Operations Vehicle demonstrator, but this one is plain green and only has three side door openings. The ring mount from the first demonstrator is currently fitted to this one. Can anybody shed any light on the history of this vehicle, whose existence I was unaware of until a couple of months ago. **LRM**

life on the ocean wave

In last month's issue, Shaun covered the development of the winterised and water-proofed variant of the Defender XD for Britain's 3 Commando Brigade and her contingent to ACE Mobile Force (Land). In August, Land Rover's project manager Graham Archer officially signed the fleet over to the Ministry of Defence, while at that very same moment many of the vehicles were being loaded onto Royal Navy ships for their first foreign deployment. Naturally **LRM** was there to watch.

Exercise ARGONAUT 99 is scheduled as a four-month deployment around the Mediterranean and the Black Sea to fly the flag for Britain and to give the Royal Navy an opportunity to work in close co-operation with both our NATO naval partners and a number of friendly states in the Middle East region. If all goes to plan, the seventeen ships will visit fourteen countries before their return at Christmas. During the exercise, the large contingent of Royal Marines and their commando-trained British Army support elements will participate in several amphibious landings.

Many of the units deployed on ARGONAUT 99, particularly the lead commando elements, have now been re-issued with the wading Wolves, so this exercise is the type's official in-service baptism (no pun intended). Most are carried on vehicle decks of the flagship commando carrier

HMS *Fearless* and the amphibious transport ships *RFA Sir Bedivere* and *RFA Sir Galahad*, but a few have also been driven onto *HMS Ocean*, which is Britain's new Helicopter Assault Ship.

The largest Royal Navy ship at sea at present, *Ocean* can simultaneously land two company battlegroups of commandos ashore, one by helicopter and the other by landing craft. The ship's four Mk V on-board landing craft have been specifically designed to carry a Wolf and trailer combination to the beachhead and her twelve Sea King helicopters can also transport Land Rovers ashore as underslung loads.

Incidentally, *Ocean* also carries a Discovery as the Captain's official transport while in foreign port.

During amphibious operations, dozens more waterproofed Wolves can be brought to the beach by the larger utility landing craft, which are transported in the large flooding dock at the stern of *Fearless*. In the follow-on phases even more Land Rovers will arrive on Mexeflote powered pontoons from *Sir Galahad* and *Sir Bedivere*. On the Egyptian phase of the deployment in particular, where the gently shelving sandy beaches can prevent the landing craft getting in as close as might be wished, the sight of all these Wolves wading ashore through several feet of surf should be particularly impressive. **LRM**

what's in a name?

If I were to take an old 70 Series Toyota Landcruiser and stick Land Rover Defender badges all over it, it might fool some of the general public, but I doubt if many readers of this magazine would fall for it.

Being an enthusiast first and foremost, I check out the other two Land Rover magazines for articles of interest, and I am sure many of you do too. It was therefore with some surprise that I came across a feature bearing my name in the November 1999 issue of LRO.

I say surprise as, other than the articles already in the pipeline at that time, I have not contributed to LRO since receiving a pleasant little letter last Christmas informing me that my regular monthly contributions were no longer needed due to the "forthcoming recession".

After more than ten years as a military correspondent for the magazine I was slightly sad to be dumped so unceremoniously, but as Richard Howell-Thomas almost immediately offered me this regular column in **LRM** I quickly cheered up. You see, on this magazine I can pretty much write what I like, when I like, as a like.

Anyway, let's get back to this mysterious article in LRO. It certainly appeared to be some of my scribbling, but my memory of it seemed slightly hazy. Too many beefburgers?

Fortunately, a quick scan through my hard disc soon found the answer. This work was actually an additional feature that I wrote in September 1996 for a Discovery Special in the October 1996 issue.

As is only to be expected of a three year old piece, it is now horrendously out of date, but LRO must have been happy enough to publish it in this form as they did not ask me to revise it.

As for the photographs, two of them also date from 1996. The photos originally submitted with this article, and there were no less than a dozen of them, actually showed Discoverys in more conventional military use, better illustrating the original feature.

As for the photo of Kosovo-bound vehicles, these vehicles actually gifted by Land Rover for non-military use.

I hope this outdated article, as published in LRO, has not caused embarrassment or offence to the officers and/or individuals in the photos, and has not misled any readers.

Just in case any other lost articles appear in LRO bearing my name, I would like to take this opportunity to publicly state that **LRM** is now the only mass circulation Land Rover magazine that I write for under the name of Bob Morrison.

■ While on the subject of other Land Rover magazines, you might have noticed that one of them claims to have been exclu-

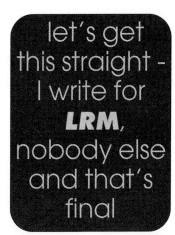

let's get this straight - I write for **LRM**, nobody else and that's final

sively invited to the launch of 16 Air Assault Brigade, which is Britain's new rapid deployment force. Well if being one of eighty or so in the media pack counts as an exclusive invite, I suppose I must have had one too.

The previous day though, I must have been Billy No-Mates, as I was one of only two civilian photographers on hand to cover the dress rehearsal as well. Hence my different camera angles.

■ Finally, I'm afraid that the caption gremlin struck on my Ranger Rover feature last month. The main picture was actually of the R-SOV demonstrator as it exists today. Watch out for pix of three different R-SOV variants, on a recent exercise, next month's issue of **LRM**.

LRM

Friday

September 3 saw the formal launch of Britain's 16 Air Assault Brigade at Wattisham in Suffolk. A fusion of the British Army's former airborne and heliborne brigades, the new formation is one of the key elements in Britain's rapid deployment forces. Naturally, Land Rovers play a major part in this role.

If proof were needed, the speed with which elements of the former 5 Airborne Brigade were able to deploy as peace enforcers into Kosovo early this summer, underscored just how vital lightly equipped and well trained troops are in this rapidly changing world as we approach the third millennium. Without the superb professionalism of Britain's airborne troops, particularly the men of the Parachute Regiment and the Gurkhas, plus their supporting elements, the transition to peace in the war torn province would not have gone so smoothly.

Within just a few of days of arriving in the Balkans region, the Paras and Gurkhas were to find themselves acting as spearhead troops for the multinational peace enforcing mission, now universally known as KFOR. Under the eyes of the world's newsreel cameras, the lead elements piled into helicopters on the Macedonian border, slung their Land Rovers underneath, and leapfrogged up the main arterial road in Kosovo's capital, Pristina. Behind them, some of their colleagues

new vehicle, new role

to meet the world's ever changing **military needs the** Army and its **Land Rovers are** changing too. **Bob Morrison** investigates the new **16 Air Assault Brigade** and their **WMIK**

advanced on the ground in a fleet of Land Rovers, and within hours the capital had been liberated. For the next few weeks, Gurkha and Para Land Rover patrols would be a common sight around the British administered sector of Kosovo. Likewise, when the Australian led, and UN backed, peace mission went into East Timor to prevent civil war escalating in September, British troops with Land Rovers were among the first to arrive by air. The lead elements were from Britain's Special Forces, and they were quickly followed by Gurkhas stationed in the Far East, but the operational procedures they used were the same as some of those demonstrated by 16 Air Assault Brigade, less than three weeks before. By coincidence, a Gurkha battalion of the British Army is permanently garrisoned in Brunei, just a few hours flying time from Darwin where the international force was assembled. Had the Gurkhas not been so close at hand, it is likely that elements of 16 Air Assault would have been deployed instead.

pathfinder patrols

At the 16 Air Assault Brigade demonstration on September 3, when 24 Airmobile Brigade was formally mothballed to allow some of its component units to form the core of the new Brigade, a typical rapid deployment scenario was laid on for the visitors, including Princes Charles, William and Harry, plus about 80 members of the Press. The action part of the display

commenced with the HALO (high altitude low opening) parachute insertion of two four-man Pathfinder patrols. These highly skilled paratroopers, who would secretly glide into the operational theatre at least a day ahead of the main force, would be the brigade's initial eyes and ears on the ground.

Until recently, the Pathfinders have used stripped down and specially modified versions of the Defender 90, but they are soon to receive WMIK versions of the Defender HS model, or Wolf as it is now universally known. Likewise, all lead elements of 16 Air Assault are being issued with Wolves, and those units tasked in an infantry role will also receive WMIK versions. For this initial display, as only one WMIK demonstrator was available, the Pathfinders borrowed a couple of green painted 110 DPVs (desert patrol vehicles) of the type used by their friends based in Hereford. The DPVs were used primarily to recover the Pathfinders from the battlefield prior to the commencement of the main assault.

The demonstration scenario was based on the surprise insertion of an infantry battlegroup to capture an enemy held airfield, which could then be used as the Forward Operating Base for the brigade's paratroopers and anti-armour helicopter units. To keep the enemy pinned down, RAF fast jets bombed troop positions on the airfield, without damaging the vital runways and the supporting infrastructure. This was ➡️

Report & pictures Bob Morrison

Left: The big Chinook makes light work of this underslung load of Land Rover and rubber fuel bladder. Above: Only one demonstrator WMIK was available for the demonstration

Top: WMIK demonstrator kitted out and ready to roll, quickly, to anywhere in the world. Above left: The new brigade has a full complement of supporting units such as medics, gunners, engineers, mechanics and logisticians. Above right: This Military Police hard top Wolf is shown fully rigged for heliborne operations

followed by a mass attack by the brigade's missile-armed helicopters, today Lynxes, but the new Apache will eventually be assigned to the brigade.

As the surviving enemy soldiers kept their heads down, a brace of RAF Hercules transport aircraft swept in almost unnoticed and screeched to a halt in the classic manoeuvre known as the Khe Sahn approach. Before the defenders had time to react, a Scimitar armoured vehicle and a Land Rover shot out of the back of each firing weapons and closely followed by a platoon of paratroopers. One of the Land Rovers was fitted with the WMIK prototype and carried both a forward firing GPMG (general purpose machine gun) plus a Browning .50cal heavy machine gun on its pulpit mount. This method of capturing an airfield - even a grass strip gliding club airfield could be suitable as an operating base - is known as a tactical air-land operation or TALO, and was perfected by the old 5 Airborne Brigade.

armed wolves

With the airfield's defenders defeated, a second wave of troops was flown in by RAF Chinook and Puma helicopters. To demonstrate the brigade's mobility, a hard top Wolf was flown in underslung from the Chinook, along with a rubber fuel bladder for refuelling the helicopters. After the demonstration a Military Police hard top Wolf, fitted with radios, was displayed fully

rigged for heliborne operations. Several other Wolves belonging to the supporting arms were also on show.

In addition to two parachute battalions, the new brigade also has a third brigade of infantry soldiers, as well as supporting units such as medics, gunners, engineers, mechanics and logisticians. All of these men and women are trained in heliborne operations as a matter of course. The gunners, and those sections of the other units tasked primarily with working in close support of the brigade's two parachute battalions, are also qualified paratroopers. To give all of these units maximum battlefield mobility, all are equipped with a small number of Land Rovers, mainly Defender 110HS models. The Parachute battalions also field their own version of the Defender 90HS, which has removable rear sides and is capable of being double stacked on a medium stressed platform (MSP) for parachute insertion.

As **LRM** goes to press, 16 Air Assault Brigade has deployed on its first full scale training exercise. Under operational control of the newly formed Joint Helicopter Command as of October 1, it is now ready for deployment to any crisis region, should the need arise. Hopefully though, the new brigade and its equally new Land Rovers will never have to be deployed in anger, and the next millennium will see less strife than the last century of this one.

LRM

fightback

Land Rover are beginning to win back markets lost in the early eighties

From the mid eighties until quite recently, Land Rover lost a lot of military sales ground in Europe to the Gelandewagen or G-wagen, built by Steyr Daimler Puch in Austria, but badged and sold as a Mercedes Benz for NATO markets. Recently, however, the Defender has begun to fight back.

Unlike their army colleagues the Dutch Marines, who train closely with Britain's Royal Marines, have remained loyal to the Land Rover marque since about 1985, and they are now beginning to field some of the latest Wolf models. Another old military Land Rover customer in Europe has recently returned to the fold, and these vehicles have just rolled off Solihull's production line as this column goes to press.

However, it is the Italian Army which is converting to Defenders faster than anyone else at the moment.

Since the fifties, the Italian automobile industry has always been able to produce competent light utility 4x4 vehicles for its own armed forces, plus the armies of a few friendly foreign governments. When it entered service in the mid-seventies, the 1107AD version of the Fiat Campagnola was actually better in some respects than the Series III, and for a while it caused a fair bit of concern at Solihull. Today, though, the market for military specification light utility vehicles has shrunk to such an extent that production of a new type purely for national use is no longer a viable option, and countries are having to consider either buying off the shelf, or assembling foreign vehicle kits locally to achieve at least some degree of national labour input. When looking for a replacement for their now long in the tooth Campagnolas, this time the Italian forces bit the bullet and decided to buy foreign for once.

It was actually the Italian Carabinieri, a sort of internal security force, who first procured Defenders in quantity, but their army colleagues were not far behind. The latest Italian users of the brand are the Special Forces, Italy's equivalent of our SAS, who have just procured a batch of twenty Tdi-powered Defenders, fitted with a variation of the Weapons Mount Installation Kit or WMIK.

This kit was originally designed to meet a British Army requirement for a means of mounting a forward firing machine gun ahead of the vehicle commander, and a heavy weapon on

a ring mount over the rear load bed. The main provisos of the specification being that the kit could be quickly and easily fitted to a standard Defender 110HS (Wolf) and that the design dimensions did not exceed the base vehicle's airportability envelope. In other words, it should still be able to fit inside aircraft and helicopters for rapid deployment.

The Italian version of the WMIK, or the Rapid Deployment Vehicle (RDV) as Land Rover calls it, is based on the standard Italian military specification Defender 90, to ensure full compatibility with the rest of the fleet. Converted by Ricardo Special Vehicles, who jointly developed the WMIK concept with Land Rover, these vehicles are devoid of windscreen, side doors and top hamper. A specially-constructed, low profile roll cage both provides crew protection in the event of a rollover and acts as a base for the pulpit style ring mount for the main armament. The forward machine gun is mounted on a post beside the front passenger side forward door pillar. Though not shown, a removable foul weather protection kit has also been specified by the Italians, hence the unusual lashing points.

The vehicle's third crew member is accommodated on a rearward facing seat, with four point harness, off set to one side of the load bed. Tie down points are provided along the other side of the bed. At present the Italian vehicles only have a standard front passenger seat, but it is understood that the contract may be modified to include the neat, elevating, commander's seat found on the prototype British Army vehicles. Other modifications include a side swinging rear stowage basket in place of a drop tailgate, and soft mesh panniers over both wheel wells.

It should be noted that the vehicle we photographed was in the final stages of assembly, and the complete gun mounts were not fitted. The rear ring mount had only just been attached, specifically for our photo session, and was only loosely held in place with a couple of bolts. Naturally, as the vehicle only had a handful of kilometres on the clock when we borrowed it for the photos, we were not able to give it a thorough road test but, like all 300 Tdi Defenders, it was both light and responsive. During normal cornering, the heavy duty roll cage and weapon platform seemed to make little appreciable difference to road handling. **LRM**

Report and pictures Bob Morrison

LRM would like to express thanks to Ricardo Special Vehicles for their help and their time. A feature on the British Army WMIK Wolves will follow once the type is fully in service.

Top: The Italian Special Forces, their equivalent of our SAS, have just procured a batch of twenty Tdi powered Defenders, fitted with a variation of the British Army's Weapons Mount Installation Kit or WMIK. Top left: The third crew member sits on a rear facing seat and is restrained by a four point harness. Centre left: The forward machine gun is mounted on this post beside the front passenger side forward door pillar. Left: The vehicles were converted by Ricardo Special Vehicles who with Land Rover jointly developed WMIK

world sales

I was interested to read some gossip about military sales in Southern Africa in the October issue of the Ex-Military Land Rover Association's newsletter. It appears that one of the club's contacts in South Africa spotted what he took to be a Defender 90XD (Solihull name), TUL HS (MoD name) or Wolf 90 (squaddie name) at a car show. The vehicle was one of a small fleet ordered by Botswana, for defence duties, and somebody took a chance in passing it off as a standard Defender on the assumption that nobody would know the difference. Wrong.

Actually, the vehicle in question was built on a South African specification Defender chassis, not the special eXtra Duty chassis built in Solihull, though it did have some Wolf body panels and some of the additional strengthening associated with the latest batch of British Army vehicles. My sources, however, who are 100 percent reliable, assure me that it was not a Wolf as such, but a Defender tailored to the client's specific requirements. I believe that Botswana is about to replace quite a large number of its light and medium utility vehicles in the not too distant future. I will be keeping an eye on the situation as it develops, and have no doubt that their experience with the reliability and flexibility of this small fleet of hybrid Defenders will work in Land Rover's favour.

Incidentally, New Zealand is also about to replace its ageing fleet of military utility vehicles. These are 1982 vintage Land Rover Stage One V8s, which have now exceeded the twelve year life expectancy by some five years. Numbering 567 in total, the Land Rover fleet has given excellent

> ## spotted in South Africa, a Defender dressed in Wolf's clothing

service, but it is now proving to be expensive to maintain. Nowadays diesel is the standard operating fuel for most armies and the New Zealand MoD says that petrol is often not available in the area of operations, so the replacement will have to be diesel powered.

As part of a NZ$500 million re-equipment programme, which includes armoured personnel carriers and fire support vehicles, the Land Rovers will be replaced by 423 Light Operational Vehicles. Of these 115 will be civilian specification pick-ups, but the remainder will be to full military specification, with 51 having armour protection and eight being ambulances. It is believed that Land Rover is actively chasing this contract. However, due to the sudden involvement in East Timor, 30 Holden Rodeos (Isuzus) were purchased off the shelf for NZ troops participating in peacekeeping operations. These vehicles will form part of the 115 vehicle 'white' fleet.

Many military purchasers attempt to achieve a degree of national labour input when buying military vehicles. It was therefore with interest that I read the following words from the NZ Minister of Defence, the Hon. Max Bradford. "This project has potential to offer New Zealand industry work in the areas of assembly, testing, training and on-going maintenance." Fortunately, the construction of the Defender lends itself easily to kit assembly.

It had been my intention to go to Egypt to cover Britain's amphibious forces in exercise BRIGHT STAR 99 and to see the new 'Wading Wolves' come ashore, but circumstances ruled it out. Just as well that I didn't go, as a colleague tells me that Egyptian troops came ashore instead.

LRM

In November we looked at the origins of the elusive US Rangers Special Operations Vehicle. This month we bring you exclusive photos of these intriguing vehicles on a recent training exercise in the United States.

It's the little questions that are always the hardest to solve. For example, are the US Rangers Special Operations Vehicles black or green?

Of course only a military Land Rover 'anorak', or should that be Land Rover 'fleece', would actually care. So it must say something about my peculiar mental condition that I have actually let this trivial question bother me for the last six or seven years. Recently, I thought I was about to find the definitive answer, in the form of a dozen photographs of the elusive beasts, but I'm afraid I am now even more confused. It appears that the answer is yes; they are black or green.

A few weeks back, my American military journalist colleague Joel B. Paskauskas II spent some time on a training exercise with the Rangers and was allowed to photograph their fully equipped R-SOVs. When Joel's transparencies arrived, I was so interested in them that I immediately set up my slide projector so that I could view them at maximum resolution, but on the colour scheme this posed more questions than it gave answers. In no two shots were the colours identical, and without seeing them in the flesh, so to speak, I cannot give a definitive answer. The best that I can come up with is that the standard vehicles have either a very dark green base coat which has been completely over-sprayed with black, which has then worn off on some areas of some

dark secret

we publish exclusive pictures of **the elite US Rangers** at work **with** their unique **Land Rovers**

vehicles, or that they were originally painted in two-tone black and very dark green camouflage, and this has now weathered. I favour the second option.

Until receiving Joel's slides, the only three photos that I had seen of in-service R-SOVs were of a standard vehicle on display at an Association of the US Army (AUSA) show, published in the limited circulation company magazine Land Rover Fleet World three or four years ago, and a couple of Myles Murphy photos of the 'Shark' communications variant. This first photo was so small and dark that it showed little of the vehicle's detail, and I could not find out very much about the hard top 'Shark', because of its role. Careful examination of these recent photos has yielded a treasure trove of new information for the military enthusiast.

basic configuration
We now know that there are at least four variants of Land Rover in use with the Rangers, who are considered to be the elite of the US Army and are rated second only to Delta, which is the equivalent of our SAS. The bulk of the R-SOV's are of standard configuration - what I will call the rapid intervention variant for ease of identification - and are similar in basic configuration to the Demonstrator featured in the November 1999 issue of **LRM**. The ambulance version is also of quite similar body shape, that is it is open topped with a roll cage, but it has no weapons mounts and is configured to carry up to six stretchers. The third variant, nicknamed the 'Shark' because of its small fin-like blade antenna, is a three-door hard top for command and communications

duties. The last version discovered to date, but of which we do not yet have photos, is the mortar carrier.

From close examination of the photos, it is evident that the basic body construction of the rapid intervention variant is virtually identical to the demonstrator, being based on a door-less Defender 110 Station Wagon lower body and having a seven point ring mount support frame which doubles as a roll cage. There are two small stowage boxes, with perforated sides, above the front wings and supported by a brushguard frame extending up from the front bumper. This brushguard has an expanded metal mesh panel to protect the radiator grille area, and a pair of infra-red driving lights are fixed to the top, inboard of the boxes. Racks for three jerrycans are fitted to each of the rear side body panels, which are cut down to below the level of the usual barrelling. Though not readily apparent from Joel's photos, it would appear that the spare wheel is carried on the rear load bed floor.

The vehicle's main armament is carried on a ring or pulpit mount, similar in type to that found on the Humvee. Weapons carried on this mount can be either the .50cal M2 heavy machine gun or the Mk19 40mm grenade launcher. A tripod for the M2 is carried on the bonnet. The vehicle commander is armed with a forward firing machine gun, which in these photos is a 7.62mm FN MAG. This is the Belgian medium machine gun used by the British Army under the GPMG designation. The Land Rover R-SOV demonstrator was usually configured with weapons manufactured by Royal Ordnance, and it also had various weapons ➡

Report
Bob
Morrison

Pictures
Joel
Paskauskas

Far left top: Typical rapid intervention variant of the R-SOV with .50cal main machine gun. Far left centre: The ambulance variant, with two stretchers on the bonnet frame. Far left bottom: The Shark command and communications vehicle is top secret. Above: Typical two-vehicle R-SOV patrol - the one on the left totes a Mk19 launcher

transit racks around the body and roll frame; this stowage concept does not seem to have been carried through to the American vehicles. There is also no evidence of the anti-armour weapons carrier on the rear of the cage and other minor details such as the canvas and velcro light covers are not on the production vehicles.

seven on board

In its original form, the Demonstrator was configured to take six personnel, two in the cab, two outward facing behind them and two inward facing to the rear. There was also a simple strap seat under the main armament, which I assumed would be manned by one of the rear four personnel. In one of Joel's photos a vehicle is fully crewed with seven men, but I suspect that this would not happen operationally. I suspect that vehicles would actually work in pairs with four, or maybe five at a stretch, personnel on board each.

As previously mentioned, the ambulance version appears to be quite similar to the rapid intervention variant, but it is actually built on a standard three-door Defender lower body, with rear sides cut down to the same level. The roll cage is also of slightly different configuration, with two central, longitudinal rear members instead of the four-point rear frame, to allow two stretchers to be carried down each side. Two more stretchers can be carried crosswise on the bonnet.

Presumably a medical orderly would travel on the rear load bed between the tubular frame. Various medical packs are slung about the stretcher support racks, which have quick release catches to secure the stretcher handles. No winch is fitted to the ambulance, and its spare wheel is carried on the front.

The 'Shark' is a command, control and communications vehicle attached to the Rangers unit's headquarters. Its precise role is shrouded in secrecy, and it even has sideways pointing infrared lights. It is festooned with antennae, both pole and blade types, and carries cable drums front and rear. Like the rapid intervention variant, it has a front-mounted winch and it also carries a tow cable coiled on the front bumper. The upper rear body of this version is more rectangular than the Solihull design, and the roof has square edges. The rear third of the roof is slightly sloping, presumably to allow it to fit comfortably inside a Chinook helicopter (on the standard soft-top 110, the rear canopy frame has to be dropped if the vehicle is carried internally). No side doors are fitted, but it is safe to assume that the rear body is totally self contained to allow personnel to work with lights on. Body colour appears to be all-black over a green base, but some of the black paint appears to have weathered.

Due to the nature of their work, which is mainly undertaken well away from the glare of TV lights and out of range of cameras, and often in the dark as well, it

is unclear whether the R-SOVs have ever been deployed operationally. With what is believed to be as few as fifty or so Land Rovers available to 75th Ranger Regiment at any one time, it is clear that not all units can be equipped with the type, so their use must be pretty specialist. When Company B of the 3rd Ranger Battalion deployed to Somalia in 1993, on what is believed to have been the Rangers' last major operational deployment, there was no mention of them having taken any of the R-SOV fleet, though it is believed that the type had been accepted for service well before this date. This tends to lend credence to the belief that they are only intended for deep interdiction 'in and out' missions.

we want to know more

Although the R-SOV Defenders have been in service for over six years, and are probably past the mid point of their intended life cycle, little has appeared about them in print. It will be interesting to see what they have actually been up to for this period, because the photos clearly show that they have not been sitting around in dry storage. If any of our American military readers, or for that matter any British Army personnel working alongside the US Army, have come across these interesting vehicles we would love to know more.

■ Thanks to Joel B Paskauskas II for going out of his way to capture the R-SOVs on film for us. **LRM**

INTERFET
Discoverys

After the initial blaze of publicity when the Australian-led International Force East Timor (INTERFET) successfully deployed under UN mandate in late September to restore peace and security, media attention has dropped off. British military personnel, mainly from the Brunei based 2nd Royal Gurkha Rifles, are still operational with INTERFET, however, and naturally they have been using Land Rovers for patrolling.

In addition to their standard Defenders, the Gurkhas have also made use of a fleet of Discoverys for a variety of duties. Although the precise origin of this fleet of civilian specification vehicles is not known, though being right hand drive they could have emanated from Australia, they are the ones that were used by UNAMET personnel supervising the independence elections at the beginning of September. They are first series Discoverys in stock civilian colours, but with white bonnets carrying the UN initials and logo, plus white UN letters on the roof.

The Gurkhas must have quickly realised that these Land Rovers would be an excellent addition to their vehicle pool, because they

had hardly established themselves on the island before they were putting them to good use.

The first one that I spotted, pressed into Gurkha service, seen on a TV news clip, had its rear windows removed and a couple of loudspeakers installed, so that information could be communicated to the civilian population.

A couple of days later, the first UN relief convoy of trucks to Cairui was headed up by five Discoverys and a Defender 110. The lead Discovery sported the crossed kukri insignia of the Gurkas as a window sticker.

■ Another interesting Land Rover spotted in service in East Timor was a Perentie ambulance. Other than the trials and demonstration vehicles, this is the only occasion that I have seen an ambulance body on the 6x6 Perentie chassis. Unfortunately though, only part of the rear body appears in the photo of Australian medics evacuating a wounded civilian, but it is still instantly recognisable. Standard Aussie Perentie Land Rovers have appeared from time to time on newsreel coming out of theatre, but I am still searching for good still photos.

If any of our antipodean readers can help, I would be much obliged. **LRM**

Crown Copyright photo: Sgt Ian Liptrot

Australian MoD photo

if only...

Last month's article by James Taylor on those special Swedish Series Ones set me thinking. It was a subject I was not too familiar with, though I had seen photos of Anna-Clara and thought she was a one-off. Like the Tickford Station Wagon, also covered in the last issue, the aesthetics of these post war period vehicle designs really appeals to me.

If I come up with all six numbers on the National Lottery, I think I'll try to buy myself one of the pick up models. Incidentally, if any readers know of photos or illustrations of the Swedish Navy prototype, please get in touch.

While on the subject of my oft-dreamed about lottery win, I have started to make another wish list. Top of the list in the military division has got to be the Defender 90 Multi Role Combat Vehicle (MRCV) demonstrator. I know exactly where this vehicle is stored, and my bid will go in at ten past eight on the night that my numbers come up.

To keep the MRCV company in Bob's Private Land Rover Museum, I will also have to persuade the Australian SAS to part with one of their Perentie 6x6 Remote Area Patrol Vehicles. Nearly ten years ago I got the chance to drive one of these off-road in the UK, and the memory lives with me to this day.

A Series IIa 88 Lightweight and a Series III 109 Portee, complete with Wombat anti armour gun, would come next, closely followed by a GS 101 and deactivated 105mm Light Gun.

Well, I can but dream.

Then, of course, I would have to track down one of the Wadham Stringer Crash Rescue ambulances used on Royal Naval Air Stations before the introduction

of the One-Two-Seven. To accompany this, I would have to pick up a Gloster Saro TACR1 fire tender. Oh, and then, the collection would not be complete without a Series IIB Army Fire Service 110 tender and a Series III 109 TACR1. I don't think I'll bother with an SAS pinky as they are now getting to be just a little common, but an SAS Minerva would be a different matter.

If I won all that dosh though, I wouldn't let it affect me. Well not much, anyway. I certainly would not give up my day job as I love writing about military Land Rovers too much.

However, I would make life in the field a little bit more comfortable. My daily transport would be a stretched Discovery, built by Special Vehicles along the lines of the Discovery Ambulance. In the back, it would have a bed along one side, opposite the passenger side rear door and a computer workstation, complete with modem and satellite phone, on the other side.

Hang on a minute, if I keep adding to the list I won't have any money left to put fuel in their tanks. I reckon I had better call it a day - though if a Series One Royal Review vehicle comes up for grabs, I could well be tempted

■ By the way, ignore all that rubbish about haggis John Hong was sprouting last month. Scotsmen know that the beast is a three legged creature that resides on the upper slopes of the Cairngorms. And to prove it, I have got a stuffed example sitting on top of my computer monitor as I type this.

Also, proper whisky is spelt without an e.

Sassenachs!

LRM

> I won't have any money left to put fuel in the tanks

the Series III will soon be history as far as the British Ministry of Defence are concerned

In August 1997 the UK Ministry of Defence announced that the British Army's fleet of Series III Land Rovers was shortly to be withdrawn from service. By the end of the year, somewhere in the region of 4,500 vehicles had been gathered in from garrisons and establishments around Great Britain, Northern Ireland and Germany, ending an era that lasted for more than a quarter of a century.

When Solihull introduced the cosmetically improved Series III Land Rover model in the autumn of 1971, the marque was already firmly established as Britain's prime light and medium utility vehicle in both the quarter ton and half ton payload categories. A large number of Series IIa military specification vehicles based on the standard 88 inch wheelbase chassis, plus a quantity of the 1967 model 88 inch airportable version, fulfilled the light utility requirement, but the majority of the Army's Land Rover fleet at the time were military specification 109 inch wheelbase Series IIa models. By the mid seventies, the vast majority of this Series IIa fleet was withdrawn from service, though some specialist variants soldiered on until 1997. As anticipated, the first batch of Series III 109 inch models proved to be perfectly adequate for its required military role, and for some twelve years this model continued to roll of Solihull's production lines to keep Britain's armed forces mobile around the globe. The standard 88 inch military model was, however, phased out in favour of the airportable Lightweight model on the same basic chassis.

During the seventies, the British Army did not participate in any major wars overseas, but countless minor

honourable discharge

campaigns saw Her Majesty's soldiers in action around the globe. Some of these, such as the part played by British soldiers in keeping Oman from falling under communist influence, drew little public attention. Other actions, like the defence of British interests in Cyprus during the 1974 Turkish invasion, hit the headlines. In all instances, the humble Land Rover was usually to be found beavering away in the background. However, it was closer to home in Ulster and on the continent with the British Army of the Rhine (BAOR) that most of the new Series III fleet was to see most service. Eventually, the security situation in Ulster was to deteriorate to such an extent that only armoured Land Rovers could be used on the streets in any great numbers, but in Germany the Series III fleet performed sterling service right up to, and beyond, the fall of the Iron Curtain at the very end of the eighties.

electrically supressed

In standard form, the military Series III 109 was available as either a three door hard top or a two door soft top with drop tailgate, though in time other variations entered service for specific duties. Both the hard and soft top versions could be found in either the fitted for radio (FFR) or the general service (GS) roles, and later in the production run a less heavily militarised civilian (CL) variant was also produced for rear echelon duties. The FFR version could usually be easily identified from its GS counterparts as it had provision for antennae box mounts on the front wings and posts for mounting two more antennae on the upper body sides between the

front door pillars and the rear wheels. As a rough rule of thumb, early GS versions had 12V electrics and most FFR variants had 24V provision with a 90 ampere rectified and suppressed electrical system, but as ever more variations entered service, specifications varied widely. In nearly all cases though, the FFR carried a removable radio table behind the rear bulkhead, under which could be found a pair of 100 amp radio batteries in a large metal box.

In addition to the special electrical systems and the radio antennae mounts found on the FFR variants, the military version of the Land Rover also had numerous specification changes to suit its demanding roles, though most of these were not instantly noticeable. The special IRR matt paint finish which aided concealment from infra red observation devices and the common two tone (usually) green and black camouflage scheme were instant clues to the vehicle's military ownership, as were the two digit/two letter/two digit registration plates, but there were other less obvious clues, such as bumper pattern and stowage clips for pick and shovel.

At the front of military spec Land Rovers, the bumper usually sported two additional short sections on top as wing protectors. These allowed unladen Land Rovers to be close parked head to tail without body panels being damaged and also enabled one vehicle to push start another without causing damage. At the rear, a parallel profile strengthened rear cross member was nearly always fitted, and the swivelling NATO towing jaws fitted to this allowed an impressive towing capacity. It was not uncommon for RAF and ➤

Words and pictures Bob Morrison

Above left: Rare windowed hard top FFR, with side windows painted out, umpiring an exercise in Germany.
Above: A late model CL specification in Germany, 1998, identifiable by stepped rear cross member, filler cap and grab handles

➤

Clockwise from top left: Though hard tops were more common on air bases, the RAF also use some soft top GS models, like this one at RAF Chivenor; REME hard top GS, on attachment to the Honourable Artillery Company; Stripped down Yeomanry soft top FFRs snake out of Keilder Forest; The Gulf War was the Series III's last major combat outing; A typical soft top FFR during an exercise on Salisbury Plain. Inset right: 5 Airborne Brigade soft top FFR, stripped down, being loaded onto a pallet for parachute drop

RNAS Land Rovers to be used as tractors for aircraft weighing eight tonnes or more. A pair of bumperettes on the rear cross member, instead of the grab handles found on civvy vehicles, prevented the NATO tow hitch from one vehicle denting the bumper of the one behind.

Another external give away that a vehicle was to military specification could be the lack of a petrol filler in the rear right body side. Most military spec Land Rovers had twin under seat fuel tanks, filled by removing the seat cushions, but once again this was not a hard and fast rule, as some later small batches procured for specific tasks had hybrid specifications. Incidentally, although the vast majority of Series III Land Rovers were petrol powered, some diesel Series III military models also saw service. The standard army way of differentiating fuel requirements was to paint the filler cap red for petrol and yellow for diesel.

nothing fancy

The engine almost invariably fitted in British Army Series III Land Rovers was the 4 cylinder 2286cc model which produced 70bhp at 4000rpm and 120lb/ft of torque at 1500rpm. Maximum road speed was usually given as 65mph or 105km/hr, and operating range on two ten gallon (45 litre) tanks was expected to be in the region of 350 miles (560km). Small quantities of V8 and 6 cylinder powered vehicles did see army service in

special roles, though usually not with the standard hard top or soft top body designs. Most diesels were used by the Royal Navy and, occasionally, the Royal Air Force, plus it is believed that the Army had a few for use in explosives handling areas.

The other major specification difference between military and civilian Land Rovers was the lighting system. On the battlefield at night, nothing gives away a vehicle's position quicker than accidental turning on of the lights. To alleviate this, all front line military Land Rovers have a special dual role lighting system, operated by a large turn switch on the dashboard. The normal sidelight and headlight states are used for peacetime day-to-day driving, but on the battlefield these can be over ridden. When wartime operation is necessary, either low visibility convoy lights or complete blackout state can be selected.

Dependent on precise settings, the brake and indicator lights can be made inoperative to prevent accidental illumination. Driving in these conditions at night requires intense driver concentration and a fair bit of skill. Nowadays, night vision devices can be worn by drivers operating in blackout conditions, but reduced perspective calls for equally high driving skills.

The CL version of the Series III 109, which entered service much later into the production run, was essentially a civilian specification vehicle painted in military

Below: The galvanised single bumper is the first indicator that this Royal Naval Air Station 109 is to CL specification.

colours and with a bare minimum of militarisation. Civilian pattern front bumper and rear grab rails were standard, as was the normal stepped rear cross member. The lighting system was identical to that of the ordinary Land Rover, as were the electrics, and many vehicles were even finished in standard glossy dark blue or dark green paint finish. However, bonnet mounts were usually fitted for the carriage of the spare wheel.

the wheel turns

Just as in due course the Series III replaced earlier models, it too has now been replaced by a more modern Land Rover design. The introduction of the One-Ten in the mid eighties, and the 110 Defender at the end of the decade, heralded the demise of the Series III 109 and saw the type being increasingly relegated to rear echelon duties. Some units though, particularly the Paras, hung onto their petrol powered 109s right up to the end. The Gulf War was really the Series III 109's swansong, and very few were to see service in Croatia or Bosnia, though small numbers were operationally deployed to African countries for peacekeeping missions in the nineties.

In preparing this feature, I took a look back to the section of my photo library that covers the late eighties period. At that time, just prior to the demise of the Warsaw Pact, Britain's armed forces were at their zenith. Land Rovers feature in almost every scene, and though the One-Ten was slowly relegating the Series III to quieter duties, the old workhorse was still very much in evidence. **LRM**

buy one now

Since about November 1997, when the first bulk quantities of the last serving Series III Land Rovers were demobbed, prices have taken a tumble and it is now possible to buy a runner with just one previous owner for under a grand.

If you are prepared to shop around though, and can spare a bit more dosh, there are plenty of good condition, well maintained 109s to be had through the specialist dealer network, and just £2,000 can buy a reasonably tidy example.

Readers with the time and skills to refurbish their own vehicle might find that purchase direct from the official disposal agents, MVS of Lichfield, suits them best. If, however, spending countless hours in a cold garage and losing the skin off all your knuckles in the process does not hold much appeal, the specialist ex-military dealers could well have something in stock to suit your needs. All can offer fully prepared, registered and taxed 109s off the shelf, and most are able to tailor vehicles to the customer's precise requirements. Of course, buying a refurbished, taxed and certificated vehicle from a dealer will cost you a lot more than a direct release vehicle that has stood out in the elements for anything up to two years, but think of the time and

effort you will be saving yourself. If, though, you are on a budget, and are prepared to have a go yourself, that massive fleet of demobbed Land Rovers might be just up your street.

My look at the Series III has concentrated purely on the long wheelbase Series III 109 soft top and hard top models, but windowed hard tops and Station Wagons on the same base chassis are also available in reasonable quantity, if you shop around. Series III, and earlier Series IIA ambulances are as common as leaking door seals, and can be had almost for a song. A few of the rare Carawagon commander's vehicle conversions can also be spotted lurking about, but prices for these are much higher. The most often overlooked of the Series III bunch, the 88 inch soft top, is also available in small quantities, but prices are much higher than 109s, due to their rarity and popularity.

Dealers who are currently offering a choice of Series III 109s include: Automotive and Cross Country Vehicles; P.A. Blanchard of Skiptonthorpe, Yorks; David Crouch of Kibworth, Leics; L. Jackson of Bawtry, Nr. Doncaster; South View 4x4 of Orston, Notts; TRS of Pentre, Glamorgan; Witham Specialist Vehicles of Colsterworth, Notts; WJA Automotive of Edgware, London. **LRM**

the little things

While discussing with a colleague just how much our collective knowledge of our favourite 4x4 has expanded over the last twelve years, in effect since our esteemed Editor started the first monthly magazine dedicated to Land Rovers, it occurred to me that specialist writers like myself live in a world of our own.

We vacuum up every snippet of information on our chosen specialist subject, and then spend hours discussing our findings and theories. Little things like the type of wheel used on the new Santana PS-10 may turn out to be irrelevant in the grand strategy of the world of Land Rovers, but on the other hand they may just hold a clue to something much larger.

I know from my postbag, my electronic mail and my contacts with club members, that some of you have read my scribblings for many years, and as a result know just about as much as I do on the general subject of military Land Rovers. Others have a much more specialist knowledge than I do on maybe one sub-type or on a particular facet of Solihull's products. But for every person like them and me, there are hundreds of you who are newcomers to the saga.

Hence the reason for last month's back-to-basics story on the Series III military 109 and this month's one on the Lightweight. I have also got another in the pipeline on the Forward Control 101, but that might have to wait for a couple of issues as my German military photo-journalist colleague Carl Schulze has just sent me some recent pictures of British and Kenyan Army Land Rovers, taken in Kenya.

Many of the photos which accompany the following Light-weight article are from negative film shot in the mid eighties, in the days before I converted to transparency film. Searching back through my archive for these older photos I unearthed a couple of forgotten gems, such as a Series IIA signals line-layer still in service round about 1983. I also rediscovered my photos of a Lightweight being armoured in the Northern Ireland Vehicle Depot in 1988. Wonder what else is lurking in that old box?

When looking back, almost with a tear in my eye, at photos of the Lightweight which I ran in the last millennium, I also spotted a connection that I found intriguing. The three girls most photographed in the passenger seat, and very occasionally behind the wheel, were named Hazel, Heather and Rowan; the latter being the Scottish name for the mountain ash. Weird.

■ Lastly, I'm afraid the gremlins got into last month's column and the feature article on the Series III. The six-wheel Range Rover conversion produced for RAF crash and rescue teams was designated TACR2 not TACR1, and the photo on page 79 was taken in Germany in 1988 during exercise IRON HAMMER, not in 1998. Sorry.

To some this correction might seem like splitting hairs, but I feel that it is important that anything of a factual nature which appears in print should be as accurate as possible. So if I inadvertently write something which you know to be incorrect, or if the typographical gremlins get into my work again, please let me know. My E-mail address is bob@lrm.co.uk.

■ Anyone looking for a genuine WOLF roll cage and canopy, for either Defender 90 or Defender 110, should have a word with Keith Gott, as he still has a few for sale. Call 01420 543210.

> living in a world of his own, Morrison recalls the girls in the spare seat

In the early to mid 1960s, when the Cold War was at its height and large sums of money were being allocated to equipping Britain's new all-professional armed forces, several experimental Land Rover designs were conceived. The special airportable variant, now more commonly known as the Lightweight, built around the short wheelbase military chassis, was by far the most successful of these designs.

Back in the sixties, the government's Fighting Vehicle Research and Development Establishment (FVRDE) at Chertsey, later known as the Military Vehicle Engineering Establishment and now part of the Defence Evaluation and Research Agency, was the driving force behind military vehicle design, trials and testing. Manufacturers like Rover, Morris and Austin worked very closely with the boffins at Chertsey, but most initial experimental work on military vehicles was either undertaken or commissioned by this wing of the civil service.

If the armed forces had a requirement for a vehicle to undertake a particular task, they would set FVRDE the challenge of finding the solution, rather than going directly out to industry with a draft requirement, as is done today. Dependent on precise requirements, the guys at Chertsey would then produce prototype or experimental designs, based on either off-the-shelf vehicles and systems, or from a mix of existing and all-new componentry and technology, before issuing a highly detailed specification for manufacturers to work to.

The Series II/IIa Land Rover, because of its simple, bolted, modular construction plus its proven durability and mechanical reliability record, was an ideal base vehicle for most experimental light utility truck-based

LRM

cold war warrior

The Red Arrows

ROYAL AIR FORCE

it's thanks mainly to communism that Rover and the FVRDE developed the lightweight

Words and pictures Bob Morrison

designs. As a result such eccentricities as a fully amphibious light cargo vehicle, complete with inflatable sausage-like flotation bags, and a hovercraft variant were built and trialed, though neither went into full production. However, it was a much more basic variant from this period, the Lightweight Land Rover, which would eventually see long term and worldwide service with all three of Britain's armed services.

rapid deployment

The initial Lightweight design evolved from a specific requirement for a vehicle which could be used by Britain's out-of-area and rapid deployment forces. The British Empire, which had traditionally been represented in pink on world maps, atlases and globes, was shrinking on an almost weekly basis, often to be replaced by the red tide of Communism. Whereas in the past, garrisons and bases in almost every region could be relied upon to provide back-up troops to assist in quelling any uprising or minor invasion of Empire soil, backed up with a little bit of Royal Navy gunboat diplomacy, some parts of the Commonwealth were beginning to look extremely isolated. To counter this, and to complement the relatively small British amphibious forces pre-positioned in regions of both assumed future and current troubles, a means of long range air transportation of both men and material was seen as an urgent necessity.

Long distance air transportation of vehicles is expensive in fuel and by the very nature of their design aircraft are severely limited in the weight of cargo that they can carry. Any dead weight that can be saved will either increase a planes operating range, or allow a higher proportion of more vital cargo, such as men,

ammunition and rations, to be carried over a fixed range. By the sixties, helicopter lift capability had now also reached the stage where is was just about possible to undersling a light vehicle for use by rapid insertion heliborne troops, so the military logisticians were also trying to tailor future requirements to take this factor into account. When the FVRDE team from Chertsey sat down with Rovers designers in 1964 to look at future requirements, they already knew that the next light utility vehicle procured for the British Army and the Royal Marines would have to be considerably lighter than even the current Series IIa 88 inch wheelbase soft-top model.

Space is also always at a premium inside transport aircraft, and though designers were no longer tied by the ludicrously small dimensions of the side-loading Douglas Dakota on which Parachute Regiment Land Rovers were carried in the early days, any width and length savings that could be found would be appreciated. One factor which was noted early in the design brief investigations was that if a few inches could be shaved off the width of a Land Rover, vehicles could be transported side-by-side in pairs inside the then current Argosy transport aircraft.

On the naval side, any width and length reduction that could be made would also be most welcome. Though the weight factor is never a problem at sea, even comparatively large ships such as assault carriers suffer from stowage constrictions, and every cubic foot that can be saved leaves more room for supplies and personnel. It was also noted that if a slightly narrower version of the Land Rover could be manufactured, it could be shoe horned into even the smallest of Royal Navy landing craft. This would allow small ➡

Top left: Typical Lightweight in the utility role being used by an Aldershot based field ambulance unit in the mid-eighties. Centre left: This Lightweight wears the sand and green camouflage used on Cyprus. Above left: Rear view of the Aldershot vehicle with Red Cross markings. Top right: This windowed hard top flew all over the world with the Red Arrows. Above left: A rare signals line-layer conversion

Above: Possibly less than a dozen Lightweights were converted like this for recce duties by the Parachute Regiment.
Below: This Commando Lightweight is rigged with chains as it has just been flown in by helicopter during a demonstration.

Above: Royal Marines Lightweight with trailer splashes ashore in Norway.
Below: Commando Helicopter Operations Support Cell used a small nimber of tiger-striped Lightweights during the Gulf War

 Opposite page top: The Royal Air Force were probably the biggest users of hard top Lightweights. Opposite page above: This RAF Police Lightweight has Station-wagon-style sliding rear windows and full height rear door Below: Royal Military Police duty vehicle photographed in Cyprus

teams of Royal Marines specialists to go ashore with their own vehicle on even the most cramped of landing beaches, without waiting for the heavily loaded larger and utility landing craft to come ashore.

weight loss regime

It was 1967 before the results of the early feasibility studies and experiments matured into the final trials vehicle, and the following year before a bulk order was placed, with first examples entering mass service in 1969. To meet the specified weight and dimensional requirements, the design team had pared down every oversized part of the vehicle and discarded anything heavy that was surplus to requirements. Little could be done away with on the rolling chassis, but by short-ening the frame and making a simplified and removable front bumper, minor weight savings could be achieved.

Removal of the canopy and its support frame, plus doors and tailgate initially brought the body weight down slightly, but even then the Land Rover was still far too heavy for the desired helicopter transportation weight of 1135 kg (2500 lb). However, by greatly simplifying all body components, and making the upper portions of the rear body removable, the team eventually brought the weight down to a slightly more acceptable 1198kg (2640 lb).

The new simplified, slab-sided rear body design gave a width reduction of about 150mm (6 inches), but this would have left the ends of the standard axles protruding outside the dimensional envelope, so track was reduced slightly to avoid this problem. A narrower front bulkhead was produced to match the body width and the new front wings were little more than angular wheel boxes with a flat upper surface. A simple, deep cross section, angular, one piece bonnet was designed to compensate for the new lower front wings. Overall width, when stripped down for transportation, was now just 1524mm or 60 inches.

By the time that the Lightweight entered service, contemporary helicopter lift capability had increased markedly, so the slightly above specification weight no longer posed a problem. When stripped down as an underslung load, doors, body tops, canopy with sticks, windscreen, bumper and even spare wheel were packaged up as a follow-on load. Over the next few years though, helicopter capacity increased even further and it soon became very unusual to see a Lightweight in stripped down form during exercises. However, on odd occasions when additional aviation fuel was needed for extended range, strip-down was still practised.

Shortly after the first batch of Lightweights entered service, changes in lighting regulations dictated that future headlight positioning would have to be in the wings. To accommodate this, the wings were slightly redesigned, and although superficially these hybrid models look like Series III Lightweights, they were other-wise built to Series IIa specification.

From the early seventies though, full Series III specifi-cation Lightweights were manufactured, and bulk manufacture continued periodically to meet British and foreign military requirements until 1985. Just like the

standard Series III model, the last Lightweights were scheduled for withdrawal from service by 31st December 1997, but a fair number soldiered on until well into the following year with units who had not yet received their full quota of replacements. Even as recently as December 1999 though, reports were still coming in of odd survivors lurking in far flung corners and of a handful being kept on reserve by specialist users.

a vehicle for all reasons

Over the three decades that the Lightweight saw service, just about every major unit of all three British armed services appears to have used the type. Its main market though, was with the specialist amphibious, airborne and airmobile brigades. Lightweight Land Rovers have been waded ashore through five feet of surf by the Royal Marines, dropped in pairs by parachute from C130 Hercules aircraft by the RAF for use by the Paras, and flown forward by helicopter for a variety of specialist and conventional Army, Navy and RAF users.

The type first saw active service in Ulster, where it was later to be fitted with GRP armour, small numbers fought in the Falklands conflict many thousands of miles from home, and a not insubstantial number made it out to the Persian Gulf for the 1991 war to liberate Kuwait. Shortly afterwards, the Royal Marines took them into northern Iraq on Operation Haven, and a very small number even made it out to Croatia and Bosnia under UN colours.

Today, hundreds have found a new lease of life on the civilian market, where their compact dimensions and good power to weight ratio make them more popular than standard ex-military Series III 88 inch and 109 inch models. **LRM**

prices falling

Except for a couple of very rare exceptions, the Lightweight was never made available to the general public, and so the few good early examples which came out through the military surplus auctions always commanded much higher prices than comparable civilian or standard military specification models. Even today, you can expect to pay several hundred pounds more for a poor condition Lightweight than a fair condition 109 of comparable vintage.

By the very nature of their use, wading in salt water, jumping out of aircraft, tobogganing in arctic Norway - a large proportion of the Lightweight fleet disposed of before the late eighties was in less than pristine condition. However, the introduction of the winterised and para-drop 90 models, for commando and airborne use respectively, saw later production Lightweights seeing out a good proportion of their service life with less demanding units. By the early nineties, although the market was by no means flooded, recently demobbed good condition Lightweights could be found without to much difficulty, albeit at a price premium.

All but a very small proportion of the British specification Lightweight fleet left the factory with soft tops and petrol engines. Hard top vehicles with one piece rear doors were mainly issued to Royal Marines and Army units tasked in the NATO northern flank reinforcement role, where they could be expected to encounter arctic conditions, but other units could request them for specific duties.

Various small batches of windowed hard tops were also procured, mainly for RAF use where all round visibility on airfields can be a necessity, but some of these trickled out to the other services. A very small number of diesel powered Lightweights was also procured by the Ministry of Defence, possibly for use in potentially explosive atmospheres, but at least a couple of these saw Royal Marines service in the eighties. Some foreign armies, most notably the Dutch, also bought diesel Lightweights.

With the mass 1997/8 casting of the Series III Land Rover fleet, the market is now awash with Lightweights and prices have dropped to a more realistic level than previously. Two of our advertisers, Craddock's, South View and Witham (Specialist Vehicles) Ltd, each have in excess of a hundred direct release vehicles, at prices ranging from £1000 unregistered to about £2500 with tax and MoT certificate. Three or four of our other advertisers have small numbers of good condition or reconditioned road taxed vehicles in the £2500 to £3500 range. On the private market you can find old, but well cared for examples priced from £2500 down to £1250, but anything going for less than this is quite likely to be a bag of nails.

If you come into serious money though, I know where you can find the more pristine ceremonial Lightweights used by the Honourable Artillery Company at the Tower of London. **LRM**

can't say much

I usually meet Land Rover's Government and Military Operations team at shows and exhibitions, but as I always seem to be passing their office in the dead of night on my way to cover a dawn event, or on my return from a long day out on assignment, I never get the chance to catch them at their desks.

To compound matters, the members of this compact team are often spread to the four corners of the earth at any one time, so it's pointless just dropping in for a chat. However, a call to their private line at HQ is often redirected to their mobile phones at home or abroad, so they are seldom out of touch if I desperately need an answer to a particular query.

On flying into Birmingham Airport on my return from a recent assignment, however, the team's boss and I found that we both had some clear time in our respective diaries; so I popped in for a chat. Naturally, I did my usual ferreting about what is new in the military Land Rover sphere, both at home and abroad, and he replied as truthfully as he could.

Confidentiality clauses, written into military purchase contracts by governments to protect their national security, can be a pain in the backside, but Land Rover and journalists like myself have to respect them. Very often these smokescreens thrown up around military deals are purely political, and serve no purpose whatsoever, but just occasionally lives might be jeopardised by a seemingly innocent fact leaked to the mass media. Having seen first hand how careless talk really can cost lives, I always err on the side of caution, and seldom press home a point.

Other information garnered by or leaked to the press can also have hidden adverse consequences on the commercial front, so one has to be careful what one puts into print. Land Rover is a comparatively small player in the international vehicle manufacturing field, and any advance notice of new developments that can be gleaned by larger foreign competitors could well give them that added edge in a head-to-head procurement battle.

One message which Government and Military Operations are eager to pass on, however, is that the military Defender as we know it is definitely here to stay for some time yet. Land Rover's contractual commitments to the Ministry of Defence and to foreign governments dictate production facilities for the XD (Wolf) model must be maintained for several more years. Naturally, I pushed to find out how the much-awaited new Defender model might affect military sales but, as expected, I ran into a brick wall here.

There has been much speculation over the last decade about relocation of Defender production. Without doubt the Solihull site could make better use of the space taken up by the Defender line for more cost-efficient mass appeal models, but finding a politically accepted alternative site poses all sorts of problems.

A number of eastern European countries, with the low wage costs and overheads that would make these labour-intensive vehicles more competitive have been suggested, but all have now been eliminated. For a while a proposed assembly plant near Ankara might be on the cards, and South Africa has been heavily backed too, but these schemes now seem to be dead.

I wonder if maybe the production line will actually be reduced to a simplified government and military customers only built-to-order operation in the UK. **LRM**

> be careful what you write, be careful what you say

Last month in Military Scene we took a brief look at the history of the Series IIA/III Lightweight Land Rover, which was designed primarily to give Britains out-of-area forces an airportable light utility vehicle. Today there is no need for a weight saving Land Rover as both transport aircraft internal capacity and helicopter lift capability have increased dramatically, and as a result the standard military Land Rover, the Defender, can be routinely transported to the far side of the globe.

Since the Lightweight's conception in the 1960s, Britains military sphere of influence has shrunk drastically, but as a nation we are still committed to supporting our Commonwealth partners in times of crisis. The outbreak of many predominantly localised or internal conflicts since the end of the Cold War period, and the resultant trend of committing multinational peace-keeping troops to attempt to restore a degree of normality, has also seen Britain's armed forces deploying overseas several times in the last decade or so. Naturally, wherever British troops go, Land Rovers go too.

Ideally, in the first instance the spearhead troops on any international rapid deployment would be the Paras or the Marines, but the increased trend to towards airmobility means that any infantry battalion could easily find itself committed to peacekeeping or deterrent operations overseas. The supporting arms, such as gunners and engineers, also have to be prepared to

in Kenya you can...

... train in a wide variety of climatic and terrain extremes

deploy as part of a mixed battlegroup, so they too must be trained to the same standards. The post Cold War manpower reductions throughout the armed forces, and the constant cycle of training requirements mean that there may not be sufficient infantry battalions available to meet all our commitments at any one time, should a sudden crisis such as Kosovo or Bosnia arise. However, all British Army soldiers, irrespective of trade, undertake basic infantry training and regular refresher exercises, support troops like the gunners can also find themselves on the front line as peacekeepers.

hot and cold

To enable our troops who are tasked to these international military fire brigade actions to operate efficiently in all climates and temperature ranges, a number of foreign training areas are used on a regular basis. Jungle training is mainly carried out in Belize or Brunei, arctic warfare training is practised each year in Norway, the Sovereign Base Areas in Cyprus allow hot climate training to be undertaken in the summer, and regular joint or multinational exercises in Arab countries give troops the opportunity to train for hot desert warfare. One country, however, actually provides nearly all of these varied climatic and operational terrain training opportunities within its national boundaries. On the nine separate areas made available to the British Army in Kenya, virtually all types of out-of-area military training can undertaken, with the obvious exception of arctic operations.

Under a long-standing agreement with the Kenyan Government, each year three infantry battalion battle-groups participate in six-week exercise programmes to acclimatise them for operations in equatorial and tropical regions. Called Exercise Grand Prix, these training packages allow troops to undertake live firing in desert and rain forest environments, as well as conducting basic jungle training and high altitude scrubland operations. Soldiers on the exercise also gain the opportunity to learn the basics of Swahili, a key language understood by many throughout the African continent, and they get to experience African culture at close hand. A Royal Engineer squadron usually also deploys as part of the battlegroup, and the civil engineering projects which they undertake as part of their exercise package give something back to their hosts as well as providing realistic operational training conditions.

Although all current Land Rover models used by the British Army can easily be carried inside long range RAF Hercules transport aircraft, it makes little sense to despatch a complete battalions worth of vehicles down to Africa three times each year. Instead, a permanent vehicle pool is kept at a logistic base on the edge of Nairobi. As each battlegroup flies in, it collects sufficient vehicles to bring it up to operational readiness status, before deploying up-country. The specialised nature of the training programme, and the lack of need for armoured personnel carriers on the exercise, mean that Land Rovers play a much larger part

Words
Bob
Morrison
pictures
Carl
Schulze

Opposite page top: Soft top 110 with trailer in tow is workhorse for anti-armour training exercise. Opposite page below: Factory fitment capstan winch is useful for civil engineering projects. Above: Soft top FFR in use as artillery command post

in day-to-day operations than on a comparative exercise on say Salisbury Plain. A small permanent administrative cell, designated British Army Training and Liaison Staff Kenya (BATLSK), coordinates the training packages and ensures that the pool vehicles are maintained to the same high standards that they would be at home.

huge distances

The Defender 110 accounts for the vast majority of the Land Rover fleet, in both soft and hard top variants, but a small number of Defender 90s are also available for command and liaison duties. The reason for the 110 being preferred over the 90 is pretty straightforward; it can carry more personnel and cargo. Distances on and between training areas in Kenya can be vast, and the more capacious 110 allows a lot more comfort space for personnel travelling in the rear over unmade roads and rough tracks. The varied range of pre-exercise and refresher training carried out, often at unit or sub-unit level, sees small teams and groups of soldiers working at different locations in the bush, so the Land Rover is also more economical and convenient than a four tonne payload truck.

As battalion training is carried out in so many different locations and over much larger distances than back in the UK, good communications are important. Live-fire training has to be carefully coordinated to ensure that blue-on-blue, or as the Americans say

friendly fire, incidents do not occur. It is also important that radios are on hand in case routine training accidents occur and casualty evacuation or additional has to be requested. To this end, a higher than usual percentage of the Land Rovers is fitted for radio (FFR). These vehicles, identifiable by antennae mounting boxes on top of the front wings, and vertical tubular antennae mounting brackets on the body sides behind the front doors, carry additional batteries to power permanently fitted radio sets. Man-pack radios can also be plugged in to the system. However, if performance of the standard issue radios is as bad as is suggested in the leaked reports on sets used by the Paras in Kosovo, I would hate to be dependent on them in a real crisis.

Terrain conditions across the nine training areas used, four of which are on private land made freely available to the British Army by the landowners, are varied to say the least. For example Archers Post and Ol Kanjao, situated 140kms north west of Nanyuki, comprise 1500 square kms of scrub bush desert at an altitude of 3000ft.

Temperatures range from 17C to 34C, the vegetation is thorn bush and cacti, and the soil is red murram sand. In comparison, Gaithiuru is an area of thin rain forest on the lower slopes of Mount Kenya , bounding with the National Park. It is an area rich in flora and fauna, and an ideal training area for basic training in jungle operations. Temperatures reach 24C and the rainfall in April is around 1500mm (60ins), which

Above left: Both 90 and 110 models, in hard and soft top versions, are used in Kenya. Above right: Where would the tea urn be without a Land Rover in the bush. Right: Unusual hard top 110 FFR with side windows. Opposite page top: The BATLSK team field a small number of white 110 Station Wagons. Opposite page below: Series III, with what appears to be a British number plate, being used by the Kenyan

equates to the annual rainfall on some of the wetter parts of Western Britain. Kathendeni, on the other hand, sits on the southern slopes of Mount Kenya between 5000 and 8000ft above sea level. Rainfall and temperature are not as high as Gaithiuru, but the foliage varies from thick jungle to impenetrable bamboo on this excellent high altitude training ground. Further contrasts can be found at Ol Pejeta, where most of the 20,000 acres available for artillery live firing and other exercises are covered by open grassland between rocky outcrops.

old, but in good nick

To blend in with the varied terrain and foliage in Kenya, a two-tone sand and green camouflage has been adopted for the Land Rovers. Other than this however, the vehicles look just like any other British Army ones and even carry their UK registration plates. Close inspection of these shows that some of the fleet is about twelve years old, though a few are nearly new. Externally, all appear to be in pretty good condition, irrespective of age.

My good friend Carl Schulze, who took the accompanying photos while covering 1st Battalion Royal Gurkha Rifles on exercise in Kenya late last year, also photographed a couple of Series III Land Rovers in use with the Kenyan Army. One of these appeared from its registration plate to have been an ex-British Army 109 dating from around 1982/3. Despite showing cosmetic signs of age, it appeared to be in sound condition after at least 17 years service in this demanding environment.

Other non-standard vehicles spotted, in the Nairobi compound but not out on the ranges, included white civil specification Station Wagons used by the BATLSK team. These were fitted with brush guards which had tubular side struts acting as sill protectors along the lower edge of the body sides. Carl also spotted a ten year old white military specification hard top, also used by BATLSK, which had twin rounded windows in each body side.

LRM

camera shy

In addition to the BATLSK fleet of military Land Rovers, Kenya is also second home to a small number of very special Defenders. These camera-shy beasts are the Desert Patrol Vehicles (DPVs) used by the 22nd Special Air Service Regiment the fabled SAS.

Successors to the Series IIA Pink Panthers of the mid sixties, the first DPVs entered service around 1987, and a small number were soon despatched to Kenya for training purposes. The pair seen in this photo, taken by SAS Gulf War veteran and author 'Yorky' Crossland, were being used for driver training before an exercise. As with all new bits of kit, it is prudent to trial every facet of their capability prior to deployment, and here the troopers are testing winching techniques. Unlike their predecessors, at least a quarter and maybe as many as half of the DPVs were fitted with self recovery winches. As Yorky comments in his book Victor Two, these winches were found to be a necessity in the harsh operating conditions of the Iraqi desert.

We will cover the SAS DPVs in more depth in a future issue, so I wont go into too much detail here, save to say that the base vehicles were V8 powered One Tens with Hi-Cap rear body trays and a plethora of armaments and stowage. Though not immediately apparent from this black and white photo, the two camouflage colours applied over the stone base coat were grey and brown. Like their predecessors, the DPVs seem to have left the factory finished in standard NATO Green paint, but many were over painted by the users for desert operations. The primary scheme, as used during the Gulf War, was grey stripes over a stone base coat, and the brown paint seems to have been added as required for African operations. The only green DPVs that I have seen have been in depot, but I am told that vehicles still sporting their factory finish have been used for training in Wales and on UK exercises. The small post war batch of Tdi powered replacement DPVs (several were lost or badly damaged during the 1991 Gulf War) appears to have left the factory painted in a more sandy shade.

■ Incidentally, in a bid to attract more recruits the Ministry of Defence has just run a competition called Operation Kenya. The main prize was a week-long adventure training package in Kenya with the next infantry battalion to take part in the Grand Prix exercise series. By the time you read this, the lucky winner will be just about on his or her way. One hundred runners up will also have won a weekend with the Paras. If you are under 28 and considering a career in the British Army, check out the www.bethebest.co.uk or www.army.mod.uk websites for future competitions.

SAS Desert Patrol Vehicle in Kenya (Yorky Crossland photo)

conundrum

I do appreciate a good conundrum, and writing about military Land Rovers provides plenty of these. When I first covered the US Rangers Special Operations Vehicle or R-SOV for **LRM** (November 1999 issue), I mentioned that I had uncovered what I thought was a second demonstrator, finished in plain green and with only three side door openings. I now believe this to actually be a third demonstrator.

Memory is a funny thing, and when researching the main feature for this month, I suddenly realised that a vehicle which I recalled as being a Multi-Role Combat Vehicle was no such thing; it was actually a second R-SOV demonstrator! Close inspection of photos taken back in 1993 showed that this second demonstrator actually belonged to Marshall of Cambridge and, more glaringly, it was right hand drive. The vehicle, now in private hands and featured in my November article, is left hand drive and has all the right accessories, which means it is almost certainly Land Rover's original demonstrator. The green three-door is also a left-hooker, and though it does have some of the minor body details of the original, it is nowhere near as complete. As it is highly unlikely that the right hand drive Marshall vehicle was converted, we must conclude that there were actually three built in addition to the Ranger fleet.

While on this subject, I have recently had a look through some more of the photos from Joel Paskauskas' collection, and can confirm that at least six Rangers seem to travel on the R-SOV on training exercises. One of the shots also shows the front end of what is clearly an R-SOV exiting one of the Chinook helicopters used by the US

> **a riddle that turns on some fanciful resemblance between things**

Special Forces. This confirms what I have said in the past about the Defenders' ability to be carried inside a Chinook being one of the prime reasons why the Rangers opted for the Land Rover.

Changing tack completely, I have just spent a couple of days on the Balearic Island of Formentera, taking some photographs for a book project. While there I kept an eye open for the old civilian version of the Lightweight, the Ligero, which was manufactured in Spain by Santana. I did not spot any at all, though I did eventually find one on neighbouring Ibiza.

When I first visited Formentera in 1987, old Santana Land Rovers were very popular with both fishermen and farmers. The sleepy islands' tiny police station also had an old 88 almost permanently sat outside, and rumour had it that the island's fire engine was also a Land Rover, though I never tracked that one down. Today the farmers and fishermen drive shiny new Patrols, Pajeros and the odd Discovery, plus there are a few highly polished soft top Defenders outside holiday homes. Tourism has brought wealth to the island, not to mention a second filling station. But the police force has also grown drastically, and as well as having moved to bigger premises, they now have their own fleet of Spanish-built Nissan Patrols and Santana Suzukis. Even in the Balearics times are changing, but at least the gas and electricity company have bought 110 Defenders. After centuries of fighting off pirates and invaders from around the Mediterranean, this beautiful island no longer needs a regular military presence, which is just as well as I hate to think what the salt atmosphere would do to steel bodied light utility vehicles. **LRM**

Above: *It looks like a Wolf, but the 110 MRCV was just a demonstrator mock-up*

Above: *The 110 MRCV in private hands.*
Main picture: *A Sea King delivered the 90 MRCV to the RNBAEE93 mobility display*

it's amazing says Bob Morrison, what those 'in the know' know

Land Rover cannot always disclose to whom or where it sells its military products, but the demonstrators displayed at military exhibitions can provide many clues. I made my first visit to a British Army Equipment Exhibition in 1978, and over the years I have seen many changes in the company's demonstration line-up. The most radical of these changes happened in the first half of the last decade, in response to the thawing of East-West relations and the changes in military doctrines as a result.

With the exception of the three Australian six-wheel Perentie demonstrators, which we will look back at in a future issue, the vehicles displayed by Land Rover at the 1990 BAEE were relatively conventional. The armed variants included a 90 Portee with 106mm recoilless rifle, the sand and brown camouflage 110 Desert Patrol Vehicle demonstrator and a mini-gunship 90. This garish little vehicle, which toted a pair of twin general purpose machineguns (GPMG) on a central pintle mount in the rear load bed and a forward firing one for the commander, was painted in pink, sand and light brown three-colour camouflage which was reminiscent of Neapolitan ice-cream. All three were left-hookers, as was only to be expected of demonstration models aimed primarily at Arab markets. There was also a genuine right hand drive

no great secret

SAS 110 Desert Patrol Vehicle (DPV), in sand and grey camouflage, on show at the Mobility Demonstration, but this Land Rover drew little attention as it was now old hat.

The vehicles which caused the greatest stir at the show were the dune buggy type Longline Light Strike Vehicle (LSV) and the slightly smaller Wessex Saker. Two examples of the former were on show, one inside the pavilion and the other in the Mobility Display, and it was freely admitted behind closed doors that they had been designed in principle and bought by the SAS.

private venture

The Saker, on the other hand, was a private venture which never entered service, despite much hype by its manufacturers. The design team at Longline was headed by a father and son partnership, on security grounds we will just refer to them as Ralph and Paul, who had been heavily involved in experimental vehicle work for the Ministry of Defence. Their two-man, 4x2 LSV used a bought-in tubular space frame, powered by a Volkswagen engine, and could carry either a MILAN anti-armour missile launcher or a heavy machinegun above the crew on its special roll-cage universal mount.

Little did we know it at the time, but within a few weeks Saddam Hussein's forces would invade Kuwait, leading to the greatest multi-

Above:
**A rare shot of
both R-SOVs and
the 90 MRCV
demonstrators
together**

Below:
**The sand-
coloured
90MRCV was
fitted with a
pop-up MILAN
missile launcher**

national military operation since the Korean War. Both the Land Rover DPV and the Longline LSV would be deployed to the Gulf region by the SAS before the end of the year, but only one actually went to war. Despite the promise that it had shown in trials, the arduous desert conditions that the LSV encountered during work-up exercises in a neigh-bouring country, plus the need for the SAS to deploy deep behind enemy lines for a period of weeks without support, all conspired against it and none made it as far as Iraq. In contrast, several fighting patrols of Land Rover DPVs deployed deep into Iraq for prolonged periods, and though a few were lost in accidents, on the whole these vehicles performed as admirably as their crews. American Special Forces working alongside the SAS in the 1991 Gulf War were so impressed by the Land Rovers' performance that soon after they ordered their own unique variant, the Special Operations Vehicle or R-SOV (see November 1999 and January 2000 issues).

To avoid the traditional clash with the French Euro-Satory military expo and the Farnborough Air Show, the next biannual BAEE was held over until 1993 and renamed the Royal Navy and British Army Equipment Exhibition. At this show the R-SOV made its first major UK appearance, though its

official debut had been at Euro-Satory in 1992, but it was upstaged by a pair of weapons-toting demonstrators. The Multi-Role Combat Vehicle (MRCV) was on display in a big way. Conceived by Land Rover's Government and Military Operations team, the design of the MRCV had been fine-tuned by Paul of LSV fame, working in a consultant role to Solihull. These new vehicles, based on the Defender 90 model, were essentially concept vehicles designed around the lessons learned in the Gulf War, when even Series III Land Rovers with impro-vised machine gun mounts had to be pressed into service.

I had actually been aware of the new vehicles for a couple of months, but was sworn to secrecy as Land Rover wanted their debut to have maximum impact. As a reward for keeping my big trap shut, which is not an easy job, a senior member of the Military Ops team at Lode Lane (hello Brian, its about time you got your name in **LRM**) journeyed down to my Devon office to explain the concept. Using a series of sketches on acetate, he showed how a basic Defender with a cut-down rear body could be transformed into countless military variants. The base vehicle, which could be on any of the three production wheelbase versions, though I do not believe any 130 demonstrators were ever built, was essentially a standard chassis and front end, but no doors or windscreen were fitted. The rear body was a simple load tray, based on the standard item but with flat sides which terminated at wheelbox level. A drop-in cab roll-cage was common to all three versions, and a number of interchangeable rear roll-cage modules could be bolted to this to achieve the desired weapons fit. Various removable and interchangeable side and rear racks and panniers could be clipped or strapped into place to provide ammunition and kit stowage for the relevant weapons fit or role.

dramatic colours
The two new vehicles on show at RNBAEE93 were kitted out for completely different weapons systems. The 90MRCV which fronted Land Rovers' outdoor display area, alongside what I now realise was the second (Marshall) R-SOV demonstrator, was finished in a sand, green and black three-colour camouflage scheme and toted a 40mm Mk10 Grenade Launcher on its pulpit (ring) mount. Incidentally, this highly effective multi-theatre camouflage scheme has its origins in a late 1980s design by Press Officer Mike Gould, who was a member of the G&MO team at the time. A 7.62mm machine gun was also carried by this left-hand drive vehicle, clamped to the forward roll-cage pillar on the commander's side on a special adjustable swivel mount. It was this vehicle which appeared in the press release action photos and in the MRCV brochure, though without the self-recovery winch that was fitted in time for the show.

The second MRCV 90, which was right hand drive and finished in a plain sand paint scheme, took part in the mobility display alongside the original (Solihull) R-SOV demonstrator. Instead of the rear roll-cage extension and pulpit weapons mount of the first vehicle, this one had a

esting prototypes in his private collection, the 110MRCV is in pretty much the same configuration as its first public appearance in June 1995, though it is not rigged with weapons yet. At RNBAEE95 it sported a .50cal machine gun on its pulpit mount and a forward firing 7.62mm machinegun in front of the passenger. Two removable panniers were carried over each wheel box, and the spare tyre was strapped into a rear pannier. The reason that this vehicle has two side panniers was that one could be removed and used on the 90MRCV, with the other small one making up the length for use with a 110MRCV, in keeping with the original interchangeability concept. As for the roll-cage, it was essentially the same as that seen on the 90MRCV with grenade launcher, but it was extended to run the full of the vehicle. Today the 110MRCV is in a three-colour sand, brown and black camouflage scheme, but originally it was finished in just sand and brown. **LRM**

pop-up mount for a MILAN missile launcher in the rear load bed, and removable racks for three reload missiles over both wheel boxes. When not in use, the MILAN launcher mount could be folded backwards to drop the weapon to floor level, where its relatively delicate optical system was less likely to be damaged during harsh off-road adventures. In addition to offering protection, this collapsible mount also allowed the vehicle a comparatively low profile and made the anti-armour version of the Land Rover harder to differentiate from lower value targets. A removable rear pannier was provided to carry the normal two-man crew's personal kit.

Although the 90MRCV demonstrators attracted much interest at the show, the type did not go into series production. For the RNBAEE95, Land Rover had to come up with something a little bit different to hold the attention of potential customers. The Wolf (TUL/TUM) or Defender XD was on show, along with one of the second batch of SAS DPVs, but to the average watcher these appeared to be just the same old Land Rovers. As enthusiasts, we appreciate that the Wolf is a faster, tougher and more versatile vehicle than any of its predecessors, but this may not be particularly noticeable to the average defence procurement officer or executive. What Land Rover needed was a sexier version of the Wolf to attract attention. Their solution was to produce a 110MRCV, which looked like a Wolf and bristled with machine guns.

The 110MRCV which appeared in the Mobility Display at RNBAEE95 certainly looked to be Defender XD based, but was it? It had the distinctive intake baffles on the front wings, pioneer tools on the bonnet, and the characteristic rear-up pose of the second trials batch, but my sources at Land Rover tell me that it was actually a sheep in wolf's clothing. Cosmetically, through the use of spare components, it may have appeared like a Wolf, but they say it was actually just a standard production line chassis cab with an MRCV rear body. This may explain why it had the special bonnet with alternator bulge, which is more usually associated with the older TUM(HD) gun tractor trials model. Tyres fitted were standard military issue Michelin XCLs, rather than the Goodyear G90s found on the early trials batch Wolves.

Now owned by Douglas Landy, who also has the original R-SOV demonstrator and a few other inter-

THE CONCEPT of armed light utility vehicles stretches back to David Stirlings' Special Air Service of WWII, who used Willys Jeeps armed with Vickers and Browning machine guns in the Western Desert campaigns. After Normandy, they fitted some of their vehicles with armoured panels and small bullet proof glass windscreens, for use behind German lines. In the fifties the Belgian SAS fitted these kits to their Minerva Land Rovers. At about the same time, the reformed British SAS converted a small number of Series One Land Rovers for deep reconnaissance duties, and fitted them with machine guns too.

In the sixties, they experimented with long range desert vehicles, culminating in the procurement of the special batch of Series IIA 109 Land Rovers known as Pink Panthers. In the eighties these were replaced with the 110 Desert Patrol Vehicles, which earned their place in history during the battle to pin down Iraq's mobile Scud missile launchers in the 1991 Gulf War. The MRCV demonstrators were the link between these vehicles and the WMIK Wolves now entering general service with the British Armys' rapid response formations.

Above:
Marshall R-SOV demonstrator and 90MRCV on Land Rovers RNBAEE93 stand

Below:
The classic SAS Pink Panther actually entered service in dark green

military future

As I write this, a month after the not unexpected news (unless you are the Trade & Industry Secretary) that BMW has cut and run from loss-making Rover, it is still unclear who will now own our favourite 4x4. It was actually back in January that Ford made a serious bid for the Solihull part of the operation, and not long after that when its arch rival General Motors made it clear that it, too, was interested. Who can blame them?

For decades Land Rover was the Cinderella of British motoring, but today the company is the one major jewel in its crown. Former owners British Aerospace and BMW have both been instrumental in taking the marque into the 21st Century, and although I would have preferred it if ownership had stayed in the UK, I would rather see the company prosper under a foreign owner than be dragged down the drain by Longbridge. But why are two of the World's biggest automobile players interested in this comparatively small operation?

Don't kid yourself that they are just after the nostalgia side of the business, epitomised by the legendary Land Rover name. The decision makers are hard-nosed executives, who are not going to throw away £1.75 billion on a world-wide reputation made in the fifties and sixties, but lost to the Japanese in the seventies and eighties. They are trying to buy Solihull because it either fits a gap in their current product range, or because it clashes with it. My belief is that the first applies to Ford and the second to GM, so I have my fingers crossed that old Henry's mob are allowed to complete the deal.

Looking at the current Ford range, neither the Maverick (badge-engineered Nissan Terrano) nor the bland Explorer are doing particularly well in the internationally buoyant civilian 4x4 market. I reckon that Ford will be only too happy to replace the Maverick with the Freelander, both in the US and around the world. They will no doubt retain the Explorer for the folks back home, as it is as American as apple pie, but they will promote both Discovery and Range Rover as prestige brands on that side of the pond.

On a global scale, they have the necessary clout to promote all three models to an extent that BMW never could, and that is no bad thing. GM, on the other hand, are doing okay internationally with their Isuzu range, which is sold under different badges and which often competes head on with Land Rover products. Vauxhall Discovery? I don't think so!

What will happen to Defender though if Ford wins? As the company does not have a successful light or medium military utility vehicle in their portfolio, I believe the future of the (New) Defender is probably secure. Ford's long tradition of producing light military vehicles effectively ended after they manufactured the first batch of M151 MUTTs (Military Utility Tactical Transport) in the sixties. The original Ford Bronco, built between 1966 and 1977, was the last civilian vehicle which could have made a name for itself in this class, but the US military never really took to it.

If Ford is allowed to conclude the deal to buy Solihull, I believe they will be only too happy to promote the military Defender both at home and abroad to recapture this important market.

Watch this space! **LRM**

> ## better in the hands of an overseas owner than down the tube with Rover

Land Rover started with a clean sheet of paper when designing the FC101 - they had to...

For more than two decades a very special batch of Land Rovers was thrown out of aircraft flying at 800 feet, waded through salt sea up to five feet deep and suspended from helicopters flying at tree-top height. Once on terra firma, these unique little vehicles were expected to tow their own weight, at the same time as carrying a ton of ammunition and anything up to a dozen strapping paras or commandos. Is it any wonder that many consider the 101 inch wheelbase Forward Control to be the best 4x4xfar?

First conceived in the mid-sixties, the Truck, General Service, One Tonne, 4x4, Rover was designed from the outset to be capable of transportation under Royal Navy helicopters. Its primary role was to be gun tractor for a proposed new 105mm light artillery piece, and to tow ammunition resupply trailers for this gun. Entering service in 1975, after a protracted design and test period, the vehicle was to serve in this role until the mid-nineties with Britain's crack airborne, amphibious and airmobile forces. When the Rapier anti-aircraft missile system entered service with the Royal Artillery and Royal Air Force, this compact Land Rover was converted for the job, and fifteen years after rolling off the production line it deployed to

twenty-five years later

the Gulf War in this specialist role with the Army.

Known to troops as the One Tonne (pronounced One Tunny, plural One Tunnies) and occasionally as the FC101, the new Land Rover was the most compact ever produced by Solihull. Sitting on standard 9.00 x 16 tyres, the 101 gives the initial appearance of being a large vehicle, but when stood next to a soft top 109 its true size becomes apparent. Measuring just 4125mm long (13ft 6in), its length sits squarely between that of 88 inch and 109 inch Series Land Rovers, and it is only about 160mm (6in) taller and wider than them. Despite these 'bijou' dimensions, the vehicle's forward control design and basic rear body construction give it a load bed area of approximately 2500x1700mm. As can be guessed by its official military designation, design payload is 1000 kilogrammes, but this figure was regularly exceeded in operational conditions.

When the draft specification for the One Tonne was laid down, it was anticipated that the new artillery piece it was being designed to tow would have a powered axle. A special ammunition trailer with powered axle was also developed to accompany it. To suit this then experimental concept, the first prototypes were engineered to provide six wheel drive, but it eventually became clear that such a drive train configuration for a light vehicle and

trailer combination was inherently unsafe off-road. The requirement was dropped before full production commenced, but it did prove its worth on the first east-west vehicle crossing of the Sahara Desert.

q quarter century

The One Tonne made its public debut at the 1968 FVRDE show, but it was to be another four years before the pre-production batch was completed for user trials. (Incidentally, although I have press releases from this show on both the One Ton 109 and the Lightweight, I have yet to find one for the FC101. Can any reader help?)

The first production batch was accepted for general service in 1975, and batch manufacture was completed during the following year. Though intended only for British military use, Luxembourg ordered between fifty and sixty vehicles at this time to equip troops dedicated to NATO's multinational ACE Mobile Force, and it is believed that a small number were procured by Egypt. It is believed that the Egyptian 101s were used as anti armour vehicles, mounting the British Aerospace Swingfire system, but I have only ever seen one blurred and grainy photo of these vehicles in print. Terry Gander of Jane's Defence publications has also stated that Iran bought some, presumably before the

Story and pictures Bob Morrison

Above left: Brace of Gun Tractors suspended under an RAF Chinook

Above: Commando One Tonnes roll off a landing craft in Cyprus

Shah was deposed.

Although the FC101 was conceived as a gun tractor, its high load capacity but compact dimensions made it an ideal choice for carrying the mortar platoons of battalions tasked in the light infantry role. Such units included the parachute and commando battalions, plus rapid response troops such as the Gurkhas. The mortar version had inward facing seats for four over the rear wheelboxes, containers and clamps for the mortar on the load bed, and mesh ammo baskets behind the bulkhead. Para mechanical engineers also rigged up a pair for repair and recovery duties. One carried a tuck-away one tonne crane jib on the load bed, and the other had a hand operated hoist in the rear for effecting engine changes in the field. However, the largest batch of variants was the fleet of battlefield ambulances, re-bodied on General Service chassis around 1980. As this batch is worthy of an article in itself, we will pass them by until a future issue.

So why was the One Tonne such an unusual and, consequently, long-serving vehicle? In essence, the design team got it just about right from the outset, if you ignore the powered trailer red herring. Although Land Rover had tried various attempts at providing both airportable and high capacity vehicles to meet several military specifications, they had tended to stick closely to the traditional layout and drive train configuration.

Even the Forward Control 109 and 110 models of the sixties used pretty much standard chassis and body panels, with the result that they always looked like a compromise. With the FC101 model they had to go back to the drawing board. The Fighting Vehicle Research Development Establishment (later Military Vehicle Engineering Establishment and now

Defence Engineering Research Agency), which was then at its peak at the height of the Cold War, also had a hand in the design, and for once their input was of a more practical and less experimental nature.

driver up the front

To meet the required transportation dimensions, while still achieving the desired load bed area, it was pretty clear from the outset that the new vehicle would have to be of forward control design. Volvo's Laplander, produced in great numbers since the early sixties, had already proved that a forward control design was feasible. The Austrians were also hard at work on a slightly larger vehicle to replace the tiny Haflinger 4x4 light utility, and by 1965 they had produced the prototype of what would become the Pinzgauer. If the British Army were to continue to by British -they evaluated the Volvo as a possible light gun tractor - Land Rover would have to start with a clean sheet of paper.

The new vehicle was designed with a simple, no frills ladder chassis, to which was bolted an extremely simplified cab formed from aluminium sheet and mild steel. Driver and front passenger sat either side of the engine, which was enclosed with relatively easily removable aluminium panels. The rear load bed was of simple flat construction, and the body sides were constructed in such a way that they could be stripped off in a couple of minutes. Even the corner posts could be unbolted and set aside to bring the weight down for air transportation. The double tube roll protection bar behind the cab was also quickly removable, as were the front doors and windshield. When completely stripped for helicopter transportation, but carrying sufficient

Clockwise from top left: Typical drop zone load of eight Paras, all their kit and a tonne of ammunition; Royal Marines vehicles backloading during an amphibious exercise; Parachute failure broke this one's chassis, but it still drove off the pallet; Rapid artillery deployment in Turkey; Just off the pallet after a parachute drop

1800kg of artillery piece over rough ground. And this is after being buffeted around inside an aircraft flying at low level for several hours and then being thrown out on parachutes from a height of eight hundred feet.

The para gunners may have been rough on the vehicles, but at least they did not subject them to 1500mm (5ft) of salt water at regular intervals, and then drag them off to the Arctic for a couple of months each winter. The Commando gunners did though. They also regularly slung them under Sea King helicopters for ship-to-shore transfer, as well as deploying with them to both desert and jungle theatres on training exercises. The basic, but sturdy, One Tonne gamely soldiered on.

The RAF might not have been quite as rough with their vehicles, but they expected a pair of One Tonnes to tow a complete air defence system plus crew, and carry several reload missiles as well, in their role as mobile airfield defenders. No, the One Tonne did not exactly lead a quiet life.

around the world

The first operational deployment for British One Tonne Land Rovers came in 1982 when a Task Force was dispatched to the Falklands. Although it had been decreed that the islands were unsuitable for wheeled vehicles, a few were taken by the paras and commandos. One even featured in some of the earliest footage from Port Stanley after its liberation.

Their next large-scale deployment was to Saudi Arabia in 1990/1, where as Rapier Tractors they provided the last line of defence for British troop concentrations preparing to recapture Kuwait. Soon after, a small quantity deployed to Northern Iraq with the Royal Marines tasked with protecting the Kurds. A small number made it out to Croatia and Bosnia in the first half of the nineties, but by the end of 1998 almost all had been withdrawn from service.

In addition to the soft top general service fleet, produced in both 12V and 24V versions, there were also a number of hard top conversions. The most numerous of these were the four-stretcher ambulances, but specialist communications and electronic warfare hard top versions were also manufactured. However, these are a story in their own right and will have to wait for a future issue.

Despite their hard life, and despite now being around a quarter of a century old, a surprising number of the One Tonne fleet has passed on to civilian ownership. Possibly as many as one third are already in private ownership, and there is even a thriving collector's scene in the United States. The type has its own club the 101 Forward Control Club & Register, who produce the excellent magazine Six Stud. Check out their website at www.101fc.co.uk.

The Ministry of Defence eventually issued a requirement for another FC101 replacement in the nineties, after having to prolong their in-service life as a result of the disastrous Reynolds Boughton gun tractor procurement fiasco at the end of the eighties. It is believed that Land Rover offered to refurbish the fleet, complete with Tdi engines and ergonomically redesigned cab, for a fraction of the price of complete replacement. Their offer was declined, and the One Tonnes were eventually unloaded onto the ever-keen civilian market. The only taxpayers to benefit from this were the ones who bought themselves what many consider to be the best small military 4x4xfar.

fuel for 100 miles running, unladen weight dropped from 1924kg to 1580kg (3500lb).

No doubt when the Solihull team started work on the project, they knew that the 3.5 litre V8 petrol aluminium engine scheduled for the Range Rover was waiting in the wings, but at least one of the first prototypes was powered by a Ford Falcon engine. The new military vehicle also had permanent four wheel drive, a feature that the standard military Land Rover would not get for another fifteen or so years, but despite the Range Rover clearly having some influence on the design, leaf suspension was used instead of coils.

It is intriguing to think what might have resulted if the Ministry had just held back for a couple of years before issuing the One Tonne specification. With an almost assured order potential of two to three thousand vehicles, they might have been tempted to invest in a common coil-sprung chassis for both the new military model and the revamped Series III military models.

When it eventually entered full service in 1975, the One Tonne was by far the most powerful vehicle in its class. The V8 engine produced 128bhp at 5000 rpm, which was 85 percent up on that of the four cylinder engine in Series III 109, but even fully laden it weighed only 20 percent more. Speed had to be pegged back to 120 km/hr (75mph) to prevent accidents. As for the requirement to carry 1000kg, it did so easily, and the troops soon found that the vehicle could be abused with impunity. On 5 Airborne Brigade exercises it was not unusual for gun tractors to carry 1000kg of simulated ammunition, eight gunners with their bergens and full equipment, a couple of spare jerrycans of fuel and camouflage nets for the gun line, all while towing

LRM

Sierra Leone

For decades the Land Rover was the world's most ubiquitous military and police light utility vehicle, but over the last two decades Japanese and, to a lesser extent, European trucks have stolen this market. But times are a-changing and the company is slowly and relentlessly clawing back its market share, as has been only too obvious on our TV screens recently.

It's not widely appreciated, but with the exception of the SAS, British Army soldiers have never had a proper heavy machine gun mount on their Land Rovers - until last year. Ever since the Second World War, in even the poorest and most ill-equipped of countries, it has been standard practice to fit either NATO or Russian designed 0.5inch calibre weapons on any available light utility 4x4 or pickup truck, to give the infantry a degree of close protection and air defence. Some wars in the Third World have been fought almost exclusively from the back of pickup trucks toting machine guns. At long last, the Ministry of Defence has latched on to this idea and, as you may have seen on your TV, the guys from 1 Para have have now deployed WMIK-equipped Wolves to Sierra Leone.

The WMIK, an acronym for Weapons Mount Installation Kit, allows a heavy machine gun, close support automatic grenade launcher or anti-armour missile launcher to be operated accurately from the back of the vehicle. A ring or pulpit mount, attached to a full-length roll-protection cage, allows full 360 degree traverse, and unlike a simple pillar mount, the gunner can move freely and safely around the load bed. A forward-facing secondary general purpose machine gun, operated by the vehicle's commander allows a withering rate of fire to be laid down

> ## some may consider the Land Rover as a weapon of war

if necessary. By simply lowering the main armament, the WMIK retains the Defender's full airmobility capability, and this allowed the Paras to fly straight into Lungi Airport by RAF Chinook helicopter.

At the time of writing, a week into Operation Palliser, the Paras have not yet had to fire their weapons in anger, but they have already been responsible for the safe evacuation of over three hundred British, Commonwealth and European citizens from the war zone. It is early days yet, and a week in war is even longer than a week in politics, but it seems that the mere presence of British troops has been enough to make the rebels of the RUF have second thoughts about attacking Freetown, the capital city. Also, for the first time ever, an SAS 110 DPV team has appeared operationally in newsreels. Driving a NATO green 'Pinky', they were filmed with Nigerian forces operating 25 miles east of Freetown. Despite the bad press that they were initially subject to, the UN peacekeeping troops seem to be trying to rally the situation too. It was interesting to see a joint Sierra Leone and Nigerian Army team using Defenders with machine guns on pillar mounts to fight back against RUF rebels ambushing one of the main lines of communication. Other African troops committed to the UN operation in Sierra Leone are also using Land Rovers, as do the Jordanians who are working closely with the British Paras.

As this column goes to press Royal Marines of 42 Commando, diverted from a NATO exercise in the Mediterranean, are ashore with their waterproofed Wolves to boost the Paras. Some may consider the Land Rover to be a weapon of war, but once more it is earning its spurs as a weapon of peace. **LRM**

By peacetime military procurement standards, the design and trials process for the Forward Control 101 was not a particularly long one, but it still took eight years to bring it from prototype to service issue. During this development period, the British Empire was fading fast and military roles were being reappraised to better cater for the needs of the large standing army in Germany. Britain still needed a lightly equipped rapid reaction force for long range deployments, and does even to this day as the Parachute Regiment have just proved in Sierra Leone, but the bulk of British Army manpower was now focused on deterring the massed Warsaw Pact armies. Heavy modern armour, rather than light artillery towed by softskin trucks, was the prime requirement for the British Army of the Rhine (BAOR) and the FC101 order now seemed to be excessive.

In the late seventies, the Central Vehicle Depots at home and on the Continent were not exactly awash with surplus-to-requirements One Tonne Land Rovers, but it was clear that other roles would have to be found for some of the excess stocks. Conversion to Rapier Tractor configuration, for both the RAF and the Royal Artillery, was both a cheap and effective solution for a small quantity, but that still left several hundred pristine, high

the largest batch of Forward Control 101 variants had ambulance bodies, but there were other hard top variants, too

red cross and vampires

performance and high capability off-roaders gathering dust. The solution, a flash of inspiration, was to convert them to compact dimension battle-field ambulances to support the lightly equipped rapid response formations such as the Paras, the Royal Marines, and the Spearhead infantry battalions, plus the ACE Mobile Force units committed to NATO Northern Flank deterrence.

upwardly mobile
The casualty clearance chain developed by the British Army, which took a wounded soldier from battlefield to field dressing post to field hospital to hospital, was a complex but very efficient system. Highly mobile mechanised frontline formations, that is those with tanks and armoured personnel carriers, were equipped with tracked, and occasionally wheeled, armoured ambulances to carry their wounded back to the comparative safety of the rear echelons. Formations slightly further back from the action, lightly equipped rapid intervention troops, and static defenders, on the other hand, were equipped with small numbers of 109 Land Rover ambulances down to individual unit level, so that they could cater for their own day-to-day medical transport. The larger of these formations also fielded transport squadrons equipped with Land Rover 109s, for

transportation of casualties from second to third line medical facilities.

By the late seventies, the oldest of these four-stretcher Series IIa ambulances were well past their pension age of twelve years, though the last of the breed actually survived until at least 1998, and the FC101 chassis seemed to offer an excellent base for a replacement. Eventually, in excess of 500 surplus One Tonne soft tops would be delivered to Marshall of Cambridge for conversion, and by 1980 the first was undergoing final user trials.

The new vehicles, though slightly taller than the 109s they would either replace outright or relegate to secondary roles, were more compact and offered better conditions for crew and casualties. Inside the casualty compartment it was almost possible for the medic to stand up straight when tending his patients, and the upper stretcher racks were of a design that was both easy to load and raise. However, it was the smoother ride and better off-road capability of the FC101 ambulance which really set it apart from its predecessor. The power of its V8 engine also gave it excellent on-road performance, a factor which a fair few peacetime accident and exercise casualties were thankful for.

Though the driving compartment of the 101 Ambulance was just as cramped as the ➡

Report and photos Bob Morrison

Above : BRITMEDBAT FC101 ambulance cruises the war-ravaged streets of Vukovar in 1992. (Photo: Arthur Thompson)

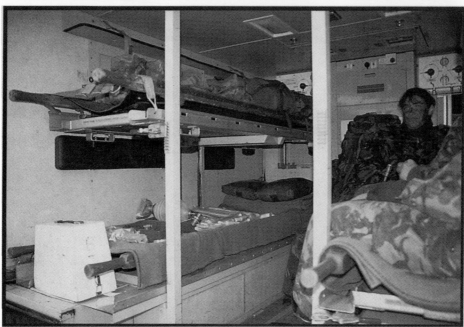

 Gun Tractor variant, crews soon grew to like the vehicle. Its high insulation properties and the powerful space heater behind the cab bulkhead, designed primarily for use by troops committed to Arctic and Northern Flank defence, made it one of the snuggest vehicles of its day. Indeed on New Year's Day 1996 in Bosnia, I even came across one FC101 ambulance driver who had slept in his vehicle overnight in preference to his camp bed in a heated tent inside a factory building, despite temperatures that were well sub-zero and there being two inches of solid ice on the ground underneath.

do you know?

The initial IFOR deployment to Bosnia in 1996 was the FC101 ambulance's last operational deployment, but it was by no means the first. Although I have no definite documentary proof I believe that the Paras took at least a couple of the new ambulances with them to the Falklands in 1982 for Operation Corporate. My memory is not as good as it used to be - no doubt because I ate too many dodgy beefburgers as a teenager - but I am pretty sure that I recollect seeing one on newsreel driving through Port Stanley just after the Argentinean

surrender. If any reader can provide confirmation (please e-mail *bob@lrm.co.uk* or drop a line to the magazine) I would be most grateful.

The marque's first peace-keeping deployment was to Cyprus, where a small number were used to provide medical cover for the Blue Beret peace-keepers patrolling the island's Green Line. As late as December 1993, a pristine white ambulance with UN plates and markings, was permanently on-call outside the British HQ in Nicosia. At the same time, other FC101 ambulances were deployed with the infantry battalions garrisoned in the two Sovereign Base Areas on Cyprus. These vehicles sported the two-tone sand and green camouflage scheme which is so effective on the island, and which has also been used by units tasked with playing Opposition Forces (OPFOR) on British and Canadian training ranges. Both of these OPFOR units also used sand and green FC101 ambulances to provide medical cover in case of training accidents.

In 1991, nearing what had originally been planned as a twelve year service life, a number of FC101 ambulances went to war against Saddam Hussein, in the battle to liberate Kuwait. Although by this time much newer and more capable

Defender-based ambulances were in service, several British Army and RAF formations deployed with the FC101, and they performed admirably in the desert environment. One of these machines, owned by Laurie and Helena Wright and christened Mabel, resplendent in gaudy, hand-painted, two-tone camouflage, has been a familiar sight at shows around the country for many years.

signals vehicles

Incidentally, the other hard top variant on the Forward Control 101 chassis also saw active service in the 1991 Gulf War. Normally referred to as signals vehicles, most of these were used by REME as Radio and Optronics repair vehicles, though a few also served as command posts and communications vehicles. Their body shape is different to that of the ambulance version - they can be recognised by their small twin doors in the side of the body and their single back door.

After the Gulf War, it was assumed that the FC101 ambulance fleet would eventually be mothballed, but the flare-up of conflict in the Balkans put paid to that. In June 1992, 24 Airmobile Field Ambulance deployed to Croatia to provide medical cover to UN personnel. Known as

BRITMEDBAT, the unit deployed four self-sufficient detachments, each with four ambulances, to regional locations around Croatia. As Britain's UN contribution in the former Yugoslavia grew, so did the number of 101 ambulances. Although they did the job well, these vehicles were no longer the best ones available on the British Army inventory, and they were certainly a bit long in the tooth for their allocated task. Questions were asked about this in Parliament, and modern Defender 127/130 ambulances were eventually taken out of mothballs and dispatched to replace them. But it would be at least five more years before the last one returned from neighbouring Bosnia.

Elsewhere in this issue, James Taylor is looking at the overall development, history and international sales of the entire FC101 range, so I don't plan to bore you too much on this subject. However, it is worth noting that Luxembourg also deployed a handful of hard-body ambulances and signals vehicles. Also built by Marshalls, they are of a slightly different body shape, though the ambulances are reasonably similar inside. One of these, owned by Darren Parsons, has been doing the rounds at shows for the last couple of years, and hopefully I'll get around to

Above left: Red Cross flaps dropped for tactical reasons, an ambulance rolls ashore during an amphibious exercise

Above right: The very rare sight of an FC101 ambulance being flown forward under an RAF Chinook

covering it in a future issue.

The last of the British military Forward Control 101 Ambulances should have been demobbed at the end of 1997, but a handful still soldiered on well into 1998. I have recently been told that at least one unit is still hanging on to one, tucked away in a hidden corner of their vehicle pool, but the vast majority now seem to have been released for public sale. The high construction standard of their bodies make them highly desirable for off-road camper conversions, and if a replacement Tdi engine is shoe-horned in, they can be economical vehicles for long range excursions and adventures.

Twenty five years after production, and twenty years after conversion, many FC101 Ambulances are getting a new lease of life in civilian hands. And all after a combat record that few other vehicles in this class can equal. **LRM**

cloaked in secrecy

THERE IS one last hard top FC101 variant which deserves mention, but which must still remain shrouded in secrecy because of its role. The Vampire, of which less than twenty were built, was used for very specialist Electronic Warfare duties in BAOR during the 1980s.

I first tracked these elusive beasts down on exercise in a forest close to the inner German border in 1989, if my memory serves me well. I had been tipped off of their presence, by a Land Rover enthusiast in uniform, and fought my way through thick undergrowth along a long disused forest track to reach their location deep in the forest. As I broke out into a clearing, just a few hundred metres away, the startled Belgian troops providing outer perimeter defence of my objective, flagged me down and ordered me to a halt. On seeing my camera, they politely but firmly ordered me to turn around. When I told them that I only wanted to photograph these Land Rovers with giant communications antennae, the officer in charge looked me straight in the eye and asked "What Land Rovers? There are no Land Rovers here." I got the message.

It would be another eight years before I got close to one in the field again. This one had a tent along one side and tarpaulins around the other three to break up its outline. Its unique rear access ladder betrayed its identity and I quickly banged off a couple of shots, before a Para signals sergeant spotted me and told me what to do with my camera. Some of the equipment originally used on the Vampires is now fitted to a later vehicle type, so I will have to wait a few more years before telling their story.

Top left:
The FC101 ambulance was much shorter than its SIII predecessor

Top left:
Royal Marine ambulance outside a field dressing station - note the folding rear step arrangement

Far left:
One of only two shots the author ever managed to take of Vampire on exercise.

Left:
Demobbed Vampire, recognisable by roof line and single door in right side, but without rear cable drum and telescopic mast

deployment

In the good old days of the Cold War, when the superpowers were terrifying both themselves and everybody else on the planet with the prospect of total nuclear war, we lived in a remarkably peaceful world. Okay, we had local troubles like Ulster and foreign flashpoints like the Middle East, but on the whole most of the smaller nations were too busy sucking up to Uncle Sam, the Soviet Bear or the Chinese Menace to bother with each other. Nowadays, it seems as if just about every minority ethnic group around the globe, not to mention a couple of ethnic majorities, is hell-bent on picking a quarrel with their countrymen.

In the last six months of the second millennium and the first six of the third, British military personnel have been deployed to the conflict zones of Bosnia, Kosovo, East Timor and Sierra Leone. Others have been despatched on UN peacekeeping missions or as ceasefire observers to many other countries. Yet more have found themselves helping out with disaster relief missions from Turkey to Mozambique. Others have been on standby for at least two possible British citizen rescue missions, similar to the West African one recently undertaken by the Parachute Regiment and the RAF. All with manpower levels only about a third of that available during the Cold War.

Total military Land Rover numbers are also now probably around a third of their Cold War figure, but a little Land Rover goes a long way. It looks like only about a dozen or so WMIK (pronounced 'wimmik') Wolves were actually available for the Paras to deploy to Freetown, but by all accounts they did an excellent job and were clearly seen flying the

flag by both the locals and the world's media. A leaked report on the practical lessons learned by the Paras during the Kosovo crisis allegedly highly praised the Pinzgauer over the Land Rover, as the forward control Austrian vehicle offered better off-road capability and load carrying capacity than the Defender. It was being suggested that the Paras, now reduced to just a small part of 16 Air Assault Brigade, might trade in the majority of their Land Rovers as a result. The performance of just that small clutch of WMIKs on Operation PALLISER seems to have changed a lot of minds.

The Royal Marines who deployed as follow-on troops have also been equipped with their own winterised and waterproofed version of the Wolf for amphibious operations, but it appeared that they would not be getting the WMIK version. Instead they are to be issued with the long-promised armoured version of the tracked BV206 over-snow and all-terrain vehicle, and as a result of this purchase it was claimed that the Commando battlegroup tasked in the rapid reaction role would lose a large portion of their Defender fleet. Operation PALLISER seems to have proved how short-sighted this decision was, with the Paras leaving their WMIKs behind for their Royal Marine colleagues to use. Rumour has it that 3 Commando Brigade now plans to indent for its own WMIKs.

■ Changing topics, last month Shaun commented on how my favourite Top Gear presenter, himself a died-in-the-wool Stage One Land Rover fan, reckoned you get a lot more Cherokee for five grand than you get Discovery. You can get even more Lada for this amount, and I might just be tempted by the Ruskie. Must be sad to own a 4x4 with submarine-like depreciation rates. **LRM**

fewer Land Rovers are doing more in more places

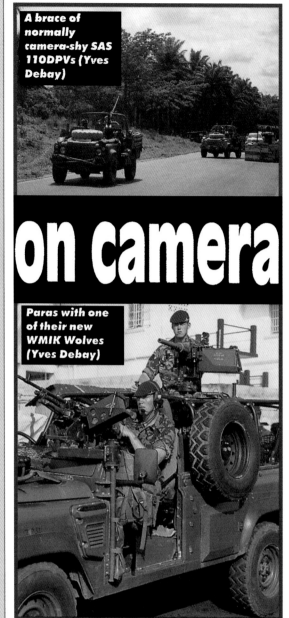

A brace of normally camera-shy SAS 110DPVs (Yves Debay)

on camera

Paras with one of their new WMIK Wolves (Yves Debay)

The British JRDF (Joint Rapid Deployment Force) mission to rescue British, Commonwealth and European nationals from strife-torn Sierra Leone, Operation PALLISER, has now terminated. During the month-long operation, the international airport at Lungi was secured, several hundred civilians were repatriated, rebel leader Foday Sankoh was arrested to be handed over to the Sierra Leone police, and the presence of British troops in the country effectively bolstered the United Nations peacekeeping mission. Naturally, Land Rovers featured prominently in this rapid deployment action.

operational deployment

In last month's Military Scene column, we mentioned that the new WMIK (Weapons Mount Installation Kit) package, fitted to the latest 110 Wolf Land Rovers had seen their first operational deployment with 1 Parachute Regiment battle-group in Sierra Leone. Despite many of this battalion's personnel being deployed overseas on exercise, the Paras and their RAF support were able to mount one of the most rapid long-range non-combatant evacuation missions ever conducted.

Continued on next page

on camera

Continued

the normally camera-shy SAS were clearly visible in Sierra Leone recently

Indeed, it has been said that the Chairman of the US Joint Chiefs of Staff has let it be known that he doubts whether even US airborne forces, with all their resources, would have been able to move as quickly. To bring 1 Para up to full operational strength, units from 2 Para and the Gurkhas were drafted in at short notice, and the Pathfinder platoon from 16 Air Assault Brigade deployed with the battlegroup as forward reconnaissance.

It is for rapid deployments just like this that the Paras are so lightly equipped, though they carry heavier firepower and more ammunition than comparable-sized infantry units. This is where the WMIK Wolf proves its worth as it gives a great degree of mobility to the battalion's heavy machineguns, at relatively low weight penalty. In Sierra Leone, the area of ground which had to be covered to provide security for the airbridge, the port facility and approach road network was so vast that only vehicle-borne troops could effectively patrol it. We have not yet received any reports of total distances covered by the Land Rovers during the deployment, but they featured in just about every newsreel clip broadcast. When the Paras were relieved by Royal Marines from 42 Commando, who travelled by sea on HMS Ocean

and other logistic vessels, they left them their WMIK Wolves. Although the Marines have their own version of the Wolf, specially rigged for wading ashore, they have not been issued with the WMIK yet.

Designed for Land Rover and the MoD by Ricardo Special Vehicles, the WMIK can theoretically be fitted to any 110 Wolf, though for full installation some minor drilling and strengthening modifications are necessary. For example, cleats need to be added if fabric doors are to be used for weather protection, plus some bodywork has to be modified for various small fitments and brackets. This work can either be done by a specialist contractor such as Ricardo, or by base workshops. The kit is modular and easily removable, which allows it to be fitted to another base vehicle should the original be damaged in an accident or immobilised due to battle damage.

special forces
Britain's SAS, or to be more precise 22 Special Air Service Regiment, have used the 110-based Land Rover Desert Patrol Vehicle (110DPV) as their primary combat vehicle for around thirteen years, but until very recently none have been

Report
Bob
Morrison

Above:
First sighting of
an SAS 110DPV
(Yves Debay)

filmed in action. In May of this year, however, one of these specially modified Land Rovers made a highly public debut in Sierra Leone, as British troops helped restore calm to the Commonwealth nation plagued by civil war.

When a 110DPV and its three-man crew pulled up in front of a television news camera, many miles inland from Sierra Leone's Lungi Airport, some thought that the highly secretive SAS had blundered. In reality, they were almost certainly announcing to the world in general, and the rebel Revolutionary United Front (RUF) in particular, that Britain meant business. At home the Government seemed to be unsure exactly what its precise intentions were in the West African state, but on the ground the British commanders were getting on with the job of returning an air of normality to the area. These days there is no surer way of getting this message across, especially to those whose basic military training was along British lines, than by announcing that the SAS are in the vanguard.

conventional role

In addition to their specialist anti-terrorist role, which was highly publicised in 1980 when they dramatically secured the safety of 26 hostages held in London's Iranian Embassy by the Democratic Revolutionary Front, the SAS also have a more conventional military role. During the 1991 Gulf War small patrols initially deployed deep behind enemy lines by helicopter to monitor movement of Iraqi long range Scud missiles, which were being fired at both Saudi Arabia and Israel. These clandestine reconnaissance operations were followed by eight-vehicle patrols of heavily armed Land Rover 110DPVs, which roamed the deserts of Iran for a number of weeks, striking at communications centres and mobile Scud launchers which were such a major part of Saddam Hussein's

military strategy. In this role, the SAS returned to their roots of deep penetration vehicle-borne missions, of the style of those undertaken against the Germans and Italians by David Stirling's original team in the deserts of North Africa in 1942.

To enable 22SAS to carry out its conventional tasks, each of the Regiment's operational combat squadrons is sub-divided into four 16-man specialist troops. Each troop has a specific method of insertion for conventional warfare, though all personnel are trained to operate by any means. The Air Troop specialises in high altitude parachute insertion, Boat Troop uses rubber inflatables and collapsible lightweight kayaks, Mobility Troop deploys by Land Rover and Mountain Troop climbs. Though their initial method of insertion may be by parachute, boat, vehicle or on foot, once behind enemy lines the SAS usually melt away into the terrain to gather intelligence unseen or strike at key targets.

The Regiment operates from its own discrete base on a former RAF base in England and has direct access to specially modified transport aircraft and helicopters, to allow it to deploy world-wide in utmost secrecy. In Sierra Leone, however, their presence was distinctly overt as they liased with United Nations troops up-country and undertook probing reconnaissance missions. There was some speculation, no doubt well founded, that they were preparing to assist in the rescue of UN personnel held hostage by the RUF, but the rebels eventually released them before any action was taken. No doubt the presence of Britain's elite, who have an unequalled hostage rescue record and a reputation for beating off enemy forces of vastly superior numbers, caused the rebels to consider their options a little more carefully.

It was during one of the high-profile SAS patrols that combat photographer Yves Debay came across

Above: Deployment of the new WMIK 110 allowed the Paras to mount wide-ranging and highly mobile armed patrols (Yves Debay)

The first batch of 110DPVs was procured by the SAS in the mid-80s to replace their 20 year old Series IIA Pink Panthers. These were powered by the 3.5 litre V8 petrol engine and, when expertly tuned, were the fastest Land Rovers then in British service, despite the massive amount of fuel, ammunition and equipment carried.

a new derivative of the 110DPV that has not been seen in public before. At first glance the new 110DPV variant, which I will designate the Type 3 for ease of reference, looks quite similar to a WMIK Wolf as it has a rear compartment roll-cage with ring mount for a heavy weapon. However, a quick check of the front wings shows no evidence of the distinctive air intakes of the Wolf model, known as TUM[HS] or Truck Utility Medium (High Specification) by the British Army, so the vehicle must be based on the older Defender 110 chassis. This is borne out by the standard SAS 110DPV body construction of HCPU (High Capacity Pick-up) rear cargo bed plus the numerous minor fittings such as commanders seat base lift, side jerrycan racks, smoke dischargers, sand channel mountings and forward firing GPMG (general purpose machinegun) mount.

Armament was one forward firing GPMG for the commander and either twin GPMGs, a .50cal heavy machinegun or a Mk19 grenade launcher on a rear load bed pintle mount for the radio operator. This third crew member sat on a rearward facing seat, with his back to the roll bar and rear bulkhead, his heavy weapon providing more than 270 degree covering fire plus air defence.

main role

The main role of these Land Rovers was long range patrols and deep penetration surveillance, primarily in desert environments, so they had to be completely self-sufficient for extended periods. If necessary, the 110DPV could be transported internally by RAF Chinook helicopter or pairs could be parachuted from RAF Hercules transport aircraft. Incidentally, the 110DPV was the

only version of the pre-Wolf 110 which was cleared for parachute insertion, though the standard Defender 90 was regularly air-dropped. It is believed that every available original batch 110DPV (we'll call them Type 1) was deployed into Iraq at some stage during the 1991 Gulf War.

replacements

The 110DPVs performed admirably during the Gulf War, but several were lost or severely damaged during operations. At least one had to be destroyed behind enemy lines after being disabled in an accident, but as the vehicle was being driven in complete darkness over unsurveyed rocky desert terrain, this was understandable. To bring the Regiment back up to full complement, a second batch of vehicles was procured after the war. These vehicles (Type 2), of which only a very small number were ordered, had Tdi engines and minor fitment differences from the originals. Very close inspection of Yves' photo of the new (Type 3) 110DPV reveals a splash of yellow on the filler cap, which suggests that the vehicle has been converted from a diesel Type 2; British Army convention dictates red cap for petrol and yellow for diesel.

This latest variant of the 110DPV, actually has a welded rear compartment cage to carry the pulpit ring, rather than the bolted frame of the WMIK.

The vehicle's normal roll-bar is omitted and a single forward tube is bolted between the rear cage and the dashboard, in similar fashion to the R-SOV. I suspect that the entire rear frame is mounted to the upper sides of the HCPU load tray and can be lifted off the vehicle in one piece. This non-standard vehicle is believed to be one of a small batch of conversions produced by a specialist workshop which has undertaken a number of low quantity design and manufacture projects for the MoD. **LRM**

ON JUNE 12 the British Army handed over responsibility for the security of Lungi Airport to the United Nations mission in Sierra Leone (UNAMSIL) and Operation PALLISER was wound down. By this time the Paras had returned to the UK by air and the Royal Marines were preparing for embarkation on HMS Ocean. An infantry training team, drawn from 2nd Battalion of the Royal Anglian Regiment, then assumed responsibility for training the Sierra Leone Defence Force under the codename Operation BASILICA. At time of writing it is unclear whether the WMIK Wolves have been left in-theatre for use by the Royal Anglians.

middle age

They say that when policemen start to look young, it's a good sign that one is hitting middle age. I thought I had skipped that particular milestone by moderating my driving habits when I hit the big four zero, ensuring that my run-ins with the boys in blue were cut to a minimum. Signing up for an Arts Degree at University a few years later, and submerging myself in a social life - which I had missed out on first time around - also seemed a good way of hanging onto my near-forgotten youth. Then, out of the blue, reality jumped up and bit me.

I was chatting to a reader at the Range Rover 30th Anniversary bash, reminiscing about the early days of the model, when he pointed out that his memories did not stretch back quite as far as mine. In fact, he was actually born after the marque, and his first recollections dated from the late seventies, when he was but a boy. It was then that the penny dropped that I had actually left school before the Range Rover was seen by an incredulous public. I even have dim memories of seeing one in a Design Council showroom - the first vehicle to achieve such an award. More to the point, I worked on some of the very first chassis assemblies as part of my basic workshop training. Yep, I have definitely hit middle age with a vengeance.

Way back in the salubrious seventies, when Glam Rock was in its infancy and I still had a full head of coiffured, shoulder-length hair, the National Lottery had not been invented. Littlewoods Pools was then seen as the answer to a poor man's dreams. It was around this time that I ventured on my first Spanish holiday, and fell in love with both country and lifestyle. Near three decades on, I still remember a conversation I had with my best mate Rudi, as we sat on a beach at midnight with a couple of girls and his guitar. Induced by copious quantities of San Miguel and Sangria, the talk turned to what we would do if we came up with eight score draws on the Pools. All agreed that a Spanish villa would be first purchase, then a flash car came next on the list, but here our views diverged.

I remember that Rudi fancied a BMW, but then that was the Germanic side of his parentage showing through. Fiona fancied a Ferrari, as was only to be expected from someone with such a love for four-legged thoroughbreds. What the other lass in our group suggested escapes me, as does her name I'm afraid - sorry. My choice? Though a throwback to the flower power era, VW beach

> a kind of beach buggy on a Range Rover chassis? Tempting

buggies were still quite popular, so I came up with the concept of a fibreglass body from one of these mated to a Range Rover chassis. I reckoned that this would have even more street cred than my mate Dave's Clockwork Orange Bond Bug. How I wish I had patented my idea.

As I sit here in Spain writing this column, the long hair is long gone, but some of the dreams are slowly maturing. The Range Rover beach buggy has not yet materialised, but maybe it will next summer. I wonder how long it would take Klaus and Donja, owners of my local in Es Canar, to notice that their black Range Rover had morphed into a fibreglass-bodied totty magnet.

Don't tempt me. **LRM**

a closer look at one of the least known special variants of the FC101

The 101 inch wheelbase Forward Control Land Rover, or One Tonne in military parlance, had three great advantages: it was compact, capacious and capable of tackling the most demanding conditions. The type was deployed from the Arctic snows of Norway to the baking desert of Oman by Britain's armed forces, and served with distinction on operations as diverse as the 1991 Gulf War and peacekeeping missions in the former Yugoslavia.

Several variants of the One Tonne were produced for specialist duties, but one of these tended to slip past, unnoticed by all but the keenest eyed observers. This shy workhorse was the Rapier Tractor, which served with both the British Army and the Royal Air Force as a prime mover for an anti-aircraft system. Now demobbed, these light trucks were packed literally to the underside of their canvas hoods with surface-to-air missiles and electronic equipment, plus they towed heavy trailer units as well. However, as a fair proportion of these spent much of their lives in warm, dry airfield hangers and seldom ventured much off tarmac, good condition examples abound. Do not

surface to air

assume that all Rapier Tractors left service in pristine condition though, as some in Royal Artillery service saw extensive exercise action in Germany throughout the 80s and 90s, as well as deploying to the desert for several months during the Gulf War.

Rapier Tractors

To be precise, there were actually two Rapier Tractor variants, known as the Tracking Radar Truck (TRT) and the Fire Unit Truck (FUT), but externally both were essentially similar. Designations were basically down to their particular role, but slight differences in their internal racking and fittings prevented them being completely interchange-able. The TRT and FUT invariably deployed as a pair, usually accompanied by a conventional long wheelbase Land Rover, but in an emergency a lone One Tonne could tow and carry enough of the Rapier package to keep the unit mobile and operational.

So what was Rapier? Still in service, though in a modernised and heavier version, Rapier was a second-line mobile air defence missile system. The

Royal Air Force used it for last line defence of airfields at home and overseas, and the Royal Artillery deployed it to protect military formations in the field. Manufactured by British Aerospace, the weapon came to prominence in the Falklands, where it was used to protect the Task Force in the bomb alley off San Carlos. Due to the extreme terrain - it was both boggy and rocky - launchers were flown into position on mountain tops by Royal Navy Sea King helicopters rather than being towed there, but that is no reflection on the One Tonne. Even fully tracked vehicles like the BV202 over-snow vehicle and the Scimitar reconnaissance vehicle had problems with the severe terrain.

Capable of hitting aircraft flying faster than the speed of sound and at heights of up to 10,000ft, the original version of the Rapier was a compara-tively lightweight system. In towed form - there was also a tracked version to accompany armoured formations - its two main components were a launcher and a radar tracker, both of which were transported by trailer behind a Land Rover. Each of these vehicles also carried four missiles in special racks, and four more were towed by ➡

Words and pictures Bob Morrison

Above: With canvas canopy in place, the TRT looked no different from any other One Tonne

the third, or Admin, vehicle. If missiles were trans-

Top:
Rear view of launcher in travel configuration towed by an FUT (Fire Unit Truck)

Above:
Canopy rolled up and upper body sides lowered to show empty missile reload racks in a TRT

ported on the launcher, as would be done in combat conditions, a team of seven gunners travelling in three Land Rovers had the potential to shoot down sixteen state-of-the-art ground attack aircraft. Conversion of the base vehicles to TRT or FUT specification was straightforward, as the configuration of the One Tonne could best be described as minimalist. To cater for airborne, airmobile and amphibious operations, the FC101 had been designed to be as light and compact as possible, while still retaining the basics of bodywork to provide weather protection in non-combat use. Unlike the much later Supacat 6x6 ATMP (All Terrain Mobile Platform) used as an airborne cargo resupply vehicle, which left its crew completely exposed to the elements in a trade-off between weight and cargo capacity, the One Tonne had a full length canvas hood plus demountable side body panels, doors and windscreen. However, these canopy frame and rear body components were so basic in construction and design that they gave a virtually uncluttered cargo

area. With the exception of the small wheel boxes on the rear bed, the back of this compact Land Rover was basically a large empty box, with every corner virtually at right angles.

unique design

By pure coincidence, as the vehicle was designed long before the missile crate, the One Tonne was almost exactly the correct length to carry reload rounds running fore and aft. By simply inserting a rudimentary, removable frame constructed from box section along each side, above the wheel boxes, four missile containers could be transported under cover. On top of each frame there was sufficient space under the canopy to carry ancillary kit, and more could be stowed under the frames, forward of the wheel boxes. A lightweight removable false floor was added between the missile racks to provide more stowage space. The unique two-part design of the vehicle's drop-sides allowed easy access from the outside to the equipment stowed under the racks.

In addition to towing either the launcher or

Blindfire radar trailers, the FUT and TRT carried an optical tracker and a TV camera optical group plus collimator unit electronic pack respectively. These were stowed in tubular handling frames on the false floor, which slid forward on rails for ease of unloading. Even with all this kit fitted, plus jerrycans, radios, tripods and ground anchors, there was still sufficient space left for a third crew member to travel in the rear of either vehicle in war-time configuration, though to travel in this manner would have been claustrophobic. The crews belt order, day sacks and helmets were carried aboard the tractors, but their bergen rucksacks and other personal equipment were usually carried by the Admin Land Rover to free up the maximum amount of space for the ancillary equipment. The great beauty of the Towed Rapier concept was that a full radar tracking and launch package, complete with towing vehicles, could be transported inside one of the Royal Air Force's stretched C130 Hercules transport aircraft. This meant that no matter where British forces deployed by air world-wide, adequate air defence

could be provided to guard the airfield they were operating from. Had a situation such as the recent Sierra Leone operation to repatriate UK and EC citizens arisen in a country where the potential enemy had an airstrike capability, Rapier teams would have been flown in to provide protection. Until its disbandment last year, Britain's 5 Airborne Brigade regularly practised for just such a scenario, though in the 90s the FC101 Rapier Tractors had been replaced by their Defender 130 (actually One-Two-Seven) successors.

anonymity and commonality

Other, less obvious, advantages of using near-standard forward control Land Rovers as Rapier Tractors were anonymity, interchangeability and commonality. At the height of their career, during the last days of the Cold War in the 80s, most unarmoured military convoys and groups of parked vehicles contained at least a few One Tonne Land Rovers in their ranks. The fact that the Rapier Tractors were virtually indistinguishable from their more ordinary companions gave them a ➡

Top:
Special trailers towed were (left to right) radar tracker, spare missile and fire unit

Above:
RAF registered TRT (Tracking Radar Truck) with towing radar in stowed configuration

Below: *The optical tracker frame could be slid rearwards on rails to make it easier for the crew*

Below: *Every cubic foot of stowage space was put to good use*

Top:
A team of six men deployed in two FC101 Land Rovers could provide air defence cover in a matter of minutes

Centre:
The high power-to-weight ratio of the V8 One Tonne and its excellent off-road ability made it ideal for the Rapier role

degree of anonymity once the fire unit and radar were disconnected. This made them less likely to be singled out for attack by enemy aircraft, despite them being a relatively high value military target. If a vehicle were to be damaged in an attack, or suffer catastrophic mechanical failure, the racking and equipment could be transferred to a standard vehicle with relative ease. Finally, the fact that several thousand similar vehicles were in service ensured that replacement components were readily available in the event of a breakdown.

air force

At the beginning of this article I briefly mentioned that both the Royal Air Force and the Royal Artillery of the British Army used the FC101 or One Tonne Rapier Tractor variant. There was essentially no difference between those used by either service, although vehicles initially procured by the RAF had A-series military registration plates. Later in their service life, when the RAF replaced their One Tonne fleet with the One-Two-Seven and when, a

little later, vehicle procurement for the three services was pooled, it was not uncommon to find RAF registration Land Rovers undertaking Royal Artillery air defence duties. Both left and right hand drive versions were used as Rapier Tractors, and at least one in each pair was equipped with the standard PTO-driven self-recovery winch on the left chassis rail.

The vehicles in the featured photographs belonged to 58 Eyres Battery of 12 Regiment RA, based in Germany in 1995. This unit, which deployed to the Gulf to protect British forces, was one of the last to be equipped with the One Tonne in the Towed Rapier role. Shortly after these photos were taken, the unit was re-equipped with the Shorts HVM (High Velocity Missile) system based on a light armoured tracked vehicle chassis.

By now these vehicles, along with the vast majority of the One Tonne fleet, have been released for sale to the civilian market. It would be interesting to hear from any reader who has bought either 81AM53 or 75FL04. **LRM**

individuality

It is a hackneyed cliche, but it really would be a boring old world if we were all the same. Fortunately, we have Land Rovers to ensure that we are not only different from the others, but different from ourselves.

I got into an argument recently with an aficionado who could not understand how I could possibly write about Solihull's finest without owning a fleet of several, spending my summer weekends trialing and passing the long winter nights away in a cold and dark garage losing the skin off my knuckles. In the end I tried to bring former Page Three model Linda Lusardi, Mediterranean beaches, fresh strawberries and Devon clotted cream to my rescue. I have had a soft spot for all four for more years than I care to remember, but that does not mean I spend my entire life dedicated to trying to bring them together. Mr Fanatic still did not get the point, but then he likes Pamela Anderson, holidays at home and cheesecake; none of which turn me on I'm afraid.

That is the beauty of our hobby, interest, passion, or addiction in, for, or to Land Rovers. We all derive totally different degrees of pleasure from our relationship with one or other, or more, of the vast range of vehicles that have carried the oval badge, not to mention one or two variants that have not.

And it is the study of these Land Rovers, not the racing of them, rebuilding of them or collecting of them that keeps me occupied for much of my working and social life. Indeed, only this morning I was propping up a Spanish bar discussing the differences between the Santana Ligero and

the Solihull Lightweight with the rock musician owner of one of the former, when I should really have been clubbing at Manumission with a couple of Danish holiday-makers. But what the hell. I'm here for the summer and the island is full of Scandinavian tourists, whereas my drinking partner is the only Brit I have found who actually uses a Ligero as day-to-day transport.

If I was the sort of guy who was only interested in money, like one or two other sad souls in the Land Rover magazine industry that I have met over the years, I could probably afford to stock my garage, drive and garden with many different vehicles. Though if I were them, I would not have the time to dedicate to my fleet as I would be too busy counting my pennies and trying to make even more.

Then again, if I came up with six numbers on the same line one Saturday, or I had Ross Floyd's business acumen coupled with his contrastingly relaxed attitude to life, I would probably start my own private collection to rival those ultimate Land Rover lovers, the Bashall boys. But I'm just a humble scribbler, guv, who is happy to talk military Land Rovers 'til the cows come home, and photograph them until the sun goes down or the flashgun batteries finally die.

Over the years I have owned several different Land Rovers and even stripped one basket case down to the bare chassis to restore it, plus I have driven more variants than I could possibly remember. I have used them for work, for play, for personal protection and even for sleeping in. Just like we enthusiasts, every one is different, and I reckon the world is richer for it. **LRM**

> I have a soft spot for Linda Lusardi, beaches, strawberries and cream

the Cinderella Land Rovers

The 127 was the prime mover for RAF Towed Rapier systems for most of the nineties

last month we looked at the FC101 Rapier Tractor, this month we look at its successor, the Land Rover 127

The Land Rover 127 Rapier Tractor has got to be the Cinderella of the coil sprung British military fleet. Conceived in the closing stages of the Cold War, this extended wheelbase soft top was never needed in her originally intended role, which was to assist in the last line of defence of fighter aircraft bases, and though she should have made it to the ball during the 1991 Gulf War, the bureaucratic ugly sisters held her back.

Today, many of these capable vehicles are either sitting around gathering dust, or being used as donkeys in minor transportation roles. In the mid-eighties, as the Rapier Tractors based on the Forward Control 101(see *LRM* September) approached their theoretical shelf life expiry date, the Royal Air Force set out to procure a replacement which would carry them through into the 21st Century. Several manufacturers expressed interest in bidding for the contract, but in the end only two were picked for full competitive trials. These were a version of the semi forward control Iveco-FIAT 40-10WM, based on the militarised version of the Iveco Turbo Daily van and light truck range, and a stretched variant of the Land Rover One Ten family. Originally called the One Two Seven by Solihull, and nowadays known as the Defender 130, when built these vehicles were

Continued on next page

the Cinderella Land Rovers

normally referred to by the numerical designation of 127, though bonnet badges usually just read Land Rover.

The 40-10WM was in service as a light troop transport and cargo vehicle with Italy's armed forces, particularly its airborne and airmobile units. It would later also be purchased by Canada, in licence-built form, and by a few other armies. At this time the stretched Land Rover, on the other hand, was only really used to any great extent by public utility companies who needed either a longer load bed or a combination of double row cab and rear cargo compartment.

evaluation trials

The first batch of 127 Ambulances for the RAF were on order, but these were designed to have much more of a civilian type role. However, despite its lack of previous military pedigree, it was the Land Rover which won the evaluation trials. While these trials were going on, I tried to gain the necessary clearances to visit the unit which was carrying out the comparative evaluation in East Anglia, but this was knocked on the head by civil servants who decreed that a journalist witnessing the procedure could jeopardise its impartiality.

Fortunately, some of the officers and men involved at grass roots level were more than happy

to chat, on condition that I filed their comments away for historical reference. The general view seemed to be that the longer than usual version of the Land Rover was reasonably good for the job it was intended to do, but they would have much preferred a forward control design of vehicle, had one been available. The Llama was in its infancy at this time, but it was not suitable for the new Rapier Tractor role as its hard cab was too high to allow it to be transported inside an RAF Chinook helicopter, and numbers required were insufficient to make cab redesign a cost-efficient option.

The biggest drawback was the even greater than usual turning circle - one service user once described it to me as an orbit - and the poor breakover angle. On paper, evidently written by someone who thought that as East of England airfields were flat there would be little reason to deploy off-road, the RAF Rapier Tractors were not expected to have to negotiate particularly difficult going, so they passed the comparatively modest rough terrain tests. However, most RAF and Army drivers I spoke to in the field once the 127 was in general service echoed the reservations of those I had spoken to earlier. The turning circle in particular seemed to be a bit of an issue. Of course, as many Rapier Tractor drivers also had experience of the earlier FC101, they knew exactly

Report and photos Bob Morrison

Above: Towed Radar Truck photographed during 5 Airborne Brigade Tactical Air Land Operation in the mid-Nineties

Top:
Note the Warn
winch on the
front of this
Royal Auxiliary
Air Force 127

Above:
The seventeen
inch stretch and
long overhang
were necessary
to allow missile
containers to be
carried under
the canopy

what they were missing.

In comparison with the generally good trials performance of the Land Rover, the Iveco 40-10 fared pretty abysmally. When it was working, it drove relatively well, but a series of breakdowns dropped its overall performance levels quite drastically, and the Land Rover outshone it. Over the last decade I have encountered the 40-10 many times, both on exercises with Italian airborne and artillery forces, and with peacekeeping forces in the Balkans. They never mention any major reliability problems when I question them, and as they often give the impression of being trained by the same instructors who teach Rome's taxi drivers how to negotiate the rush hour around the Colosseum, I never get the impression that they treat their steeds with kid gloves. I sometimes wonder if maybe the batch used for the RAF tests was a rogue one.

The RAF Rapier Tractors are essentially pre-Defender era soft top One Tens with a roughly seventeen inch (430mm) chassis stretch and a wider than usual, slab-sided rear body. As previously mentioned, the cab is soft top and this is grafted onto an extra-wide and much higher than usual rear canopy, this extra height and width needed to accommodate the reload missile racks and the vast amount of ancillary equipment carried.

As with their predecessors, the 127 Rapier fleet had two slightly different configuration sub-types; the Fire Unit Truck towed the missile launcher, and the Tracking Radar Truck pulled the revolving radar antenna. Incidentally, since the last issue went to press, Darren Parsons of the 101 Club has reminded me that all Forward Control TRTs had 12 volt electrics, and the FUTs had 24 volt. I believe that the 127 fleet all had dual voltage.

maximum access

One of the beauties of the FC101 was the relatively capacious dimensions of its rear cargo body, and the ease of access offered by its demountable, hinged side panels. Land Rover were able to provide an equally capacious rear body on the 127, but due to the comparatively small quantities ordered, the lack of economy of scale prevented them from making this too elaborate. Instead, to give maximum access to stowed equipment with minimum cost implications, they designed the rear cargo tray with large, almost full-height drop-down panels forward of the rear wheels, and made the less than half-height drop tailgate as wide as possible. The rear panel of the canopy was extended well below the level of the sides to compensate for the low tailgate, and it had a transparent panel to let in light and, more importantly, give the driver just a modicum of rear vision if the loadbed was only partially full.

Unlike the vast majority, though by no means all, Land Rovers of this era, the Rapier 127 was powered by a petrol engine. This was because the naturally aspirated diesel engine had insufficient power to drag a fully laden tractor plus its trailer at the road speeds required, or over the terrain anticipated should the Rapier teams deploy into the field. The Tdi diesel engine had, of course, not yet been finalised when the trials bid was submitted.

The well-proven 3500cc V8 engine was the natural choice. As this engine was considerably thirstier than its diesel equivalents, an auxiliary fuel tank was fitted behind the rear wheels. This gave the Rapier 127 the distinction of being the only mass-produced Land Rover with filler pipes both behind the front door and in the body behind the rear wheel arch.

Although the 127 Rapier Tractors were intended originally only for Royal Air Force service, changes in doctrine later saw them also being issued to the Royal Artillery to replace their FC101 tractors. A large number were also used for the protection of US Air Force bases in the UK and, to a much lesser extent in Germany. It is understood that these vehicles were technically purchased by the Americans, as were various other specialist batches of Land Rovers used on UK bases by our Transatlantic cousins, but the Rapier crews were provided by the RAF Regiment.

With the drawdown of US Forces in the nineties, in response to the demise of the Warsaw Pact, some of these vehicles remained on the few bases still being operated by the Americans, where they were used as duty hacks. American bases in Turkey were also protected by the Rapier system, and the 127 was used to tow the systems. These vehicles were built by Otokar of Istanbul, using many local components, and are essentially very similar to the Solihull vehicles. However, as they were not expected to have to fly, a conventional truck cab was fitted instead of the canvas front canopy used on the British version. Other minor detail differences include the rear body construction and the side locker design. It is believed that the Turkish vehicles are still in service.

democracy and reunification

By 1989, when the 127 Rapier Tractors started to enter service, the face of world politics had changed beyond belief. The Velvet Revolution was bringing democracy to Czechoslovakia and the two Germanies were on the point of reunification. The Soviet bear had gone to sleep, though even a decade on the situation in the former states of the socialist union is far from settled. Just as close to home, Yugoslavia was on the point of defragmentation and bloody civil war, but the general consensus was that a

Top:
This vehicle has been demoted to general cargo duties with the Royal Auxiliary Air Force

Above left:
Brand new 127 Rapier Tractor sits forlornly at a military port as other vehicles line up to go to the Gulf War

Above right:
The end vehicle in this Turkish Air Force line-up is a 127 Rapier Tractor

lasting peace was heading Europe's way for the first time since the 1936 Spanish Revolution. No longer did so many fighter aircraft have to guard Britain's eastern air approaches, and consequently redundancy was looming for many of the RAF Regiment Rapier teams. As the situation unfolded, it was anticipated that the British Army's rapid response airborne and airmobile formations would now have a greater part to play as part of a pan-European defence structure, and as a consequence some RAF registered 127s were transferred to fast reaction Royal Artillery units.

no manual, no go

In 1990, in response to Saddam Hussein's invasion of Kuwait, Royal Artillery Rapier teams deployed to Saudi Arabia to provide last line air defence to British forces massing for what became the 1991 Gulf War. The gunners took their by now ageing FC101 tractors with them, but they looked enviously at the new fleet of under-utilised RAF 127s. At least two of the combat unproven new vehicles made it as far as a military port on England's south coast, but red tape held them there. Just before Christmas 1990 I photographed them sitting forlornly at the docks like Cinderella.

At the time I was told by an officer with some authority in such matters that the reason they could not deploy was because no official RAF instruction manual had yet been written for the vehicles bumper-mounted self-recovery winch.

The fact that both the SAS and the Parachute Regiment used vehicles fitted with exactly the same winch cut no ice - without this manual the paperwork was incomplete, and as a result the vehicle could not be dispatched for service to a potential combat zone. Stories like this often get blown out of proportion by the military rumour mill, but I reckon this particular one is probably pretty accurate.

In the meantime, a fleet of 6x6 Supacat All Terrain Mobile Platforms, borrowed from 5 Airborne Brigade, was rapidly converted with racks and canopies to give the Royal Artillery its own more modern tractors. Though ideal for the desert terrain, the Supacat could not carry as much kit as the dedicated Rapier Tractors, and though the manufacturers worked around the clock to upgrade them, their late arrival meant they saw little service in the actual land offensive. Meanwhile, back at home, the Cinderella 127s missed the ball as their older sisters soldiered on in the sand.

LRM

good to be back

Back in the UK at the beginning of September, after spending most of July and August in the Mediterranean on various photo assignments, I soon descended into a state of deep depression. It was not the lack of sunshine that saddened me, or even the ridiculously high price of fuel – on Ibiza unleaded was only 52p a litre at the end of August.

What really sickened me on my return to England was caravans.

I don't remember seeing a single chicken coop on wheels all summer long, but within three minutes of starting my first journey back home, I found myself stuck behind one of these rolling roadblocks. As usual, this lumbering, swaying, kitchen sink on wheels was being towed by a family saloon which could not pull the skin off a rice pudding, even if it dumped caravan, roof box and passengers first.

Why do people spend the equivalent of half the price of a northern terraced house on a plywood and fibreglass box, only to tow it behind an eight year old saloon with a bottom of the range engine; or worse, a naturally aspirated small capacity diesel?

Eventually, I managed to get past Mr Snail, not an easy job on the pleasant but narrow roads of Lincolnshire, only to catch up with his double a quarter of a mile further on. That is when the penny dropped. The schools were back, and the early retiree civil servants and public employees were out in droves, to enjoy the caravan parks without all these noisy children to spoil the tranquillity. Now before you accuse me of stereotyping, the old Civil Service Motoring Association stickers in the back window, are a good give-away.

For mile after mile, I got stuck

behind Mr Forty-five. Every time we reached a built-up area, I dutifully slowed down to thirty or forty in an attempt to keep my licence clean, only to watch him continue at the only speed he ever travels at. A few minutes later, back on the open road again, there he was, still trundling along at 44.823 miles per hour. No doubt he has read that this is the optimum speed for minimum fuel consumption for his particular make of vehicle. Travelling at this speed also lets Mrs Forty-five look at the pretty cows.

Now I appreciate that dragging their second home behind them allows caravan owners to visit interesting parts of the country, as and when they like and at minimal cost, to contribute to visual eyesores around our coast and on the edges of areas of outstanding natural beauty. But if they are going to drag high visibility white and cream boxes out into the countryside, where they can be used as visual landmarks on the return from their rambles along the coastal paths and into the National Parks, could they please consider using a 4x4 which is designed for towing?

It need not be a Land Rover, though even a ten year old Discovery is more suitable and probably more economic than their under-powered medium-sized family saloon, so long as it is capable of travelling at the permitted legal maximum for towing vehicles.

Alternatively, they could do what the Germans, the Scandinavians and even a few Brits do. Put a camper body on the back of a Defender and travel to even more interesting places. But if they did that, I don't suppose they would have the satisfaction of impeding everyone else's progress.

LRM

> Mr and Mrs Snail go on their holidays and upset our Bob

at a cursory glance, the CAV Defender looks much like any standard One Ten, and that's one reason why it's so popular in the world's trouble spots

This July, yet again, inter-ethnic disputes at the start of the annual Protestant marching season led to heightened tension in Northern Ireland. As we have come to expect throughout the last three decades, armoured Land Rovers were prominent in newsreel footage as the Security Forces did their utmost to prevent the situation boiling over.

The vast majority of the armoured vehicles deployed at the time were Royal Ulster Constabulary Land Rovers, and though the British Army erected barricades at Drumcree on the edge of Portadown and on Belfast's Ormeau Road, their One Ten based Armoured Patrol Vehicles (APVs) and Defender based Composite Armour Vehicles (CAVs) made no major appearance.

By mid-July the situation had quietened. However, as tension increased again during the summer, the Army had to be brought onto the streets of the provincial capital once more, for the first time in almost two years.

A few armoured military Land Rovers could be seen on the newsreels, but the much larger Saxon armoured personnel carrier was more noticeable. Keen-eyed viewers might also have noticed a smaller vehicle which looks quite similar to a Land Rover APV, but this is actually a totally new

composite

protection

armoured squad vehicle which has been discreetly stationed in the Province. First spotted on the streets in July, it is actually considerably larger than a Land Rover, and probably weighs in at around five tonnes.

armour protection

It is believed that the degree of armour protection required to combat the next generation of battlefield projectiles has now exceeded the design parameters of the Land Rover chassis, unless crew numbers are reduced. Armoured Land Rovers, currently on strength, will still serve with the British Army for many years, but it is highly unlikely that there will be any further mass-production of vehicles designed to carry six or eight men.

The streets of Ulster have spawned many different armoured Land Rover designs since the beginning of the sixties, and indeed the very first mass-produced vehicle in this class was actually designed in Belfast for police use. It is therefore fitting that what is probably the last major armoured variant to use the Solihull-built chassis, the Courtaulds CAV100, was conceived specifically to protect troops in the Province.

However, the CAV was introduced just before the Northern Ireland Peace Process started to gather momentum, and it actually gained fame for its

parts in protecting those administering aid, covering the news and, eventually, maintaining the peace in the Bosnia. Prior to the 1999 NATO bombing campaign against Serbia, a fleet of orange-painted British Army CAVs was used by the Kosovo Verification Mission Monitors, and several of these were later used by their original owners as KFOR moved in to administer security in Kosovo.

The CAV100 consists of a hi-tech plastic body mated to a heavy duty Defender 110 chassis, powered by a 3.5 litre V8 engine. Externally, from anything more than a few yards away, it pretty much resembles a conventional hard top Defender. This is a deliberate design feature as the CAV is likely to operate in environments where the deployment of an overtly armoured vehicle could be seen as an aggressive act and lead to heightened tensions or worse. In some ways the CAV is the armoured vehicle equivalent of a bulletproof vest worn under a soldier's or police officer's uniform. It offers discreet personal protection without antagonism.

The pressure-moulded composite material, called CAMAC, used to form the cab and crew compartments of the CAV is a sophisticated laminate of S2 glass fibre and phenolic resin which combines outstanding ballistic protection with comparatively low weight penalty. This unique

Report and photos Bob Morrison

Opposite page: In December 1995 British Army CAVs reverted to a more traditional green and black camouflage scheme for IFOR service in Bosnia

Above: A typical British Army CAV in UNPROFOR markings in Bosnia, late 1995

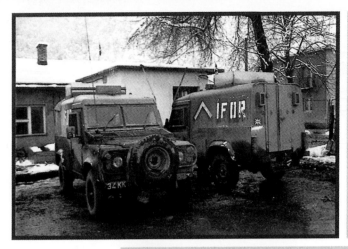

Right:
The CAV first appeared in Bosnia in early 1993 as pan armoured liaison vehicle for senior British commanders

Top left:
A brace of CAVs outside the Light Infantry command post to the north of the Bosnian inter-ethnic boundary line, January 1996

Top right:
British Army CAV in Northern Ireland markings, photographed towards the end of The Troubles. From this angle the sliding roof hatch for top cover is quite prominent

plastic armour is so light that the unladen vehicle weighs in at just 2800 kg, which gives it a troop or cargo capacity of 800kg, yet it offers superior protection to a conventional steel vehicle with the same gross weight.

In addition to being proof against 5.56mm and 7.62mm bullets, plus mortar and grenade fragments, unlike steel armour the inner face of CAMAC does not spall or delaminate. Spall is the scabs and fragments of steel which fly off the inside face of conventional armour when the outside is hit by a high energy projectile, and which can be just as lethal as if the shell had been penetrated by the bullet or shrapnel. The padded lining seen in conventional armoured vehicles is a spall liner, which hopefully traps some of these deadly steel shards, or at least prevents them from ricocheting around the interior.

The unique construction methods associated with pressure formed composites allow the rear body and cab roof of the vehicle to be moulded as a single unit, which increases its structural integrity and gives superb roll-over protection. The cab floor and bulkhead, complete with windscreen frame, is produced as another single component, which is bolted and bonded to the rear body shell. This complete assembly then drops onto a near-standard heavy duty Defender chassis.

Once the doors, roof hatch and armoured glazing

units are bolted on, the armoured personnel module is complete. The engine compartment bodywork, which is pretty much standard with the exception of a hooded air intake on the front wing, is fitted to the vehicle in the normal manner and simplified lower rear body sides are added to give the CAV the general appearance of a conventional Defender hard top.

fibreglass panels

When first introduced, the CAV was intended as a replacement for the VPK-clad Land Rover fleet used in Ulster. These were essentially standard Lightweights, plus a smaller number of 109s and a few ambulances, to which an appliqué vehicle protection kit (VPK) of fibreglass panels had been added to provide a rudimentary degree of armoured protection.

Even at the height of 'The Troubles', only a relatively small part of the Province, mainly the border regions and the cities of Belfast and Londonderry, were regularly affected by terrorist activity. The VPK Land Rovers were used primarily in the quieter areas, with the more heavily armoured steel-bodied vehicles being assigned to the hotspots.

In the Nineties the steel-bodied Land Rovers, known as Armoured Patrol Vehicles, were up-armoured to counter constantly evolving IRA anti-

Left:
This Press Corps
CAV parked at
the British HQ in
Gornji Vakuf has
the armoured
side windows
seen on many
non-military
models

armour weapons. Though the CAVs could also have become targets, it is believed that their composite plastic construction actually offered better surviv-ability from this type of weapon.

Two areas where the body construction of the CAV was shown to be equal to, and possibly even superior to that of a steel armoured Land Rover, were roll-over survivability and landmine protec-tion. The first was proved very early on in the vehicle's deployment to Ulster when one was rolled at high speed on the Province's only motorway, the M1. The vehicle bounced just like the one on the company's trials vehicle, and the crew walked away from the incident without major injury.

However, it was in Bosnia that the CAV's landmine survivability was to be tested. When an aid agency CAV detonated what was believed to be a TMA-4 anti-tank mine, which blew its wheels and front bodywork off, the three-man crew escaped completely uninjured. Later inspection showed that the integrity of the crew compart-ment had not been compromised, and not a single fragment of shrapnel had penetrated the armour.

The gradual easing of tension in Northern Ireland from the early mid-Nineties saw the CAV taking a back seat in the Province, and gradually it disap-peared from the streets. But the troubles in the former Yugoslavia were slowly drawing in more and more British military personnel on United

Nations duties, and the benign appearance of the CAV was seen as advantageous for both senior commanders, and the UK press corps which was reporting the situation on a daily basis.

press vehicle

The first CAV to arrive in Bosnia was actually the Courtaulds company demonstrator, which the BBC hired for Martin Bell and the Panorama team when they were producing the first major documentary on the unfolding situation. The vehicle proved its worth to such an extent that the BBC later bought it, and ordered a second one shortly afterwards.

The aid agencies also quickly latched on to the benefits of these vehicles, which offered the degree of protection needed by their personnel, but were also so similar to drive to an ordinary Land Rover that anyone could take the wheel. Unlike most of the earlier generation, heavy steel-bodied Land Rovers, and the hastily up-armoured vehicles procured in the early stages of the conflict, the CAV had near conventional handling character-istics and, sometimes more importantly, better power to weight ratio for getting out of trouble.

Its heavy duty coil suspension was also beneficial for travel on the country's degraded roads and improvised rough track lines of communication. The first major non-military contract placed with Courtaulds came from the United ➡

Top left:
The CAV in which
the author
travelled
through Croat,
Muslim and
Serb-controlled
areas during the
initial post-
Dayton ceasefire
period

Top right:
Red Cross CAVs
in Sarajevo –
note the
armoured side
windows, which
were also found
on UNHCR
vehicles

Road conditions were atrocious, with daytime temperatures well below zero...

 Nations High Commission for Refugees (UNHCR) for humanitarian relief duties in Bosnia. The Red Cross (ICRC) was not far behind.

liaison vehicles

At first, only a couple of British Army CAVs were deployed to Bosnia, as armoured liaison vehicles for senior British Commanders who had to negotiate with the warring factions. But by the time of the Dayton Peace Accord, in December 1995, numbers had increased quite substantially, and most units seem to have had at least one or two on hand as light armoured utility vehicles.

Incidentally, included with correspondence from Courtaulds in October of that year, I was sent an undated press release which stated that a Canadian order for three vehicles had taken the total number of CAVs serving in the former Yugoslavia to seventy. In addition to vehicles serving with British, Canadian, French and Malaysian military contingents, plus press and aid agency vehicles in Bosnia, sales of police vehicles had also been announced to British and Indian constabularies.

A few days after the Dayton Accord was signed I flew into Bosnia, courtesy of the RAF, to cover British forces deployed as part of the IFOR peace-

Above left:
A Fusiliers CAV at their temporary base in the power station under a vital dam on Bosnia's inter-ethnic boundary line

Above right:
Driver's position on a Courtaulds Demonstrator – the only major join in the two piece body is visible behind the seat

enforcing operation. On two separate occasions over the next ten days or so, I travelled in CAVs for long distances through regions occupied by each of the three recently warring factions and still nervous armed factions.

Road conditions, if you could call them roads, were atrocious, with daytime temperatures well below zero and fresh snow lying over thick, polished ice. As well as being grateful for the protection offered by the CAVs composite armour, I was also glad to be travelling in a trusty Land Rover, which I knew I could rely on in the worst that mother nature threw at us. I was also really happy to be sitting in a CAV, rather than an ordinary Defender, when an approaching coach pirouetted towards us, missing us by inches, as its bald tyres hit a patch of black ice on a steep slope outside Gornji Vakuf.

Production of the CAV is now complete, but no doubt these unique, armoured Land Rovers will soldier on for many years yet. And when the base vehicles finally get pensioned off through old age, the fact that the body can be dropped onto any heavy duty Defender chassis should see them being refurbished to extend their working lives well beyond their anticipated decommissioning date of 2005. **LRM**

the one that got away

Story and pictures Bob Morrison

Above: Restored to near new condition, only the registration plate gives a clue to civilian ownership

Richard Hunt retired from a successful career in international heavy plant sales many years ago, to spend more time with his family, but could not settle down to just pottering around in the garden, even though his Norfolk garden looks like it was landscaped by Capability Brown. Today, he and his wife Linda have what he terms a small business, importing and exporting highly specialised track-laying plant and civil engineering equipment, but he still gets the urge to graze his knuckles on vehicle restoration projects once in a while.

In his words he is "not really a Land Rover enthusiast", though when he reflected on that statement he realised that he had actually owned Discoverys and Range Rovers for more years than he cares to remember, so maybe he actually is. However, his latest rebuild project must be the envy of every Land Rover restorer, and labels him an enthusiast in my book.

Our story starts with Richard paying a visit to MVS, the Official Marketing Agents for MoD vehicle spares and Series III Land Rovers. He was only there to help a friend in the trade who was hoping to purchase a small batch of decommissioned leaf sprung Land Rovers, but a rather sorry looking Defender 90 caught his eye. Its side-mounted spare wheel and distinctive air intakes behind the front wheels confirmed that this was no run-of-the-mill Defender though, and Richard was intrigued enough to look closer at it.

The bug bit.

Vehicle LN64AA turned out to be a genuine production batch Defender 90HS, or Truck Utility Light (HS) 4x4 GS Soft Top Land Rover 2.5 litre Turbo Diesel, as the MoD class this particular model. The HS in the classification denotes that it is a Higher Specification model, to differentiate from the original eighties spec naturally-aspirated diesel Land Rover 90, or its nineties younger brother the Defender 90, and the GS describes its role as a General Service vehicle.

However, to most soldiers this model is known as the Wolf 90, a nickname which originated from the original Land Rover codename of the early nineties.

The vehicle which caught Richard's attention had

rolled and damaged, this Wolf sneaked past the system and escaped to civvy street

clearly been involved in a roll-over accident, but although the front wings were badly crumpled, the front bulkhead was distorted and the upper cab was trashed, mechanically and structurally it appeared to be pretty sound. On learning from his friend in the trade that all Wolf components can theoretically be procured through the normal dealer network, the prospect of a full and relatively easy restoration project seemed a distinct possibility.

In the past, restoration of military specials so early into their service life has not been easy, as unique parts could not be ordered off-the-shelf. Today though, in order to save costs and reduce MoD manpower levels, all warranty work and many general repairs are carried out by Land Rover's dealer network rather than through military workshops, hence the easy availability of parts.

That's the theory anyway, though Richard was to find that some ordinary Defender components turned up instead of the requested Wolf parts, leading to about five weeks delay in total during the course of rebuild. This was despite him having

access to a genuine Wolf parts microfiche through friends in the trade.

mechanically sound
Once he had forked out the sort of cash that could buy a brand new, small family car, in exchange for an accident damaged and unregistered Land Rover, Richard had it transported back to his Norfolk home, where he gave it a basic mechanical inspection. Despite the vehicle clearly having stood outdoors for some period of time, it actually fired up at the first attempt, and it was soon ascertained that it was, indeed, as mechanically sound as the cursory inspection at MVS had suggested.

However, Richard did note that the track rod was damaged, and he detected what he considered excess movement in the rear prop shaft, so both were replaced with genuine parts. Both front wings were damaged beyond economical repair, so replacement was a foregone conclusion, but the front bulkhead could probably have been repaired without too much trouble. In the past, this would have been the normal course of action so early into the model life of a military special,

Above:
Posed in front of an air defence gun at the Muckleborough Collection near Cromer. Ring 01283 588210 for times and details

Clockwise from top left: Strengthened front end of Wolf seems to have stood up to roll considerably better than standard Defender; The bulkhead could actually have been repaired, but there seemed little point in bodging; How it looked at the start of the rebuild; Damage to rear tray was minimal

but as the genuine part was readily available Richard decided not to spare the expense and fitted a new one.

Tarmac found on the damaged bodywork was evidence that the Land Rover had rolled on the road, and as is only to be expected of a soft top in such circumstances, the windscreen and door tops were pretty much destroyed. Other than this and

associated damage to the canopy, the enhanced roll cage of the Wolf had prevented any major damage behind the cab.

The lower rear body panels behind the back wheels were slightly deformed, but this may have occurred during the righting process. After inspection, Richard decided just to pull them back into shape rather than go to the unnecessary expense

registered for the road

BRINGING THE vehicle to private road registration standard took more than just the hard physical work of the rebuild. Both Land Rover and the Defence Logistics Organisation's Census Team had to dig into their records to provide Richard with the information necessary, and he would like to use this article to publicly record his gratitude.

During the searches, the following history was uncovered.

TUL (HS) number LN64AA came off the Solihull production line on October 3, 1997, and was stored by Land Rover until its despatch to the MoD depot at Ashchurch where it was officially accepted into service on March 24, 1998. On May 13 it was recorded received by 10 Transport Regiment of the Royal Logistic Corps, at the time part of 5 Airborne Brigade

but now a component of Colchester-based 16 Air Assault Brigade.

It was while serving with this unit that the Wolf had its accident, and according to records it was cast on September 24, less than a year after rolling off the production line. It then lingered in Colchester for nearly twenty months before being released to MVS for disposal.

Distance travelled by that time was just 8,572 km. Nobody has yet disclosed why the Wolf sat around for so long, but my theory is that it was possibly a victim of the restructuring of 5 Airborne into 16 Air Assault, which took place at the same time as much of Britain's airborne assets were involved with the Kosovo Crisis and other operational commitments.

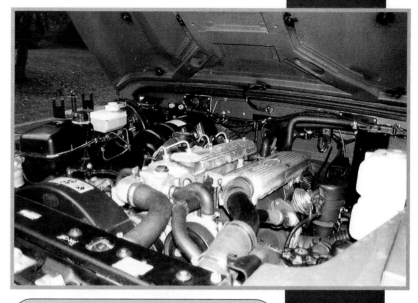

of replacing them.

On checking the damaged canopy, a manufacturer's label (Trim Technology of Bedworth) was found and Richard contacted them to see if it was possible to buy a new one direct. The company has now gained approval to sell its design direct to the civilian market and Richard was delighted to find that a replacement would cost just £225 plus carriage.

Compared with the old Land Rover canopy with which most readers will be familiar, the Wolf equivalent is a quantum leap forward in both material and fastening design. The speed lacing rear flap fastening is so basic it leaves you wondering why it was not used long ago, the rubber fasteners along the bottom edge are simplicity itself, and as for these neat little cord grips, cold and numb fingers need no longer be a problem.

During the course of the summer, Richard slowly returned the Wolf to as near original condition as possible. Other than delays caused by the supply of wrong components, the project was reasonably straightforward, though he did find that some parts were not supplied with all the minor fitments found on the original.

brief history

THIS ARTICLE is not the place to delve into the history and development of the Wolf, but brief mention is necessary to set the background for Richard's purchase. When, in November 1991, the Ministry of Defence issued its requirements for a batch of light and medium utility trucks (designated TUL and TUM) to replace its over 6,000 strong Series III and Forward Control 101 fleet, Land Rover already had a project team up and running in anticipation of the announcement.

By this stage, even the very youngest of the leaf-sprung MoD fleet was over six years old, and many other vehicles were between two and three times this age. Of course many newer vehicles from the coil-sprung Ninety and One-Ten model range were also then in service, but it was anticipated that many of these would be eight years old before the first of the Series III fleet replacements entered service; even if the proposed contract remained on schedule, which is not a very common occurrence in military procurement.

A total of nineteen companies originally expressed interest in tendering for the TUL and TUM contracts, but only two were short-listed for evaluation after bids were accepted. Land Rover and Steyr-Daimler-Puch bid to supply both vehicles, plus a separate sub-class of heavy duty vehicle designated TUM[HD], but although both companies were invited to participate in trials for this last category, only the Land Rover bid was deemed to meet the criteria for the straight TUL and TUM classes.

After Land Rover's original TUL/TUM prototypes ran into problems during these trials, the vehicle was completely reworked and resubmitted for evaluation. A handful of the original prototypes - let's call them Stage One Wolf for future ease of reference - have now made their way into civilian hands, but unlike the replacement trials vehicles and the production batch, these do not have a chassis derived from the New Range Rover.

At time of writing, it is believed that LD64AA is the only production standard Wolf in private ownership.

Top and above left:
Rear compartment left seat lowered and right seat raised to show standard troop or cargo configurations

Above right:
The wolf is powered by the 300Tdi engine, as developed for the Discovery, but with minor modification for military use

military scene

Right:
Simple but
effective wire
guards to protect
the light clusters
are standard on
Wolf

Below right:
Richard and his
new toy beside
one of
Muckleborough
Collection's
armoured
vehicles. The
museum re-
opens in time for
the February half
term holiday

Below:
All that is
missing is the
Defender badge
and pioneer
tools, though the
antennae mount
boxes on the
wings are
unwired

For example little parts such as some of the canopy tie-down eyes had to be taken off the damaged components, and the same was true of some captive nuts. Possibly minor design changes during the production run of nearly 8,000 vehicles could be the root of these problems but, as they did not affect the rebuild too much, Richard did not look into this matter in any great detail.

full inspection

In a little over three months from purchase, the Wolf was ready for its journey to the test centre for pre-registration inspection. Freshly painted, and dressed in its brand new canopy, the vehicle looked like it had just rolled off Solihull's production line. But that did not impress the examiner, who gave it the full treatment.

As always, and as every one us who has taken a vehicle for an MoT test will know, a couple of minor faults reared their ugly heads, but they were soon corrected and a relevant age-related civilian plate was issued. Ministry of Defence Defender 90HS registered LN64AA was now Land Rover R103 FNG, the first production Wolf in private ownership.

One final little snippet. My contacts tell me that it is highly unlikely that any more production batch Wolves will be allowed to slip through the net, for several more years at least, unless they are damaged completely beyond repair. This little beauty might be the only one around in private hands for quite a while, so I am keeping my fingers crossed for at least five numbers and the bonus ball before this article goes into print. **LRM**

and now...

SO WHAT is going to happen to this unique vehicle now? As far as Richard is concerned, the project was no more than a restoration task, and now that it is complete he is looking for another suitable subject. If a serious collector or enthusiast is interested in buying it, he would be willing to part with the vehicle for a sensible sum, to both liberate cash for the next project and to free space for same.

According to unclassified papers released by the MoD, the gross replacement cost of a Wolf 90 is just over £26,000 and this particular one had a net book value in excess of £22,000 at the time of its accident. So if you're thinking of making an offer, please be sensible.

If interested, ring the **LRM** office with a contact number for me to pass onto Richard, or e-mail me at *bob@lrm.co.uk*.

morrison
military scene

never enough

Over the last couple of months I have had a number of letters and e-mail messages asking where copies of the book The Modern Military Land Rover can be bought. This was a project that James Taylor and I collaborated on a few years back, with him writing the history and me providing most of the photos, plus info on operational uses of the various types.

Unfortunately, the publishers of this title ran into financial difficulties shortly after it reached the shops, and it is believed that remaining warehouse stocks may have been disposed of well below trade price to generate cash for creditors. I understand that for a short period it was possible to pick up copies in a few cut-price High Street bookshops, but I never managed to track any of these down. In fact, both James and I only have a single copy each, so if any reader comes across a dusty old pile of unsold copies anywhere, please let me know.

A couple of readers have also suggested that I bring the subject up to date, to include the Wolf in particular. I would be only too pleased to do this if a suitable publisher were to approach me, but to date this has not happened.

It appears that those mainstream publishers who pay the going rate seem to prefer to use established motoring authors with a slight knowledge of a particular subject, rather than lesser known authors like myself who have a more specialist interest. They also tend to stick to subjects which have been proven best-sellers before, hence the reason for so many Ferrari car and Spitfire aircraft books.

When writing a specialist column in a magazine like *LRM*, which is itself highly specialist, regular contributors like myself have to try not to repeat ourselves too much. As I have been writing about the Defender XD (Land Rover designation), Defender HS (MoD designation) or Wolf (what the users actually call it) since it was a shadowy Solihull project, and have published photos of the model since soon after its very first public appearance, at a military display on Salisbury Plain, I worry that I might be subjecting readers to a degree of overkill.

However, a couple of recent letters have asked me to reprise the subject. What do you want? Have you read it all before, or does the topic bore you to death?

Please drop me a line, or better still email *bob@lrm.co.uk* with your views. No promises though.

Like many readers, I keep track of the various Land Rover bulletin boards on the internet. As I have this column in which to pontificate, I tend to be a reader rather than a contributor, but just occasionally I will drop in a reply to one of the military queries if I think I have something valid to contribute to a thread.

More often than not though, I will probably just post a reply direct into the email account of the person who posted the question. The internet certainly has its uses, especially for keeping people around the globe with a specialist interest such as ours in touch with each other.

However, it never ceases to amaze me how it compresses the time space continuum. Long periods in front of the screen also leave me with a numb sensation at the base of my spine which is very similar to that caused by long road journeys in a Series Land Rover.

I really must get out more!

LRM

> **some folks just never tire of reading about military Land Rovers**

when circumstances demand, the Land Rover is often in ...

On a cold, wet, grey November day, Shaun Connors and I pitched up at the Royal Marines' Amphibious Trials and Training Unit (ATTURM) in Devon, just a few days after elements of 3 Commando Brigade had conducted a high profile amphibious landing in Sierra Leone. Both of us have been to ATTURM before, but when the Defence Procurement Agency invited the press corps down to Instow for the day to see the Wolf deep wading, we were only too happy to return.

As young Shaun was so eager to get even colder and wetter, and had a desire to swallow copious quantities of murky, oil-stained water, I gallantly stood back to watch as he joined the flock making their first foray into the dip tank, and bit my tongue to stop making comparisons with a certain Wallace and Grommit character. Just how Shaun coped with the experience, you can read in the feature that follows.

Britain's 3 Commando Brigade, which consists of the three Royal Marine Commando battalions plus supporting commando-trained British Army specialists such as gunners, engineers and logistics personnel, forms the nucleus of the land element of the country's long range amphibious deployment force. Working alongside the Royal Netherlands Marine Corps, in the UK/NL Amphibious Group, the Brigade also plays a major part in the defence of

deep water

NATO's isolated northern flank. These elite soldiers, many of whom are rated as being amongst the most highly trained infantry soldiers in the world, have long depended on specially rigged Land Rovers for their mobility.

a touch of WD40

Most readers will be aware that the off-the-shelf Land Rover has always been capable of wading through at least eighteen inches, or nowadays half a metre, of standing water with only minimal preparation. Usually this just means fitting wading plugs, checking axle breather pipes are sound and giving a quick spray of WD40 for added insurance against spray from the radiator fan. However, there are times when the Marines (or the commandos to be strictly accurate) have to cope with sea water of three times this depth, so something a little more is required. To give you some idea of the depth we are talking about, picture a line half way up the windscreen, and then think of that as being sea level. Enough said.

So why do the commandos, plus the British contingent to NATO's ACE Mobile Force, need to subject their Land Rovers to 1.5 metres or five foot of salt water, you might ask. Well, on the whole they try not to, and wherever possible they will pick assault beaches with sufficient gradient to allow them to drive straight off landing craft and

Mexeflote pontoons onto hard going. Usually a firm shingle beach, onto which aluminium roadway can be laid by special tractors in the first wave ashore, is the preferred landing site. If an undefended hard standing such as a concrete slipway can be found, this is even better.

However, there are occasions when the only suitable landing site in the area is a hard-packed sandy beach. Usually, such beaches are extremely gently sloping, and even in a moderate tidal range the sea will advance and recede quite some distance during the twice daily cycle. It is in these conditions that maximum fording depth may be required.

Even the largest of Britain's tank landing craft, the Landing Ship Logistic, has the shallowest of draught, and the smaller Landing Craft Utility needs well under a metre of water beneath its bow ramp. On a flat calm day, on a gently sloping beach, with the bows of the LCU aground, the nose of a Land Rover might meet little more than a couple of feet (600mm) of water on leaving the ramp.

However, to beat the resistance of the water a degree of forward momentum is also needed, and this has the effect of building a wave ahead, plus the nose-down angle of approach increases the depth perpendicular to the wheels. Add a couple of feet of swell, and the water will soon be chest deep in the Land Rover, and well above every ➡

Report and pictures Bob Morrison

Above: Amphibious landing, East Coast USA, 1996

Above left: For many years the Lightweight, seen here with LCVP behind, was the standard 3 Commando Brigade light utility

➡ mechanical and electrical component. The need to waterproof to such a depth is obvious.

Land Rovers have been waterproofed for wading since the fifties, just like their predecessor the Jeep was in WWII, and even back then considerable effort was required despite the comparative simplicity of both engine and electrics. In 1942, the Combined Operations Experimental Establishment was formed to investigate the problems arising from amphibious landings. One of the sites chosen for these experiments was Instow in North Devon, and as the war progressed both the Royal Navy's Amphibious Experimental Establishment and the Army's Fording Trials Branch of REME, were established in the area.

Situated at the confluence of the Taw and Torridge rivers, with an unusual combination of tidal flows and currents over gently sloping, sheltered sandy beaches, plus easy access to Severn Estuary beaches with the high surf and steeper gradients of the open sea, Instow offers all the right conditions for both experimental work and training.

Next month, vehicle historian Pat Ware will take an in-depth look at the early days of waterproofed and amphibious Land Rovers.

Top: Standard fording ability of pre-Wolf Defender range was sufficient for many amphibious tasks

Above: Amphibious landing, East Coast USA, 1996

After unsuccessful experiments in the sixties to design totally amphibious Land Rovers, the MoD returned to first principles and designed a retro-fit kit to allow the new Lightweight model to be used for amphibious landings. Most readers will know that this Land Rover model was designed specifically for use by rapid reaction forces such as the commandos and the paras, with its weight being dictated by helicopter lift capability.

Few will be aware that its narrow width was dictated by the need to fit it inside the small Landing Craft Vehicle and Personnel (LCVP) which hangs from the davits of Royal Navy assault ships. Both a Lightweight and trailer could be brought ashore in a single LCVP.

South Atlantic

In the following decade, the Forward Control 101, usually referred to as the One Tonne in military circles, was also rigged for amphibious landings. During the 1982 Falklands Crisis, when a British combined forces Task Force recaptured the islands from the Argentinean invaders, both Lightweight and FC101 Land Rovers were brought ashore at San Carlos.

As far as I can ascertain, most of the Task Force

Land Rovers were not rigged for deep wading, as the mainly shingle beaches used were relatively steeply shelving and ideal for bringing the landing craft and Mexeflotes close in to shore. However, if it had been necessary to waterproof the vehicles for a sandy beach landing, the procedure would have involved four distinct stages.

Stage A, which involved a minimum of fourteen man-hours of work on a Lightweight, is the fitting of the majority of the waterproofing kit, to a carefully followed set of instructions. In this state the vehicle could be driven ashore through normal fording depth, and driven indefinitely.

After Stage B work, which usually took less than one hour to complete, the Land Rover was fully prepared for deep wading, but could only run for fifteen minutes maximum before further action was required at Stage C. This third stage, usually undertaken once clear of the beach, or back on board after an amphibious recovery, took just four minutes to complete.

Finally, and within 25 miles of the landing if operational conditions allowed, the fourth stage of de-waterproofing took place.

In 1979, the Royal Marines took over sole responsibility for the training of personnel and trials of equipment for the amphibious role, and the Instow facility was renamed ATTURM. Staffed by a mixture of civilian and military personnel, it was internationally recognised as a leader in this field.

new problems

When the coil sprung Land Rovers entered military service in the mid-eighties, they brought a whole new set of problems with them, and the ATTURM team was presented with a major challenge. Unlike previous Land Rovers, which essentially had not been all that far removed from their fifties predecessors, the new vehicles were much closer in design to civilian cars, with many more electrical components and circuitry to protect.

Other trucks and vehicles with similar electrics had been waterproofed before by the team but, being much larger than Land Rovers, their very size put much of the potential problem above the waterline. When I visited Instow in early 1988, the team were hard at work devising solutions to the problem.

Incidentally, the Royal Netherlands Marine Corps (RNLMC) actually re-equipped with coil sprung Land Rovers well before the Royal Marines. I first photographed the initial batch on ➡

Top:
Rigged
Winterised
Defender
minutes after
coming ashore

Above:
Full de-rig after
wading and
before long
distance road
journey

THE LATEST batch of winterised and waterproofed Defenders to enter service with the Royal Marines come off the production line already modified to allow deep wading with no more than two hours preparation. The build-standard of the vehicle is Stage A, and at this it retains a 600mm fresh water wading capability. Only after the two hours preparation required for Stage B is it capable of wading to 1.5m in sea water.

The MoD requirement for deep wading at Stage B is; the vehicle must be able to operate, with no performance detriment, for 15 mins prior to and 15 mins after wading to 1.5m for six minutes. For Stage C, initial de-waterproofing following wading, 15 minutes are allowed, and within 500km of deep wading the full Stage D ten hour de-waterproofing must take place.

A full report on the trials, development and technical specifications of these latest Defenders, Winter Water, can be found in October 1999 **LRM**. Back issues are available, see page 69 for details.

 exercise on Dartmoor in 1987, where they were undertaking familiarisation training. Although these vehicles had a degree of enhanced fording capability built in, including a permanently fitted raised air intake, they were not completely waterproofed.

a short life
In fact, one of the Instow management team recently recalled that when one was put through the standard ATTURM test, it lasted only about thirty seconds before dying. Prior to the introduction of the Dutch One-Tens, all of which I believe were soft tops, the RNLMC used diesel Lightweights and Series III 109s waterproofed with British-developed kits.

After much experimentation, the project team at ATTURM finally cracked the various problems presented by the Ninety and One-Ten models. This led to the procurement of the 1991 batch of about six hundred winterised Defenders, which were retro-fitted with a semi-permanent waterproofing kit by 27 District Workshops at Warminster.

Though the fitting of this kit considerably cut down the amount of pre-preparation time needed, Royal Marines still had to go through a similar

Top left:
Dutch Marines
One-Ten
prepares to come
ashore from
British LCU in
Norway

Also pictured:
scenes from
ATTURM's
archives, in the
dip tank (top
right) and off-
shore (bottom
left)

staged procedure before and after deep wading. During the massive Purple Star combined operations amphibious exercise in America in 1996, all Commando vehicles were rigged for deep wading prior to landing on the gently sloping beaches of South Carolina's Atlantic Coast. Fully rigged Defenders have also landed in similar conditions on the Egyptian Mediterranean coast during multinational Bright Star exercises.

The latest batch of winterised and waterproofed Defenders (see Shaun's article in the October 1999 issue of **LRM** for full details) now come off the production line already modified to allow deep wading with no more than two hours pre-prep needed. This novel, joint enterprise between the MoD and the manufacturer has given Britain's joint rapid reaction forces a light utility vehicle which really is suitable for operations in all military environments. **LRM**

● *This feature would not have been possible without the help of ATTURM staff, DPA press officers and many Royal Marines over the years, not to mention Land Rover Military Ops personnel. Special thanks are also due to Fred Noyce of ATTURM.*

▲ 1a. A hard top Land Rover Wolf (Defender 110XD) pictured on Cyprus in early 1999
▼ 1b. This vehicle was being used on a driver training course on one of the Sovereign Base Areas on Cyprus

▲ 2a. Civilian specification 'white fleet' Defender 90 Tdi hard top in service with the RAF
▼ 2b. This 'white fleet' 110 Tdi was deployed off-base during operations to recover a crashed fighter in Lincolnshire

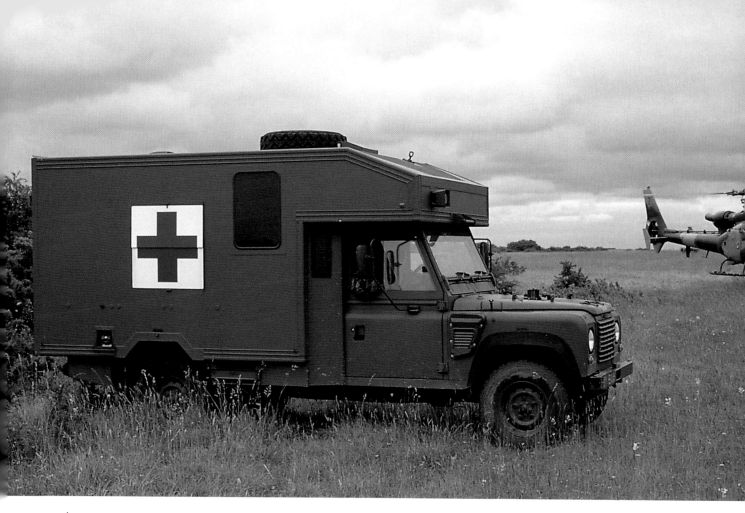

3a. Defender 130 XD ambulance on casualty standby during a parachute drop

3b. Known as Pulse, the ambulance can carry four stretcher or six seated casualties plus attendant

▲ 4a. US Rangers Special Operations Vehicle (110 R-SOV) demonstrator, now in private ownership
▼ 4b. The US Rangers procured the R-SOV after seeing SAS Land Rovers perform in the Gulf War

▲ 5a. The 110 WMIK (Weapons Mount Installation Kit) version of the Wolf displayed by Paras
▼ 5b. The WMIK has already seen operational service in Sierra Leone, Macedonia and Afghanistan

▲ 6a. Commando units use a special waterproofed version of the Wolf, identifiable by the air intake
▼ 6b. The Commandos, who are Arctic-trained, use both hard and soft top Wolves

7a. The APV (Armoured Patrol Vehicle) has now been withdrawn from the streets of Ulster
7b. An APV (up-armoured 1.5 version) with CAV (Composite Armour Vehicle) alongside

8a. As of early 2002, this was believed to be the only privately owned Wolf 90
8b. Sold off by mistake after being accident damaged, it was fully rebuilt by an enthusiast

heresy?

Following the response by caravanners to my November column, the Editor has denied me my staple winter diet of sheep's head broth; the hearty sustenance which my hielan' granny recommended be eaten as an alternative to haddock boiled in milk. I never could stand the haddock, but a good mutton broth with freshly baked, buttered bread really is a meal fit for a king on those cold winter days. Now I suppose I have upset our vegetarian readers as well, by talking about eating bits of fluffy little lambs!

At risk of having my bread ration removed as well, I just have to return briefly to the subject of towing. While covering the recent floods in Yorkshire, I spotted a notice taped to the dashboard of a Fire & Rescue Service Tdi-powered Defender. To paraphrase, it warned the driver not to use the vehicle for towing a trailer as it did not have enough power for pulling out from junctions! Other than a Unimog or Pinzgauer, I can think of few diesel powered utility vehicles that are better suited to towing a rescue trailer than a Tdi Defender. Now if everyone on our roads had to pass a practical towing test before being allowed to hitch up a trailer, instead of just having Category E automatically tacked onto their car licence, things might be different. Subject closed.

Going back to the Pinzgauer, readers might remember the fuss kicked up in both Parliament and the Press when it was thought that this Austrian-built vehicle might become the new British Army ambulance instead of the Wolf. Well, times change and the Pinzgauer is now being built exclusively in Britain. A Pinzgauer ambulance has also replaced the Defender 127/130 Crash Rescue

> **warning; do not use for towing a trailer**

ambulances on RAF Strike Command's airfields, and I welcome the move.

Before the purists hang, draw and quarter me for heresy, let me explain. The vehicle picked for the RAF is by far the best one for the job. It is a small 6x6 truck, with a wide box body which is sufficiently large to allow a trauma team to work on an injured aircrew member in transit between crash site and hospital. The Defender is simply just not big enough for this task, and no Solihull-produced vehicle over the last half century ever has been. Land Rover acknowledge this and have a very amiable relationship with Automotive Technic, the new manufacturer of the Pinzgauer. Indeed at the recent official start-up ceremony for the new production facility, the head of Solihull's Government and Military Ops team was a welcome guest.

In the past there was some criticism of H.M. Government for considering a vehicle from a non-NATO and non-EC country as a possible Land Rover ambulance replacement. The invitation to tender being issued to several other manufacturers and the subsequent trial of another European contender alongside Pinzgauer and Defender went a long way to quashing the protests in what was a relatively transparent procurement process.

The Pinzgauer 4x4 did not win the British Army ambulance contract, but it did win the 101 Gun Tractor replacement contract, after out-performing its Defender rival. It is, therefore, surprising to hear that a vehicle from another non-NATO and non-EC country might be procured for another British Army contract, without any other EC manufacturer allegedly even being consulted. Can anyone tell me more? **LRM**

armour harmer

a recoilless rifle mounted on a Land Rover can be a cheap and effective weapon for use against armoured vehicles

This month we are going to take a look at the Land Rover Gunship, a subject that I have not written very much about in the past. This compact anti-armour vehicle, which is nearly always based on the short wheelbase variant, can be a cheap and effective solution if a potentially belligerent neighbouring state has a large mechanised force at its disposal.

The weapon used on these gunships is what is usually referred to as the recoilless rifle, a type of light anti-armour weapon first produced during the Second World War. The American M40 recoilless rifle, which is the one most commonly found around the world today, is now nearly 50 years old, but it is still a highly efficient weapon against all but the most modern of Western armoured personnel carriers, and it can even destroy Cold War era tanks of the type used by many Third World armies. As the name suggests, unlike a conventional anti-tank gun which fires an artillery shell propelled by an explosive in a conventional metal shell case, the recoilless rifle is designed to produce little recoil. In the original American design, which was based on the work of British scientist Sir Dennis Burney, a special round with a perforated case was fired from a long-barrelled gun with venturi jets at the rear. The resultant low

Continued on next page

armour harmer

recoil means that the weapon can be fired from the back of a light utility vehicle like a Land Rover or jeep, without wrecking its suspension and shaking the bodywork to bits at the first round.

foolproof operation

The beauty of the recoilless rifle as an anti-armour weapon is that it is sufficiently light to be handled by two or three men, and it is virtually foolproof in operation. The weapon's firing tripod usually has a single wheel or a pair of wheels on a demountable axle to allow it to be manhandled into the firing position. Larger calibre (over 100mm diameter) Soviet-designed weapons and their Chinese copies, plus some of their now obsolete European equivalents, were designed to be towed behind light vehicles for long range deployment, but the American version is usually transported on a vehicle. Land Rovers have been used in both towing and transporting roles since the sixties, but from the middle of that decade it has been more usual for this type of weapon to mounted on the Land Rover in a manner that would allow it to be fired without the need to dismount. This gives both greater mobility and flexibility of deployment, plus it allows the crew to shoot and scoot, thereby increasing their chances of survival when facing a superior enemy.

The weapon most commonly found mounted on the Land Rover is, and always was, the American M40 series of recoilless rifle. However, after the Second World War Britain continued to develop its own recoilless weapons based on Burney's largely experimental late-war designs, and the culmination of this was the introduction of the 120mm WOMBAT recoilless gun. Entering service in the latter half of the sixties, the WOMBAT was used as a battalion level anti-tank gun by Britain's rapid deployment forces; especially the Royal Marines and the Paras. Small quantities of these weapons were mounted on commando Lightweights and Para 109s, but the new generation of hi-tech anti-armour missiles would soon render them obsolete. Having said that, it would be the turn of the nineties before the last WOMBAT was fired from a Land Rover on exercise in Germany and finally decommissioned. A friend who witnessed this final firing reported that the resulting shock popped many of the body rivets.

In many parts of the world, where the use of the latest technology is either beyond the resources of the army or outside the capability of its poorly educated conscripts, the recoilless rifle is still an extremely useful defensive weapon. Unlike the current generation of tube-launched, optically-tracked, wire-guided missiles, each

Report
Bob
Morrison

*Above:
The most recent of the gunship demonstrators had a wode firing platform and gunners seat on the mount (Land Rover photo)*

Top:
Press release
photo of the later
vehicle with
three-man crew
(Marshalls
photo)

Above left:
Second of the two
early 1990s
demonstrators
with rear crew
seats raised

Above right:
Blast plates
protect the
bonnet and wing
top, note also the
brackets for
pioneer tools

of which costs the equivalent of a saloon car, these weapons cost comparatively little, and if the state has its own armaments or ammunition production facilities, they are simple enough to be made under licence. Mounted on the back of a Land Rover or similar, which even the rawest of conscripts can be taught how to drive, these weapons then become a highly mobile defensive asset at relatively low cost.

conversions

Land Rover has never produced a recoilless rifle carrier itself, but a number of different companies around the world have modified base vehicles for this purpose. In the UK, Marshall of Cambridge has long been approved by Solihull as a converter of Land Rovers for special uses, and their recoilless rifle gunship conversions have been procured by many countries, regarded at the time of sale as being friendly to Great Britain. The first of these designs were produced on the leaf sprung Lightweight, but since the introduction of the Ninety in the mid-eighties, this model has been almost exclusively used. With a payload capability of nearly a tonne, and sufficient space for both gun crew and ammunition, as well as the weapon

itself, the Ninety and later Defender 90 models have proved to be ideal for the role.

It is very difficult to get defence manufacturers to publicly discuss their client list, as usually they are tied by confidentiality clauses in their contract. Marshalls are no different, but at least it has been possible to see what they have produced in this field by examining their demonstration models at various equipment exhibitions. During the last decade two individual demonstrators, both of which it is believed have now been disposed of, appeared at a number of invitation-only events. The first had been converted to take the ubiquitous American M40, and the second carried a slightly more modern weapon of former Soviet design. Though both vehicles essentially performed the same role, their rear mounting arrangements were different to suit their respective weapons, and there were differences in bodywork. As is to be expected of a weapons carrier like this, both were topless to give 360 degree traverse if needed.

The first of the two gunship demonstrators featured in this article was photographed at the 1990 British Army Equipment Exhibition, just a few weeks before the Iraqi invasion of Kuwait. Painted

in a light creamy shade of yellow, which was neither sand nor stone, the potential market was clearly seen as being the Gulf or Saharan regions. An American M40 was carried in the rear, and this was held in place by a simple clamp arrangement over the front, wheeled, tripod leg. A three-section channel ramp, stowed on the load bed during transit, allowed the weapon to be dismounted for emplaced firing, though as it weighed in the region of 200kgs and no self-loading winch was provided, it would have taken more muscle power than the normal three-man crew to recover the weapon.

two-piece windscreen
When travelling, the barrel faced forward and was clamped over the front bulkhead. This model had a two-piece windscreen, a feature seen on some Lightweight gunships, but no doubt this would be removed in a combat environment to reduce glare. The bonnet and wing tops were covered by plates, which I was told were to provide protection from downblast. They are not, as some observers have claimed, firing platforms. Even if the weapon was to be traversed to the rear, which would only be done in extreme circumstances, the crew would

still be able to serve the weapon from the load bed. While on the subject of the load bed, note how the seats are raised so that the weapon operators sit at firing height, and also how provision has been made to carry ammunition beneath their feet and under the left seat base. The right seat base lifts to give access to a stowage locker under it, and both rear seat backs hinge out and down for firing.

In theory there was sufficient seating for six troops, two up front and two each side in the rear, but a three-man team of commander, gunner and driver would have been more usual. As the spare wheel was fitted to the passenger side door pillar, it was not possible to have an opening door on this side, so a three-quarter height fixed panel was fitted instead. To allow the commander to access and egress his front seat, a large running board was fitted on his side.

The rear quarters of this vehicle are completely open, possibly as a result of a lesson learned on an earlier design. During live firing, a certain Land Rover press officer, who was at that time a junior member of the Government and Military Ops team, was said to have been responsible for blowing the back end off the vehicle when

Above:
The two-piece windscreen, first seen on some early Lightweights, is an easy recognition feature of 106mm recoilless rifle vehicles

he set it up to demonstrate maximum axle articulation during firing. For a long time afterwards the photo was stuck on the wall of the team's office as an embarrassing reminder to Mike, and he was not allowed to live down his blue-on-blue disaster.

specific requirements

In December 1997, when I visited Keith Gott's workshops in Hampshire, he had a similar vehicle for sale. At first I assumed that H929 RHB was the 1990 demonstrator, but close inspection shows several small differences in the rear panel, the rear compartment and the cab rear bulkhead. It is always possible that being a demonstrator it was reworked at some time, but as the original was not road registered at the time of BAEE90, I have no way of confirming one way or the other. Incidentally, it should not be assumed that production batch vehicles followed either design exactly, as each client would have their own specific requirements.

The other Marshall demonstrator featured dates from slightly later in the nineties, and has been configured to take a smaller calibre weapon of

former Warsaw Pact design. Unlike the other vehicle/s, this one has a purpose-designed post mount with operator's seat, to which the weapon is affixed. The cargo bed of this vehicle has been plated over to give a flat firing platform, and the seat boxes hinge outwards and down to extend this platform. There are stowage lockers under both seats and an ammunition locker under the load platform. A barrel clamp holds the weapon in a forward position during travelling, and there is no windscreen.

Once again the spare wheel is fitted to the front, passenger side door pillar, but in this instance a strap is provided instead of a door, though the driver's door is conventional. In 1998 I viewed this vehicle, or one remarkably similar to it, in a private collection in the East Midlands. Like the vehicle seen at Keith Gott's, it was in virtually complete condition.

If anybody has any photographs of these gunships in service with foreign armies, or for that matter of their Lightweight predecessors, please get in touch via the Editorial Office or email *bob@lrm.co.uk*   **LRM**

Top left:
The 106mm recoilless could be manhandled on and off the Ninety using the ramps strapped to the load bed

Top right:
The first Ninety demonstrator with seat backs dropped

Above:
Marshalls gunship demonstrator at BAEE90

global contact

Two readers have been in touch recently, one from the Far East and the other from the UK, regarding a suspension system which I covered in a couple of other magazines about five years ago. The patented Kinetic system by Chris Heyring, which was demonstrated on what both Phil Bashall and I refer to as the Series One trials Wolf, gave the most phenomenal pneumatically-controlled wheel travel imaginable. My latest information on this project is that a major car manufacturer has bought sole rights to the patents, and the system is currently being perfected for a next generation soft-roader

While on the subject of new technology, I spent a lot of time on the Land Rover internet bulletin boards over the Christmas break, as I was recovering from minor surgery and could not go down the pub. Although I have been on-line at home for over two years, and for some time have edited a monthly printed magazine using electronic transfer, over the last six months my use of the web has increased dramatically due to the availability of almost free access on my cable network, thanks NTLWorld. As now I no longer have to worry about soaring telephone bills or limit my surfing to off-peak hours, I am really beginning to reap the benefit of this exciting medium.

The first Land Rover bulletin board was set up around 1996 by some of our North American friends and, although very basic, it allowed a degree of contact between like-minded souls across the vast distances of Canada and America, that had never been previously possible. On this side of the pond we were a little slower on the uptake, partly because of the ridiculously high telephone

charges, but by 1998 there was a hard core of support over here too.

Christmas 1999 was probably the turning point, as computer prices tumbled and various companies offered free or low-cost internet access on local rate numbers. The amount of Land Rover lovers using the bulletin boards really took off.

Although there were a number of small independent Land Rover and off-road enthusiast forums on the web at this time, the biggest site was the Canadian-administered one which had linked up with LRO magazine. In the Spring of 2000, an off-road enthusiast with the nickname Motorhead (hello Steve) set up his own multiforum bulletin board, which also contained a Land Rover Stuff forum. Motorhead's *www.off-roader.co.uk* is an easy-to-browse site which quickly picked up a steady following, and at time of writing is the independent with the largest following.

Just before Christmas 2000, a second large independent board with purely Land Rover content was established by newcomer Chris Tricker. His *www.pepperami.redhotant.com* site grew like Topsy on steroids over the Christmas holidays, and now rates as the second independent LR site, though financial difficulties at *redhotant.com* may see this board having to be renamed and relocated by the time **LRM** goes to print.

These Bulletin Boards are a boon to anyone with an interest in Land Rovers and access to the net. Not only do they allow instant answers to be found to a whole range of problems, but they keep enthusiasts in contact around the globe, which just has to be good for us all.

I'm hooked.

> ## an almost-free phone line finds Bob hooked on the internet

LRM

it's a L

Twenty
years ago, in February 1981, the Australian Department of Defence issued an Army Staff Requirement for lightweight and light trucks in the one and two tonne payload categories, for a potential fleet replacement in the late eighties. At that time Series Land Rovers were their primary light utility vehicles.

By mid-1982, the specifications for what was by then known as Project Perentie (named after a large indigenous lizard) had been drawn up, and tender requests were formally issued that year. Seven companies responded with tenders. Fortunately, Jaguar Rover Australia (JRA) were ahead of the ball in this instance, and they were already investigating their options. Due to the vast distances covered by Australian Army units, the specification called for the vehicles to be diesel powered, but JRA also had this in hand, and a suitable engine was being investigated. Now, this is where the purists will have apoplexy; in those pre-Tdi days a Japanese engine was seen as the only serious option.

Looking through my files when preparing this feature, I came across a letter to me dated August 1989 from Ray Habgood, who was at that time Engineering Manager at the Land Rover Australia division of JRA. One paragraph read:

Right: One of the three original Army Trials prototypes with standard cab [JRA]

Right: One of the three original Army Trials prototypes with standard cab [JRA]

The Australian SAS 6x6 Perentie LRPV was designed to protect the country's most remote areas [BM]

and Rover but not as we know it

"The fuel crisis of the late 1970s spurred the decision to fit the Isuzu diesel engine. We needed a diesel to match the performance of the four litre diesel engines in Japanese Nissan and Toyota vehicles. The Isuzu 4BD1 engine was first fitted to locally assembled Stage One vehicles in place of the 3-5 V8 petrol engine."

The Stage One was essentially an early eighties transition model, produced by Solihull to bridge the gap between the now under-powered 109 and the still experimental coil-sprung One-Ten model. It was essentially just a V-8 powered, leaf sprung, Series III with a flush front end to accommodate the larger power plant. The Stage One cannot be confused with the One-Ten, as it had a mesh radiator panel rather than a slatted grille, its windscreen was two-piece and it lacked the side cheeks necessitated by the wider track of the coil-sprung Land Rover.

Although the Isuzu diesel version of the Stage One could clearly meet the Australian one tonne payload specification, there was no way that it could hope to fill the two tonne requirement. Fortunately, JRA were on the ball here too, and they already had a 6x6 Land Rover under development.

researching the options

Back in 1989 I wrote that, as a result of extensive market research conducted at the beginning of that decade, JRA had identified both civil and military requirements for a vehicle with higher payload capability than the standard Land Rover. I also said that they had considered the options of resurrecting the FC101, producing a forward control version of the One-Ten (which by then they would have been aware of) and developing a 6x6 variant, with the latter proving favourite. This is confirmed the technical description brochure published by Land Rover Australia in August 1984.

Back then, I also mentioned that the original 6x6 vehicle evaluated by JRA was one of the conversions by SMC of Bristol. These SMC vehicles, like similar ones converted by Hotspur (the Sandringham) and Townley, carried the Land Rover stamp of approval, but being after-market conversions did not appear in company military catalogues of the period. I believe that the original SMC/JRA 6x6 prototype had the standard stretched rear chassis, but by the time that the actual Project Perentie prototypes were put forward for competitive trials, a completely new rear chassis had been designed and fitted to the new One-Ten base model.

The three trials vehicles appeared identical to Solihull One-Ten pickups from the rear cab bulkhead forwards, but they had a rear dropside body which I estimate as being

Report and pictures Bob Morrison

Left top: Long Range Patrol Vehicle at BAEE90 with 25mm ASP canon fitted in rear [BM]

Left: High angle view of the left hand drive LRPV demonstrator showing side stowage and (British) motorcycle on rear pannier [BM]

Top:
Very rare shot of all three 6x6 demonstrators together after BAEE90 [BM]

Above:
The Air Defence version, rigged to tow Rapier, was a variant of the standard cargo truck with winch [JRA]

about 400mm (sixteen inches) wider than the cab body. On data sheets Land Rover usually just give chassis cab dimensions for models which have specialist rear bodies.

Although the six-wheelers were fitted with the Isuzu 4BD1T engine, the turbo-charged version of the engine fitted in the 4x4 Perentie, there was no external indication of this. However, no observer could have missed the fact that the rear chassis was unlike anything ever seen before on a Land Rover.

Although the chassis started off fairly conventionally at the front end, from just behind the transfer box it transformed into a rectangular ladder frame. This frame was constructed from MIG-welded rectangular and square hollow sections, with inverted channels running above and outside the main longitudinal members to carry the cargo bed. The entire chassis was hot-dip galvanised after assembly.

The front suspension was relatively conventional, though trim height was increased by an inch, or 25mm. The front axle was an uprated One-Ten version. Twin Salisbury 8HA axles with differentials offset either side of the centreline and wider track (1660mm instead of 1486mm) were fitted.

A coil-sprung rear suspension setup was experi-

mented with during the design phase, and an independent bogey design was also investigated, but eventually the tried and tested leaf-spring and rocker beam layout was chosen. Front and mid axle were permanently driven, with drive to the rear axle being engaged by a vacuum-actuated dog clutch when the going got really tough. This arrangement of rear axle drive output being concentric with the transfer box input was essentially that used for the powered trailer on the original FC101 design. Gearbox was the LR95, an uprated version of the LT95.

seats and cargo

Various rear body designs could be fitted to the 6x6, and several were, once production commenced. However, the prototypes had a roughly 3.2 x 2.1 metre rear tray with header board, removable drop sides and tailgate. Three aluminium bow hoops supported the heavy duty rear canvas canopy on the prototype, but this was later reduced to just two on production vehicles.

Inward or outward facing benches seated a total of twelve men, but these could be easily removed when the vehicle was used in the cargo role. A payload of three tonnes, was theoretically possible,

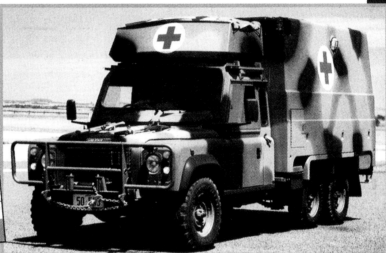

but this did include the weight of a rear body or pod. Cargo payload with the standard rear body fitted was not given in the original technical specification, but it certainly exceeded the two tonnes required by the Australian DoD.

Orders were placed for three prototype 6x6 Perenties in May 1983, and they were put in a head-to-head dual with the Mercedes-Benz Unimog U1300L, which they beat! During the trials procedure though, several alterations were suggested or proposed.

Cab ergonomics in particular, particularly if a three-man crew was to be carried, caused a degree of concern. By the time that a production order was placed, in October 1986, a new cab offering an extra 200mm (eight inches) of interior width had been designed. The cab rear bulkhead was also moved back by nearly 100mm (four inches) to give more seat movement. Now that the cab dimensions were wider, it became possible to increase the front track to match that of the rear, which further enhanced stability.

The first of the 4x4 Perenties which, other than their Isuzu engines and slightly modified bodies, look not too dissimilar to their Solihull equivalents, entered service in August 1987. It was to be

another eighteen months though, before the first 6x6 was accepted.

Original quantities required were 2,500 of the 4x4 and 400 of the 6x6, but nearly 700 six-wheelers have been procured. The six basic variants ordered consisted of Cargo Truck (250), Air Defence (70), Ambulance (100), General Maintenance (180), Electronic/Comms Repair (50), and Long Range Patrol Vehicle – all figures being approximate.

The Cargo Trucks had soft topped rear bodies, with roughly one in eight being equipped with a winch. The Air Defence variants were also winch-equipped soft tops, but they had Rapier missile racks in the rear and an auxiliary 28-Volt electrical system for the weapons system. Ambulance, Maintenance and Electronics vehicles all had steel framed fibreglass rear bodies of similar base design, but with door and panel opening differences to suit their specific roles.

The most unusual, and by far the most well-known of the 6x6 Perenties are the Australian SAS Long Range Patrol Vehicles, of which 27 entered service in November 1991. These open-topped monsters, with fibreglass bodies and crew area rollcages, fulfil the same mission as the British SAS Desert Patrol Vehicles. Crewed by ➡

Top:
Already a decade old, the 6x6 Perenties earned their spurs peace-keeping in East Timor [DoD]

Above left:
The workshop variants utilised the same basic rear body design, which was similar to that of the ambulance [JRA]

Above right:
Cab of the rhd demonstrator, photographed by Bob Morrison during a Solihull visit in early 1990

three, they have a forward firing machinegun and a rear pintle mount for the main armament; weapons carried are usually MAG58 and Minimi machineguns.

They have additional fuel tanks to give an operational range of 1000 miles (1600km) and a 250cc motorcycle is carried on a rear pannier. A substantial bullbar with integral side sill protection bars is fitted, two spare wheels are carried, and the vehicle is equipped with specialist recce, comms and navigation equipment.

canadian project

In the late eighties, JRA and General Motors submitted a joint bid for a Canadian Armed Forces contract. The proposed vehicle would have been powered by a 6.2 litre GM engine. Demonstrators were sent to Canada, and afterwards they were brought to Solihull. At the 1990 British Army Equipment Exhibition, the LRPV demonstrator had pride of place on the Land Rover stand and two Cargo variants also appeared, with the left hand drive of the pair taking part in the Mobility Display.

The SAS demonstrator, which was also left hand drive and equipped with British weapons, had a V8 engine, as did one of the cargo trucks, with the other being Isuzu powered. At the end of the show Land Rover brought all their vehicles together for a photo-call for the 1991 calendar. I was allowed to drive the LRPV around the Long Valley evaluation course to the site of the shoot, which I must say was quite some experience.

Today the 6x6 LRPV which first publicly appeared in Britain in 1990 can be seen at BMIH museum at Gaydon. The right hand drive Cargo Perentie is now in private ownership and road registered. **LRM** covered this vehicle in the January 1999 issue, when it was owned by Harwoods, and our follow-up feature can be found in this issue, starting on page 70. According to my sources in Solihull, the second Cargo Perentie was broken up, and probably crushed, some time ago. On the operational side, Australian Defence Forces six-wheel Perenties and their more numerous 4x4 stablemates played a key role in the recent East Timor crisis, and they continue to serve there under UN colours at time of writing.

When the original Project Perentie requirement was drawn up, the vehicles were scheduled to have a ten year service life and five year reserve. Though now theoretically getting close to the end of their life-span, it is unlikely that they will be pensioned off when planned, and many could well see service to the end of this decade. It had been intended to procure several hundred dune buggy type light recce vehicles to replace some of the 4x4 Perenties by the late nineties, but this project was cancelled. More recent plans call for more off-the-shelf light utilities to be procured instead of dedicated military types.

All production of the Perentie officially ended with the completion of a small batch of satellite communications vehicles ordered in late 1997.

LRM

end of an era?

It seems that despite my various jottings over much of the last decade, there is still great interest in what might just be the last conventional Land Rover designed specifically for military users. Over the last couple of months, I have had a lot of requests to cover the Wolf story, hence the feature on this topic in this issue. I will do a short follow-up on Pulse, the meat wagon version of Wolf in a future issue, but after that I am going to try to let the subject rest for a while.

Getting back to that throwaway line about the last conventional military Land Rover, as armies shrink and governments look more to leasing off-the-shelf vehicles from civilian companies, such as the ten year 'Deals on Wheels' contract announced by the UK Minister for the Armed Forces on January 29, it seems unlikely that another military project like Wolf will happen again. This Deals on Wheels programme sees a single contract lease company providing thousands of what the MoD usually refer to as white fleet (rear echelon) vehicles such as those used for utility duties on airfields and around the UK garrisons.

Many of these vehicles are trucks, vans and passenger cars, but the fleet also includes many Land Rover-type vehicles which have a secondary role in combat support. Most frontline combat vehicles, known as the green fleet, are not yet included in this Private Finance Initiative, but many knowledgeable commentators reckon that it is only a matter of time now that the thin end of the wedge has been hammered well and truly home.

As Britain saw several times in the last century, war always rears its ugly head just as soon as the strategists say there will never be another one

and the politicians respond by cutting back in armed forces and weapons. Trouble is, world peace is a long way off and the ever-decreasing ranks of the British armed forces have never been so thinly spread for more than two centuries, yet had so many overseas commitments.

We know that Land Rover has committed to supplying spares for the current Wolf fleet for about another twelve years, but with no guarantees that there will be at least a potential home market for their products, there is little incentive in militarising the New Defender. After all, with cost rather than suitability for task now seemingly being the prime factor in military vehicle supply, it will probably not be long before we find British troops deploying on peacekeeping duties with cheap and cheerful Far East pickup trucks or even Jeep replicas manufactured in the Third World.

Worse still, if Britain or Europe's interests need defending in the face of aggression, future troops might have to commandeer civilian Sports Utility Vehicles as the army no longer owns most of its own vehicles. I wonder if the small print in the leasing document rules out use in war and if severe off-road use negates the vehicle warranty?

■ Changing to more pleasant topics, thanks for all your feedback to my Santana Land Rover picture spreads published in recent issues. The information supplied by Roberto Follia Martinez in particular has been of great use. I'm taking a break from Santanas this month, but I will do a brief follow-up based on Roberto's information in a future issue.

■ The new address for the Land Rover UK Forums (what was Pepperami, see last month) is *www.planetmayan.com*

cost rather than suitability now seems to be the prime factor

LRM

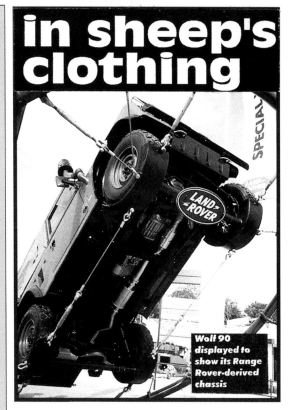

Wolf 90 displayed to show its Range Rover-derived chassis

Land Rover's Wolf project saw the company collect an important British Army contract in the mid-nineties, but the prize wasn't easily won

Nine months after the Gulf War ended, Britain's Ministry of Defence issued a requirement for a wheeled vehicle logistic support fleet with a payload range between 0.6 and 1.4 tonnes. Despite the excellent post-war report that operational commander General Sir Peter de la Billière gave the in-service Land Rover fleet, the company realised that, for the first time in nearly four decades, it could no longer assume that Britain's only home-grown 4x4 light and medium utility vehicle would be the automatic choice in this category.

When details of the Invitation to Tender were eventually published in the MoD Contracts Bulletin dated January 8, 1992, the full implications of just how much the system had changed since the mid-eighties trials of the Defender became readily apparent. No less than sixteen other European Union companies (from Britain, France, Germany, Portugal and Spain) plus Hum-vee makers AM General from the States and Steyr-Daimler-Puch from non-aligned Austria, had all been invited to present tenders by the end of February. The anticipated contract total was for 6,463 vehicles, and the prize was assumed to be worth well in excess of

Continued on next page

Royal Engineers explosive ordnance disposal teams were some of the first to receive the Wolf - note side mounted spare

in sheep's clothing

£100 million of business at 1991 rates, spread over five years of production, though the kudos gained on the international military vehicle sales market would have been immeasurable. A second requirement for several hundred battlefield ambulances was issued a few weeks later.

coincidental stumbling

Things then went very quiet for several months, partly as a result of the tender submission date being slipped back to June, but in early May, by pure coincidence, I stumbled over some information about the Land Rover contender. Far away from prying eyes, at a military range in north-east England, a new version of the Defender had been spotted. Luckily, I was covering a big exercise on this range a few days later, and my contact was able to provide me with a few interesting snippets.

As well as confirming that the vehicle appeared to be very similar to the familiar Defender body shape, and was definitely not a Discovery-based pickup along the lines of a previously 'leaked' picture, he suggested that the diesel engine sounded more like that of the Discovery than his service One-Ten. This confirmed my belief that the Tdi engine was the

likely power plant. However, the single most important snippet that he came up with was the project name - Wolf.

Armed just with the Project Wolf name and my supposition that the Tdi power plant would be used, I managed to tickle some more info out of both junior Solihull and military contacts. It soon became clear that Land Rover were not being quite so transparent and the Wolf was more than just a minor update of the Defender. However, it was to be quite some time before I learned the full details and, by then, the Second Stage prototypes were under trial. But I am running ahead of myself now.

Eventually, all bids went in, but it would not be until December 1992 that it became clear which vehicles had been chosen for competitive trials. There were actually three distinct payload categories of vehicle listed in the original requirement; these being the 500kg payload Truck Utility Light, the 1200kg Truck Utility Medium, and the 1400kg Truck Utility Medium (Heavy Duty).

Though never publicly admitted in such simple terms, this last category was introduced to give the Royal Artillery a vehicle which met their airportability and parachute drop needs

Report and pictures Bob Morrison

Above Wolf 110 FFR hard top in RAF service

116

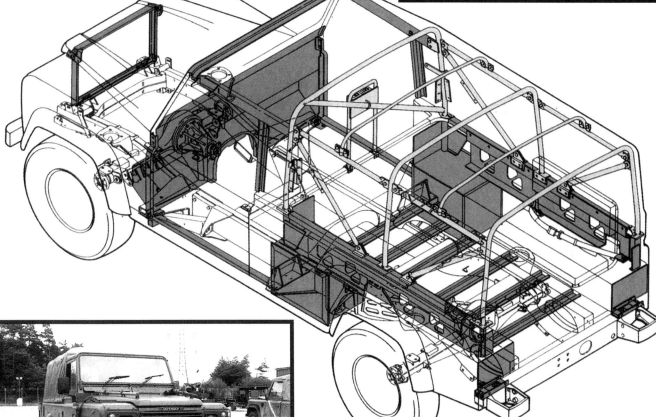

Top right:
Second Stage
Wolf prototypes
at 1995 British
Army Equipment
Exhibition

Above left:
First Stage Wolf
prototype during
trials mid-1993

Above right:
Little room under
the bonnet with
300 Tdi engine -
this is a Fitted for
Radio (FFR)
hardtop

in place of the totally unsuitable RB-44 Truck Utility Heavy that they had been lumbered with in a previous procurement fiasco.

The Defender was clearly within specification requirements for both TUL and TUM, but there was some doubt as to its suitability for the TUM(HD) gun tractor role. As the spec called for all vehicles to be commercially based, and original requirements were for less than two hundred units, there was no scope to design a totally new vehicle - especially one capable of being supported by a world-wide dealer and agent network.

Many at Land Rover would have preferred to have taken a back seat on this one, but some in the MoD were insistent that a Solihull vehicle was entered in the TUM(HD) class. To keep everyone happy, a wide-bodied 110 variant was proposed, though during subsequent trials the Pinzgauer beat it hands down, as expected. On July 28, 1994, Steyr-Daimler-Puch announced that after nine months of 'rigorous' trials, they had received a contract to supply 394 vehicles to the MoD for the TUM(HD) requirement.

With Mercedes and UMM withdrawing from the race, and both Pinzgauer and FIAT being ruled out, the TUL and TUM competitions were a one-horse

race. But this was to prove more of a nightmare than a blessing to Land Rover. As one company official explained, if two vehicles are in direct and equal competition and one hits 97 percent reliability against the other's 94 percent, it can be assumed that one is the winner. However, if only one vehicle is in the trial and is measuring up to a 100 percent benchmark, it will always be seen a loser by some, even if it hits 97 percent. After the first round of trials, somebody in the trials and procurement chain clearly saw the Wolf as a loser, and the process was suspended while Land Rover went back to the drawing board.

At this stage the question could be asked as to why the Ministry of Defence was putting a vehicle with a 45-year pedigree of British military service through the mill. Cynics might point out that the civilian side of MoD vehicle trials and experimenta-

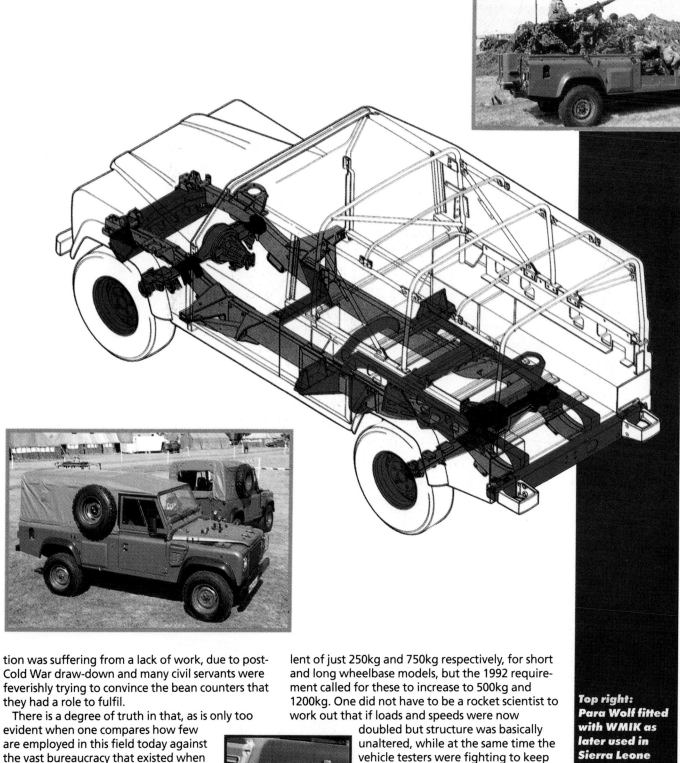

tion was suffering from a lack of work, due to post-Cold War draw-down and many civil servants were feverishly trying to convince the bean counters that they had a role to fulfil.

There is a degree of truth in that, as is only too evident when one compares how few are employed in this field today against the vast bureaucracy that existed when the original Defenders were trialed in the first half of the eighties. However, the answer is not quite that simple.

Military vehicle capabilities of the 21st Century bear little comparison to those of the mid-20th Century when the Land Rover was born, but the basic structural design remained largely unchanged from the introduction of the Series II in 1958. Back in these days, with a maximum power of 70 bhp under the pedal of the petrol version (a miserable 51 bhp for the diesel) realistic road top speeds of 50mph were seen as the norm. Today's indirect injection, turbo-charged diesel Wolf 90 can easily hit double that speed.

Military payloads back in 1958 were the equiva-lent of just 250kg and 750kg respectively, for short and long wheelbase models, but the 1992 requirement called for these to increase to 500kg and 1200kg. One did not have to be a rocket scientist to work out that if loads and speeds were now doubled but structure was basically unaltered, while at the same time the vehicle testers were fighting to keep their jobs, something would have to give. And the First Stage Wolf did.

technological superiority

Fortunately for Land Rover, the success of the Discovery model was by then bearing fruit and there was enough money in the pot to allow the new Range Rover model to be designed with the latest in computer technology. Indeed at its launch, Rover claimed that it was the first car in the world to be completely designed by computer from the ground up.

By the time that the Wolf team came to look at how they could improve their proto-types to meet the harsh - or rigorous as

opposition that failed to materialise...

IT WAS widely assumed that Mercedes-Benz would enter the Austrian-built Gelandewagen and UMM would field the Portuguese Alter II against Land Rover in the TUL and TUM classes, though in the end both companies withdrew. Off the record, a source in UMM said that they estimated that just supporting the trials would cost them over £1 million, which was too much of a gamble when competing against both Land Rover and Mercedes-Benz.

Pinzgauer's UK agents had intimated that they would be entering the short wheelbase 716M model to cover all requirements. This compact and nimble, forward control, portal axle vehicle sits midway between Defender 90 and 110 in size and slightly exceeded the larger Land Rover model in terms of both payload and towing capability. However, even with spare wheel carried inside instead of at the rear, its overall length exceeded the 3900mm TUL maximum by about 300mm, so it was no surprise when the MoD rejected it for this role. It is believed that this failure to meet specification along with the original requirement statement that a common basis throughout the range was desirable, was the deciding factor in the rejection of the Pinzgauer from both TUL and TUM.

FIAT proposed the forward control 40.10WM model, as used by the Italian Army, for both TUM and TUM(HD) categories but it is believed that this bid was rejected on the grounds of lack of commonality with TUL plus a width in excess of specification requirements.

... details and evasion

I FIRST attempted to contact all the companies on the list of those intended to tender in January 1992, by fax. Some bothered to reply, but most kept their plans exceedingly close to their chest. The Spanish Nissan plant was very forthcoming in confirming that they would not be putting forward a submission.

Mercedes-Benz of Germany dispatched details of their standard military range, as did Auverland of France and AM General of the USA. Britain's AWD Bedford intimated that it had decided "to withdraw from participation", Reynolds Boughton said they were "not at liberty to send details of this vehicle at present" and Leyland DAF declined to provide details on the grounds that there were "confidential matters that we would not wish to declare for obvious commercial reasons".

UMM of Portugal, whose vehicle had been the third Dutch Army contender alongside the Defender and the winning M-B Geländewagen, were the most open of all and offered to put a vehicle and test driver at my disposal if I was ever in Lisbon (an offer I took up within the month).

As for Land Rover, they intimated that they would be proposing near off-the-shelf versions of both 90 and 110 military spec Defender models, first introduced in 1991, but declined to provide further details until their bid had been submitted.

Pinzgauer described them - treatment doled out during the 18,000 kms long military trials, this latest computer design technology was available to them. They grabbed the opportunity with both hands and set about redesigning Wolf from the wheels and axles up.

The two areas where the prototype Wolf had not quite lived up to military expectations were chassis and axle strength and body robustness. The computers quickly provided the answer to the first problem, which is why axles are derived from those of the Range Rover with additional strengthening to suit the heavy off-road use expected in military service, and the heavily strengthened chassis is much closer in design to that of the New Range Rover than the Defender.

A sub-frame under the cargo bed was also added for better weight distribution and new heavy duty wheels were designed. As for the body, although externally all panels look virtually unchanged, the front bulkhead has been considerably strengthened and inserts have been fitted to the upper rear body panels to reinforce roll-over protection.

The top of the windscreen, door jambs and door pillars have also been strengthened plus fore and aft strengtheners have been fitted behind the side sills, to stiffen up the cab area in a crash situation. The rear tilt frame has also been increased in diameter to provide full roll-over protection.

One side effect of all this stiffening is that a heavy weapons mount installation kit (WMIK) can now be quickly added to the standard Land Rover for the first time in half a century. At the front end, a new radiator support frame not only provides more strength, but also makes radiator removal a much easier job in field conditions.

On January 18, 1996, the Ministry of Defence announced that it was to order over eight thousand Land Rovers to meet British Army Utility Truck and Battlefield Ambulance requirements. First vehicles were accepted for user trials later that year, and shortly afterwards the Wolf deployed operationally on peacekeeping duties in Bosnia.

These new Land Rovers were later to deploy with both British and Italian armed forces in Kosovo in 1999 and were baptised in combat in Sierra Leone last year. The Wolf, or Defender XD as Land Rover designates it, is also in service with the Dutch Marines. **LRM**

Top right: Cutaway Wolf 110 displayed at BAEE95 - though externally similar to Defender, it has been heavily strengthened

Above right: Fold-up seats in the rear of a Second Stage Wolf prototype, Larkhill 1995

extremes

Regular readers of this column may just have sussed out that I am a warm weather person. When I came into this world 'twas a hot summer night, and I have liked the heat ever since. Consequently, it does not take much to get me onto a plane to warmer climes to cover a story, especially in the latter part of a British winter when my old bones really feel the cold. Two periods of extreme British weather stick out in my memory; the long, cold winter of 1963 and the long, hot summer of 1976. You don't have to be a rocket scientist to work out which I preferred.

Ten years ago, though it sometimes feels like only last month, my scribblings on Land Rover topics took me to the Persian Gulf. The region was going through its coldest winter in living memory, but daytime temperatures in the desert were more like a summer day back home. Five years on, and the stage had moved to Bosnia. Cold, grey, snowy Bosnia. I went, but I did not enjoy it. Waking up in a woodshed with condensation from my breath turned to ice on my chin was a nightmare. For one three day period my boots seemed permanently frozen, and as I had 'flu as well I was not a happy bunny. I hate the cold. Give me the Sahara any day!

At the beginning of March, the Norwegians invited me up to the Arctic Circle to cover the massive multinational Exercise JOINT WINTER 2001. Against my better judgement, especially after having checked out the weather situation and discovered that -25C was about par for the course, I accepted their offer and packed my gear. The Royal Marines were scheduled to mount an amphibious landing and hopefully this would be an ideal occasion to photograph their winterised and waterproofed Wolves in their natural habitat. With luck, I might also get a chance to see how the standard Wolf fared in these extreme climatic operating conditions, so it was an invitation I really could not refuse.

There is a saying in the military that any mug can be uncomfortable. I was not aiming to be the one to qualify this, and made sure that I was well equipped with plenty of specialist cold weather military clothing, manufactured by Arktis of Exeter (01392 201614). This company was founded by a former Royal Marine officer with years of Arctic soldiering under his belt and is the mutt's nuts for keeping a soldier warm and dry. For my feet, I blagged a pair of waterproof and insulated Pro-Boots, as on general issue to the British Army and as recommended by Shaun in this mag a few months back. All my new gear lived up to expectations, and I actually enjoyed my trip.

Unfortunately though, British military participation in the exercise was badly curtailed by the foot and mouth crisis and, after just three days in Norway, British journalists were politely told that they were not welcome on the training areas because of the threat they might pose. However, I did get a brief chance to work with an RAF Regiment unit from Germany who highly praised their Wolves. Other than changing to winter lubricants and studded tyres, these vehicles were bog standard, yet started first time at -34C. Interestingly, only a few months ago they were operating in the Gulf at +34C. Unlike me, Land Rovers are made of sterner stuff. **LRM**

> the region was going through its coldest winter in living memory

In a conscious effort to ensure that government and military spending benefits the national workforce and is not a drain on their international trading balance, many countries try to arrange offset deals when buying-in foreign equipment and systems. If their manufacturing industry is not sufficiently advanced to produce, say, electronics equipment, but can turn out high quality garments, they might try to trade off quantities of combat uniforms for radios. Another alternative, where the manufacturing base is adequate but the research and development structure is less so, might be to licence-build tried and tested products with a proportion of locally produced components.

Almost since its inception, the military Land Rover has been used as an inter-governmental trading chip plus, possibly more importantly, it has also been used to develop vehicle manufacturing in countries without a national industry in this field. As even today's Defender is still little more than an automotive Mecanno kit, albeit with ever more complex electronic add-ons, the conventional Land Rover has always been well suited for local assembly. In the first instance, vehicles will usually be assembled from a straight kit of parts, but in due course it is expected that the developing in-country licensee will either fabricate a significant proportion of the simpler components himself, or source them from local industry. If, on the other hand, the chosen assembler already has a proven record in working with other automotive brands, it is possible that all but the prototypes used to validate the production sequence may have a very high percentage of non-Solihull components.

knocked down kits
From the fifties, many Commonwealth countries imported both military and civilian use Land Rovers in what was known as completely knocked down (CKD) kits, but as these nearly always consisted of one hundred percent UK components, there was no real difference from Solihull production line vehicles. However, in post-war Europe there was sufficient expertise and manufacturing capability to supply a percentage of locally sourced componentry from the outset, so hybrid vehicles such as the German Tempo, used mainly by border guards and police, or the Belgian

Turkish delights

Turkey, the land of assorted Land Rovers

Report and pictures Bob Morrison

Minerva, used in quantity by the military from the fifties until the end of the eighties, were very successful. It is probably the Spanish-built Santana range of both civil and military leaf sprung Land Rovers, that most readers will be most familiar with, but as manufacture of these was terminating, a lesser-known European vehicle builder was starting up a production line for coil sprung Land Rovers. At the opposite end of the Mediterranean, Otobus Karoseri Sonayi of Istanbul, had won significant government orders for military and public service vehicles based on the Ninety and One-Ten models.

Otokar, as the company is more usually known, is part of the vast Koc group of companies, which makes everything from household appliances

through to defence equipment, but to most Turks and visitors to Istanbul alike, the name is synonymous with the omnipresent fleet of small buses that provide transport for the majority of citizens of the only city to span two continents. These workhorses, often packed to the gills, are hammered into the ground by some of the worst bus drivers I have ever encountered, but they seem to go on for ever with minimum maintenance and virtually no rest. If they are a testament to the skills of the Otokar workforce, the Land Rover oval is clearly in good hands.

The primary Turkish Armed Forces consist of army, navy and air force personnel, but like most nations which have borders with potential enemies, the country also has a

⏸⏸⏩ paramilitary police force or gendarmerie. It is the Land Rovers used by the Jandarma, responsible for internal security and border patrols, which visitors off the tourist trail in Turkey are most likely to encounter. Normally they use either military green or police blue 5-door station wagons, with white Jandarma lettering on the sides, but they also have conventional looking green 110 soft tops for utility duties, plus green crew cab troop carriers with less conventional slab-sided rear bodies. The Turkish Army is not so dependent on Land Rovers for day-to-day duties, but they still employ a fair number of Otokar station wagons and hard tops in specialist roles. Turkish troops on peacekeeping duties in the Balkans have used camouflage painted station wagons since 1996, and I have also spotted plain green versions on the Turkish side from across the Green Line that divides Cyprus.

It was the One-Ten Station Wagon model which broke into the Turkish Army market for Land Rover. The first batch of these vehicles, which look almost identical to Solihull-built vehicles, were used as personal transport for Army officers of Brigadier rank and above. As is evident from the antennae boxes on the front wings, these vehicles are fitted for radio (FFR) models, and carry communications equipment on the right side of the rear compartment. Two radio operators can also travel in the rear on the inward facing bench seat on the left side.

seating rearrangements
Anybody who has had the dubious pleasure of travelling for any great distance in the second row of seats in a standard Solihull-built station wagon will know how poor the legroom is, and how cramped it can be if three of you are all fighting for floor space for size ten military boots as well as a bit of legroom. You don't have to be a rocket scientist to work out that senior officers will not tolerate travelling in such conditions without damn good operational reasons, so it is no surprise that Otokar ditched the standard three abreast seating arrangement for two comfortable high-back seats in the second row, mounted slightly further back than usual for improved legroom. Driver and front seat passenger, the latter being either the commander's aide or his close protection officer dependent on rank, were given more standard seats. At this point I should point out that if you assumed that the Turkish Army is a rag-tag bunch, think again - they number some of the most capable troops in the NATO alliance, and though some of the vehicles and armour used by conscripts are hand-me-down, their more specialist frontline units are as well equipped as some of their western European partners.

Top:
Turkish Army station wagon used by a brigadier, with antennae mounts on the front wings

Right:
Note the jerrycan holder, rear lighting arrangement and bumpers

used for specialist communication duties. I have only seen one of those secretive vehicles, and was not allowed to photograph it because of the sensitivity of its role. A very tall 'fish fryer' antenna in a clump of trees, and the lack of armour tracks leading into the thicket alerted me to its presence, but no amount of sweet-talking could get me inside the ring of troops guarding it. Later, I was to see the vehicle in road-going configuration, and only ventilation grilles in the sides differentiated it from an otherwise conventional hard top.

External differences between British military and Turkish Army station wagons consist mainly of add-ons such as the rear jerrycan holder, side-swinging rear wheel mount and brushguard, plus the previously mentioned antennae mounts. However, closer inspection reveals that the lighting arrangement is also different. Night convoy lights and a pair of fog lights are carried at the front in addition to the standard headlights, sidelights and indicators. The rear arrangement is completely different though, with horizontal light clusters just above the narrow rear bumpers which are substituted for the more usual military bumperettes. This military lighting arrangement, is more like the Dutch or German systems than the more basic British one. One final extra, not seen on standard British Land Rovers, is the towing bar mounted on the front bumper.

The second Land Rover variant to enter Turkish Army service was the One-Ten hard top, which was

As previously mentioned, the Jandarma also use station wagons, and it was this para-military force which actually first initiated Turkish interest in the One-Ten family. In 1986, they ordered a mixed batch of some four hundred soft tops and station wagons for use in rural locations. Anyone who has travelled away from the tourist resorts on the Mediterranean or the over-populated capital of Istanbul, will be aware just how large the country is, and how remote some of its towns and villages can be. In the more rural areas the Jandarma combines the roles of police and emergency services with border patrol and military duties, and is even used as a breakdown and recovery service. The One-Ten soft top was seen as an ideal utility vehicle for this multi-role force. Station wagons were used for command and communication roles, though without the complex radio fit that would later be seen

Top:
The Istanbul One-Ten soft top has side windows in the canopy and an Otokar badge ahead of the lower door hinge, but otherwise is near indistinguishable from its Solihull sibling

Right:
The Jandarma soft tops have side-swinging rear tailgates with integral wheel carrier

**Top:
One-Ten truck
cab with
Istanbul-
designed dual
purpose body...**

**Above left:
...and with the
canopy rolled
up, the rear
seating arrange-
ment and wide
cargo bed are
more obvious**

**Above right:
The 130 trooper
had a raised
flatbed with
drop sides and
outward facing
wooden bench
seating**

in Turkish Army vehicles.

Such was the success of the initial Jandarma batch, that more orders were soon placed with Otokar, and the company set about producing its own specialist variants. The standard One-Ten soft top is a good compromise vehicle which can carry either troops or a cargo load, but its rear bed design is not optimised for bulk cargo carrying. Otokar got around this by producing a new flat-sided load tray with simplified wheel boxes and mated this to a One-Ten truck cab. A heightened rear tilt frame and simple canvas was added to give the Jandarma a conventional, and aesthetically pleasing, dual purpose variant with near full width drop tailgate. When the canopy is rolled up, stake truck sides become evident, and these act as backs for the fold-up wooden slat seats which turn the cargo truck into a troop carrier.

local content

Right from the start, the Istanbul plant was more than just an assembly line for Solihull components, and though major body panels and drive train components were supplied from Britain, anything which could be sourced in Turkey was used on the production line. For example there was a chassis production facility on-site which produced all three of the common sizes (90/110/130) plus a heavy duty 110 inch wheelbase for armoured

variants. Unlike Solihull's, the Otokar 130 inch (actually 127) was purpose made and was not a stretched version of the 110 inch. This long wheelbase chassis was first used on Rapier tractors used to protect NATO airbases in Turkey, but Otokar soon adapted it to take a very neat drop-side rear body with a flat load bed. Outward facing slatted seats could be fitted if the vehicle was to be used in the trooper role, giving the rifle squad in the back both clear field of view and rapid egress if under attack. Until quite recently, when a hearts and minds programme eventually started to bear fruit, the Jandarma was in open conflict with PKK Kurdish guerrillas in the far east of the country.

One side effect of this battle with the PKK was the need to design light armoured vehicles for Turkish Army and Jandarma use in the conflict-torn eastern border region. Otokar first produced copies of Shorland vehicles on their heavy duty 110 inch chassis for this role, but later designed completely new vehicles along the style of the French VBL scout car, but with Land Rover drive components. Quantities of these vehicles were exported to other countries with border or internal security problems. However, the story of the armoured Otokar Land Rovers will have to wait for another day. **LRM**

on the **net**

I must confess to being a bit of a workaholic, but as I actually enjoy my job these days, this is no great hardship. For the first twenty-odd years of my working life, I was stuck in an occupation which I was fairly good at, but which bored me rigid, so these days I have no problem with burning the midnight oil when necessary.

Being my own boss, being happily divorced and having no dependents since my sweet little schoolmarm daughter took up with the biggest, hairiest and ugliest heavy metal guitarists she could find, my antisocial work practices cause offence to nobody and I am happy with my lifestyle. If I want to drive or fly off somewhere at a moment's notice to photograph Land Rovers, subject to scraping together enough beer tokens to cover the expense, there is nothing stopping me.

Well, actually, magazine deadlines do pose the occasional problem as, like an incoming spring tide, their approach is unstoppable. It is around these times each month that it can be guaranteed that I will be slaving through the night when most others are tucked up in bed.

For light relief during these long spells at my computers, and to catch up on gossip as well as sometimes doing serious research, I often drop into the Land Rover bulletin boards on the internet at weird times. (Check out *www.planetmayan.com /cthome* and *www.off-roader.co.uk* for example).

No matter what time I log in, there is always somebody else browsing. Some are nightshift workers with jobs that keep them permanently on-line and others are enthusiasts surfing from home in different time zones. Middle of the night to me in Britain might equate to suppertime somewhere in America, breakfast in the Middle East and lunchtime down-under. Without the internet I could not keep in such cheap and easy contact with such a broad church of people, all interested in some aspect of Land Rovers.

To somebody educated in the days of logarithmic tables and slide rules, when even a telephone call to America had to be booked through the operator, and only the very rich took holidays abroad, life today sometimes boggles my mind.

In addition to carrying out the activities which I try to pass of as work - I do sometimes wonder if writing about and photographing Land Rovers and military vehicles can really be considered a proper job - for the last three years I have also been trying to improve my mind by studying for a BA (Hons) degree at University. While recently finalising my dissertation on an aspect of conflict photography, I suddenly realised that I had almost missed commenting on an important milestone in the history of the Land Rover - the 50th Anniversary of its service with the United Nations. I have yet to ascertain exactly when the first Land Rover was deployed to Korea with Britain's UN forces, but I do have a brief video record of Lieutenant General Matthew Ridgway riding in one when meeting British troops under his command for the first time.

As the General assumed his new command on April 11, 1951, and the newsreel was supposedly shot not too long afterwards, it must be safe to say that fifty years in UN service must now have been achieved. Today, the Land Rover still serves around the world in UN markings, but the emphasis has changed markedly from armed intervention to peacekeeping over the last half century, I'm glad to say. **LRM**

> **a midnight oil burner takes time off to chat around the world**

information gathering

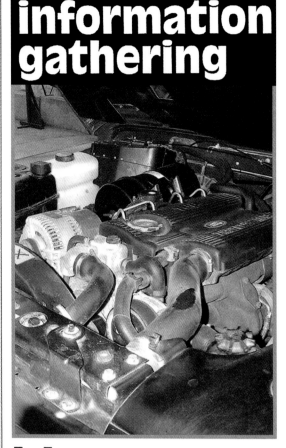

My little trip to Norway, mentioned briefly in my column last month, was made a pleasant experience by the hospitality of my hosts and the beauty of the Arctic countryside, but it was just a little bit too cold for my liking. With the onset of April showers just around the corner, my thoughts turned to photography in warmer and sunnier climes.

What I reckoned I needed was a trip that would give me a few days in the sun, combined with a chance to photograph a few Land Rovers. Macedonia, at the time in question, going through an unseasonal Spring heat-wave, looked like a suitably different place for a visit, especially as I had spotted the odd interesting glimpse of Land Rovers on the newsreels. Mind you, as it appeared as if the country might just be lurching towards the precipice of the next Balkan civil war, it was no real surprise to see half of Europe's television news teams armoured Defenders in the background.

The **LRM** budget does not, unlike those of the BBC and Reuters I'm afraid, run to a fleet of previously positioned Courtaulds CAVs (Composite Armoured Vehicles) in potential conflict zones. Instead, as my spur of the moment trip allowed no time to for sourcing a borrowed vehicle, I plumped for a good old Avis Group A hire car. The little Daewoo Tico micro hatchback waiting for me as I stepped off my scheduled Lufthansa flight may not have been my ideal choice for off-road sorties in the direction of the Macedonia-Albania border, but it had only a thousand kilometres on the clock and wore local Skopje registration plates, so it was both reliable and inconspicuous. Like most budget category hire cars, it was also in plain United Nations or press corps white. All I needed now was accreditation and an interpreter.

Skopje, once Yugoslavia's third city and now the capital of the independent state known formally as the Former Yugoslav Republic of Macedonia, first

Continued on next page

information gathering

LRM's military man has to make his own way to Macedonia

Report and pictures Bob Morrison

Above: Macedonian Police Defender. Nervous at first, they eventually allowed this photograph from a discreet distance

came to prominence at the start of the Kosovo crisis of 1998, when it was used as a base by the multitude of international civil servants and non-governmental organisations (NGOs) which seem to have multiplied like rabbits since the end of the Cold War. The nearly always pristine condition, and predominantly Japanese-made, fleet of white 4x4 utility vehicles and pick-up trucks used by this veritable army, of what seems to be mainly pen-pushers and bean counters, can be seen every-where in the Balkans and Skopje, with its abundance of good hotels and smart eating places, is no exception. The only other off-roaders that I encountered on my twenty minute drive from airport to capital were in more drab military colours, either in the used nappy mustard brown of the Macedonian Army, or the more familiar camou-flage schemes used by NATO with white KFOR markings. Skopje was also the springboard for the 1999 military excursion into Kosovo, and even today its airport and the main road up from Greece are used a primary entry routes into the troubled state to the north.

one-man navigation

On first approach, under greying skies, the city itself is little different from any other southern European metropolis of around a million inhabi-tants, excepting the fact that all the signs are written in the Cyrillic alphabet, which makes one-man navigation a bit of a handful. It is only when one ventures into the faceless

dormitory suburbs, mainly to the east of the city and away from the airport, that four decades of communist rule become apparent through the near identical blocks of multistory state housing. But, unlike in some of the equally monotonous post-war council estates of my native Glasgow and a dozen other British cities that I can think of, the occupants of Skopje's soul-less human chicken coops seem to take a bit more pride in their surroundings.

Other than the odd KFOR Wolf, heading to or from Kosovo, the only Land Rovers that I spotted between airport and hotel (the one on the southern edge of the city that was once used as HQ by British troops waiting to enter Kosovo) were blue police Defender Station Wagons, the odd Discovery and quite a few Freelanders. Now I know that some purists have an aversion to the junior member of the Land Rover family, but it does take the Solihull oval to parts that others seldom reach. As for the police Defenders, which seemed to be guarding major routes into the city, I decided that discretion was the better part of valour after twice seeing pistols drawn as I slowed down on passing them rather than maintaining my speed when waved by. Clearly these guys were nervous, and having seen on television what happened to two Albanians at a vehicle checkpoint less than a week before and only twenty-five miles away in Tetovo - admittedly they were armed with grenades which at least one was prepared to use - I decided to smile, wave a map and pretend to be a lost tourist, rather than point a camera in their direction. I was already beginning to realise that this little assignment was going to pose more problems than usual.

It would be another twenty-four hours before I got my chance to photograph one of the police Defenders, by which time I had gained my KFOR press accreditation and been given a Letter of Introduction in Cyrillic type from the very helpful staff of the country's Minister of Information. Actually, it was neither the letter nor the KFOR pass that proved the key to obtaining this picture, but a good ten minutes of bovine scatteration and pleading, aided by interesting the heavily paramilitary police, manning a strong-point alongside a main trunk road, in copies of **LRM** and Combat & Survival magazines. It was only when I had convinced the very nervous troops that I was not worried about photographing the checkpoint fortifications or their armoured vehicle, thus possibly providing their enemies with target information, that they relaxed a bit and conceded that a picture of their Defender taken in isolation would not pose a security risk.

The vehicle in question, which seemed identical to all others of this type that I saw on my visit, seemed to be a reasonably standard 110 Tdi Station Wagon, with its rear side windows plated. All glazing, including the alpine lights but excluding the windscreen, was protected by very neat fixed mesh panels. The single piece mesh to protect the windscreen hinged forward onto the bonnet, but could be quickly raised into position by wire, in similar fashion to police and army vehicles in Ulster. Front and rear lights were protected with Wolf style mesh baskets. A light bar, in a protective mesh basket, was fitted to the roof, as was a small rotating spotlight and there was a pair of occulting lights, red and blue, on the bull-bars at the front. Unfortunately, I was not allowed to either look under the bonnet or closely inspect the interior, so cannot confirm which model of Tdi engine was used, how many seats were in the rear or what kind of mileage the vehicle had done.

otokar

NATO still runs two KFOR facilities in the Skopje area. The large KFOR camp at the airport is a primarily American-run affair, but the headquarters in an industrial sector of the city is currently garrisoned by Turkish soldiers. During one of my trips to the KFOR press centre at this location, I grabbed the opportunity to take a close look at the Otokar Defenders being used by the Turkish troops as duty vehicles. After a bit of gentle persuasion, I also managed to obtain permission to photograph one of these in the compound.

Though essentially quite similar to the Otokar Station Wagon command vehicles featured in last

month's **LRM**, this batch is Tdi-powered. Externally, the main differences are rounded antennae boxes on the wings, the lack of bull-bars, no provision for a recovery bar on the front bumper, simpler side steps and fitment of repeaters in the front wing panels. In keeping with most Turkish vehicles seen on NATO deployments, these Otokar Defenders are finished in a standard three-colour green, brown and black scheme, unlike the earlier Station Wagons which were plain green. The Land Rover title has also disappeared from the bonnet front edge, but it now appears on the side wing sticker and the traditional oval badge remains on the grille. Internally, the main difference lies in the seating, with a conventional second row for three and two inward facing rear compartment bench seats, instead of the layout described last month. Incidentally, I was granted permission to photograph one of the Turkish Defenders on the express condition that the black on white registration number was removed, hence the white patch on the front bumper in the picture.

Other Defenders spotted in Macedonia were almost exclusively in use with the press corps or, to be more precise, parked up outside their four and five star hotels in the capital. During my 72-hour trip, I only actually saw one of these up near the front line, possibly because international media interest had shifted from covering the war on Macedonia's borders to watching Milosevitch being arrested in Belgrade. On the day that I arrived in the country, AP News producer Kerem Lawton died in a mortar bombardment just over the Kosovo border, and a British journalist with the French agency AFP had his unarmoured

— placed below

4x4 shot up near a village on the Macedonian side of the border, so armoured Land Rovers (or the odd armoured G-wagen) were definitely the preferred method of transport.

Several of these press corps Land Rovers, invariably painted white and being used by television crews, were Courtaulds CAVs. I covered this variant of Defender in the November 2000 issue of **LRM**, so don't propose to repeat myself, though there are a couple of extra points which bear comment. Two of these vehicles, the one with the Danish flag and the one with Reuters over-painted on its side, both had flat roofs, whereas the third one had the sliding roof hatch as seen on British Army CAVs. However, all three had twin armoured windows in each side of the rear compartment. This bullet-proof glazing allows television pictures to be taken from under cover, and usually a pair of individual forward or outward angled seats are fitted instead of the standard inward facing banks, to make the camera operator's job easier.

The plastic-armoured CAV is the most favoured armoured vehicle for press use, and there was even a G-wagen with the same type of Courtaulds bodyshell operating out of Skopje, but steel armoured Land Rovers are also used too. The two which I photographed, at different hotel locations, were of completely different designs. One of these was built around the Station Wagon configuration with five doors and the other was based on a three-door Defender 110 hard top. The Station Wagon, with its three small armoured windows down each side

Top left:
This Press Corps CAV had the British Army style roof hatch

Top right:
Another near standard TV crew CAV, with Reuters painted out on the side

Above left:
Though less overtly armoured than the Station Wagon featured, lack of windows made this steel-bodied hardtop less suitable for film work

Above right:
Tetovo - the cost of war

and shallow armoured windscreen panel appeared relatively menacing and was clearly armoured. In contrast, from any great distance only the shallow armoured windscreen betrayed the level of protection offered by the more discretely armoured 'hard top'. One interesting feature on this latter vehicle was the armoured hatch on the continental driver's side, presumably to allow papers to be presented at checkpoints.

As television crew vehicles have been deliberately targeted on numerous occasions in the Balkans, I do not propose to go any further into detail of these vehicles at this particular time. However, if and when peace and stability return to mainland Europe, which I hope will be sooner rather than later, I propose to cover the story of armoured Land Rovers in press and NGO use since the end of the Cold War in greater detail. Any photographs, stories, technical details or specifications that readers of **LRM**, and for that matter the many manufacturers in this field, can contribute would be much appreciated. **LRM**

now showing

This issue hits the UK newsstands at the beginning of June, when hopefully the Foot and Mouth crisis will eventually be under control and everybody will be heading back into the countryside at last, with midsummer but three weeks hence.

Cast your mind back about three weeks (last weekend as I write this) and savour the memory of our first burst of summer this year. The winter of 2000/2001 has been one of the dullest and dreariest that I can remember, and my memories stretch back to before the long cold winter of 1963. Hopefully, by the time that you read this the drab drizzly weather that followed the first of the annual handful of two-day stretches of summer, which now seem to be the norm, will have cleared away and spirits will have soared again. As luck would have it, that warm and sunny weekend of May 12/13 had been scheduled for the LRO Show and no doubt it would have been perfect at Stoneleigh if only F&M had not been such a problem. Funny how LRO Shows, which for the last ten years have coincided with the weekend nearest to my birthday, have almost always seen more than their fair share of sunshine. I hope that this early, albeit brief, hot spell in May does not mean that the weekend July 21/22 is cold and wet this year, as I plan to be joining all the military Land Rover enthusiasts at Beltring in Kent for the massive War and Peace Show, if I get the chance.

Talking of military shows, Shaun and I were invited by the Defence Procurement Agency to a Driving Day at the Chertsey Test Track at the beginning of May. Land Rover put on one of largest displays out of the forty or so mainly European military vehicle manufacturers

and converters present, but they had nothing on show that readers of this magazine will not already be familiar with. However, we did spot a modified Northern Ireland specification Armoured Patrol Vehicle on the stand of a company noted for both manufacturing and refurbishing armoured vehicles. Watch this space for more details later.

One thing which has become quite apparent over the last couple of years is that the standard Land Rover is no longer a suitable base vehicle for many military applications, as gross vehicle weights of five tonnes or more are now considered unexceptional. This increase in size is partly to do with armouring requirements to combat ever more powerful weaponry, but an increase in the dimensional envelope commensurate with expanding airlift capabilities also plays a part. Cases in point are the new Tavern patrol vehicle, which has been deployed on the streets of Ulster for several months now, and the Pinzgauer 6x6 airfield ambulance. Neither vehicle is particularly light nor compact. Bearing this in mind, one can but wonder what would have happened had the Llama not been binned so quickly in favour of the little-liked and problem-dogged RB44. Had Llama progressed to the production stage, maybe Solihull would have been in the position to develop Llama Mk2 on the Wolf or XD chassis, which could have been a good starting point for a larger sized and higher payload base vehicle.

I suspect we will never see anything but conventional military Defender variants come out of Solihull in the future. It's a pity, but a sign of the changing times. **LRM**

> cancelled shows, and not much that's new to see at Chertsey

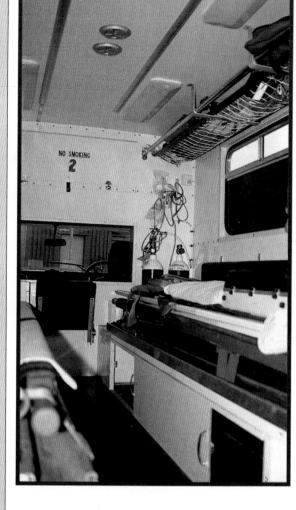

You might find this hard to believe, but a Ministry of Defence decision to purchase a fleet of around 800 military vehicles a little over five years ago caused a controversy which echoed through the very corridors of Westminster. The reason for this fuss was not the introduction of some new weapon of mass destruction on the back of a combat vehicle, but the procurement of a humble Land Rover ambulance - the Defender 130XD model, code-named Pulse.

The root of the controversy lay with the possible outcome of a programme that had seen a prospective new Land Rover base vehicle with specialist ambulance coachwork being put through a direct competition against, and evaluation alongside, two other off-road military ambulances of foreign origin. One of the competitors, the Italian Iveco 40.10WM, had soon lagged behind but, by the time that trials were complete, the Austrian Steyr-Daimler-Puch Pinzgauer had knocked the Land Rover back into second place. Both of these foreign ambulance types had UK-manufactured rear bodies and were based on chassis types that were in service with many other armies. What set the Pinzgauer apart from the others was its off-road ability, which was a result of its unusual combination of compact forward control design, high ground clearance, portal axles and large wheels. These design features and the vehicle's reputation for superb mechanical reliability came at a premium though, and it is believed that the initial unit price of the Austrian ambulance was something in the order of forty percent more

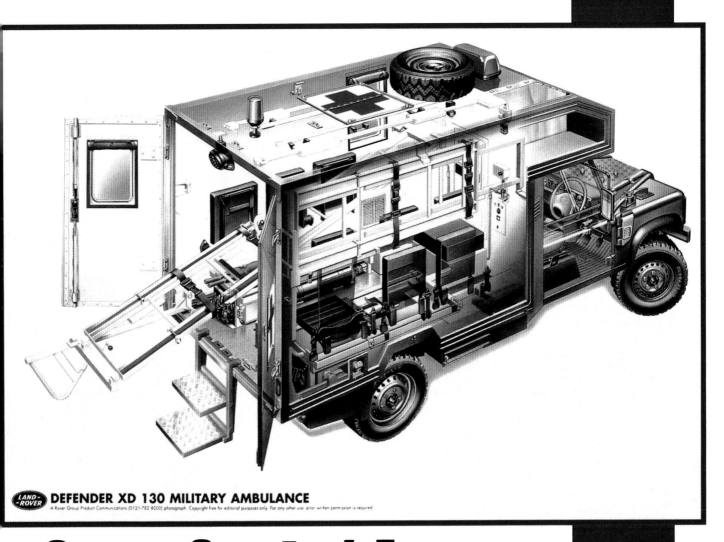

singin' the blues

almost 50 years of military Land Rover with flashing lights and sirens

expensive than its Solihull rival.

Now, although a battlefield ambulance does require a fair degree of off-road ability, it does not have to tackle conditions as severe as, say, a light artillery tractor, as the comfortable transportation of the wounded is one of the highest priorities. There is no point in collecting a casualty and then shaking him to bits, possibly complicating his injuries in the process, by driving him over the sort of rough terrain that the Pinzgauer is capable of tackling. Had both the British and Austrian vehicles been of similar price, it would have made sense to buy the one which offered the best capability, but as the Land Rover surpassed the criteria set out for standards of mobility, the purchasers would have been accused of wasting taxpayers money had they bought the Pinzgauer for this role.

On 18th January 1996 the Ministry of Defence announced that it had 'decided to award the contract for the supply of about 800 ambulances to Land Rover, subject to the satisfactory conclu-sion of contract negotiations'. Interestingly, in addition to citing lower acquisition costs, the communiqué stated that the Land Rover 'provides, in particular, excellent working conditions for the medical crew and commonality both with the new utility vehicles and the in-service Land Rover fleet'. However, a couple of years later a Pinzgauer ambulance, in the larger 6x6 configuration, would replace the small fleet of about sixty RAF and Royal Navy Land Rover ambulances used in the crash rescue role.

The new Land Rover ambulance, which the Solihull design and trials team had code-named Pulse to differentiate it from the Truck Utility Light/Medium or Wolf contract, is based on a stretched version of the same chassis. Wheelbase is approximately 3225mm, which equates to 127 inches but, as with its coil sprung stretched chassis predecessors, the company refers to it as the 130 model. Solihull's actual designation is Defender 130XD Ambulance, with the XD standing for eXtra Duties to indicate that it

Report and pictures Bob Morrison

Left:
Interior of a late model Defender 130 in RAF service

Above:
Defender XD 130 Military Ambulance

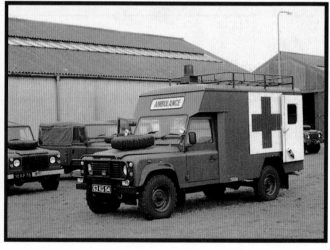

Top:
Royal Navy
Defender 130
ambulance
being repacked
after use

Above left:
The Defender
130 ambulance
was essentially
designed for
RAF use

Above right:
An early One-
Two-Seven
ambulance with
single front
panel over cab

has the stronger Range Rover derived chassis than the mass production Defender one. The Ministry of Defence, on the other hand, designates XD vehicles as HS, which stands for Higher Specification. Although there is a degree of commonality and inter-changeability between the mechanical components of the new and old 127/130 ambulance fleets, a decade of continuous model refinement actually makes them as similar as chalk and cheese from the mechanic's point of view, so precise model designation is crucial when ordering spares. On the other hand, as Wolf and Pulse are mechanically almost identical, other than the stretch and the ambulance body plus uprated suspension, the MoD decision to buy the Land Rover Ambulance at the same time as ordering 8000 Wolves made perfect sense.

airfield crash

The Land Rover's use as a military ambulance stretches back to the mid-fifties, probably 1954, when a small number of vehicles for airfield crash rescue cover were produced on the Series One 107 inch chassis. These vehicles, designated FV18005

Truck 1/4 ton Ambulance Special, were primarily designed for RAF use, but they could also be found on stations used by the Fleet Air Arm, and no doubt the odd one saw British Army service at some time in its career, though I have yet to find evidence of this. Towards the end of Series One production, the army got its own fleet, which carried the designation FV18008 Ambulance 2-Stretcher 107 inch. The rear bodies of the two vehicles were quite similar, though the navy one was taller and slightly longer, and these would set the basic rear body configuration that would see army service for four decades.

The introduction of the Series II 109 inch chassis in 1958 put paid to any further production of the FV18008, and when another batch of Land Rover ambulances was required at the beginning of the sixties, the FV18044 was introduced. Built by Mickleover Transport (later production was by Marshalls), the new Series II based vehicle had a slightly lower rear compartment to allow it to be flown inside RAF transport aircraft of the day, and in addition to the more stylish SII front end, it could be readily identified by its chamfered lower

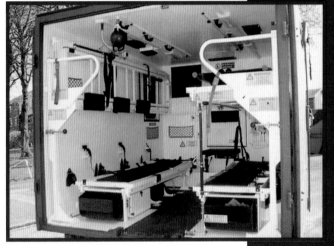

rear body, which gave increased departure angle and the degree of off-road mobility required of a battlefield ambulance. This basic body shape continued in production until the latter half of the '70s, and would be a familiar sight to British troops until almost the end of the century.

Like its army predecessor, the FV18044 was rigged to carry either two stretcher patients or up to six/eight seated casualties. When a second batch was produced around 1964 on the Series IIA chassis, fold-out rails were fitted to take a second pair of stretchers at high level, but the basic body shape was unchanged. Designation was FV18067. The external identifying feature of the earlier model is the lack of racks down both side edges of the roof for the stowage of a second pair of collapsed stretchers. A Series III version, using this same body shell as the FV18067 was produced throughout the seventies and both types continued in service side-by-side until the introduction of Pulse. The last Series IIA FV18067 that I photographed in service, being used for casualty cover during a Territorial Army parachute exercise in the autumn of 1997, was 97ER10, which was

built sometime in the 1966/7 fiscal year.

At this point it should also be noted that several hundred ambulances based on the FC101 or One Tonne chassis entered service at the beginning of the '80s, but they complemented the more traditional Land Rover ambulances, rather than replacing them. Rapid reaction formations such as the amphibious, airborne and airmobile brigades were prime users. These One Tonne ambulances deserve a feature all of their own.

peacetime
In peacetime, army ambulances always have a longer lifespan than other utility vehicles, as most seldom cover many miles during the course of the year. Airfield ambulances, frequently also used as station duty ambulances, can cover much higher mileages and, by the vary nature of their rapid response crash rescue role, they tend to be replaced quicker than their army counterparts. If my memory serves me well, the first batch of coil sprung Land Rover ambulances (excluding the very small batch of Royal Navy Range Rovers) entered service in 1986 as crash

 rescue ambulances on Fleet Air Arm stations. I seem to remember that this initial small batch had a bench seat, possibly with stretcher rails, down the left side of the rear compartment and a gurney could be wheeled into the right side. Unfortunately, I cannot find any photos of the interior of these vehicles, and would appreciate confirmation from readers on this point.

One-Ten

The new One-Ten based ambulances were bigger, faster and more comfortable for both crew and patients. It was almost possible for the attendant to stand upright in the back when treating patients and he, or she, could clamber into the front passenger seat through the rear cab bulkhead if necessary. In the Series IIA/III the attendant was shut in the back until the vehicle stopped or reached its destination. Other than possibly that small number of Royal Navy vehicles that I recollect having a gurney, the One-Two-Seven ambulances had racks for up to three stretchers, two left and one right, or eight seated at a squeeze. Six walking wounded was actually a much more manageable figure. A long, partially tinted window ran along the right side of the rear body, and there were large square tinted windows in each rear door. A few of these did serve with specialist army units, but it was more common to find them in RAF or Royal Navy use.

At least two more batches of very similar vehicles, but based on the slightly later Defender 130 chassis, were procured in the very early '90s.

These ambulances can be identified by the two-piece angular front panel over the cab. One of these vehicles, 10KJ65, famously saw active service in support of Commando helicopter operations in the Gulf War, Kurdistan and Croatia, changing colour from green, to desert camouflage, to white in a little over two years. After questions were asked by politicians as to why well-used thirteen year old FC101 ambulances were being used in the Balkans by British peacekeepers when there was a

fleet of Defender 127/130s available, the coil sprung ambulances were finally issued in quantity to army units.

Pulse

Today Pulse has replaced all leaf sprung ambulances and all but a few of the 127/130 ambulances in British Army service. Powered by the 300Tdi engine, with permanent four wheel drive and five forward gears plus twisted transfer box, it is half a century ahead of the original Series One, but it is still identifiably from the same stable. It is anticipated that the current fleet will serve well into the next decade. The Dutch Marines also use Pulse, and their ones actually entered service before Britain's. **LRM**

Top left:
Pair of British Army 1976 Series III ambulances in Cyprus

Top right:
97ER10 was probably the longest serving army Series IIA ambulance

Right:
Thirty year old Series IIA providing safety cover on an exercise

LAND ROVER OFFICIAL MILITARY AND CIVILIAN FACTORY PUBLICATIONS

Land Rover Ser. 1 Workshop Manual	4291
Land Rover Ser. 1 1948-53 Parts Catalogue	4051
Land Rover Ser. 1 1954-58 Parts Catalogue	4107
Land Rover Ser. 1 Instruction Manual	4277
Land Rover Ser. 1 & II Diesel Instruction Manual	4343
Land Rover Ser. II & IIA Workshop Manual	AKM8159
Land Rover Ser. II & Early IIA Bonneted Control Parts Catalogue	605957
Land Rover Ser. IIA Bonneted Control Parts Catalogue	RTC9840CC
Land Rover Ser. IIA, III & 109 V8 Optional Equipment Parts Catalogue	RTC9842CE
Land Rover Ser. IIA/IIB Instruction Manual	LSM64 IM
Land Rover Ser. III Workshop Manual	AKM3648
Land Rover Ser. III Workshop Manual V8 Supplement (edn. 2)	AKM8022
Land Rover Ser. III 88, 109 & 109 V8 Parts Catalogue	RTC9841CE
Land Rover Ser. III Owners' Manual 1971-81	607324B
Land Rover Ser. III Owners' Manual 1981-85	AKM8155
Land Rover 90/110 & Defender Workshop Manual 1983-92	SLR621ENWM
Land Rover Defender Workshop Manual 1993-95	LDAWMEN93
(Covering petrol 2.25, 2.5, 3.5 V8 & diesel 2.25, 2.5, 2.5 Turbo, 200 Tdi)	
Land Rover Defender 300 Tdi Workshop Manual 1996-98	LRL 0097 ENG
Land Rover 110 Parts Catalogue 1983-86	RTC9863CE
Land Rover 90/110 Owners' Handbook	LSM0054
Land Rover Discovery Workshop Manual 1990-94 (petrol 3.5, 3.9, Mpi & diesel 200 Tdi)	SJR900ENWM
Land Rover Discovery Workshop Manual 1995-98 (2.0 Mpi, 3.9 V8i & 4.0 V8 & 300 Tdi)	LRL0079
Land Rover Discovery Owners' Handbook 1990 on (petrol 3.5 & diesel 200 Tdi)	SJR 820 ENHB 90
Land Rover Military (Lightweight) Ser. III Parts Catalogue	608180
Land Rover Military (Lightweight) Ser. III User Manual	RTC9120
Land Rover 101 1 Tonne Forward Control Workshop Manual	608294B
Land Rover 101 1 Tonne Forward Control Parts Catalogue	608239
Land Rover 101 1 Tonne Forward Control User Manual	
Range Rover Workshop Manual 1970-85 (petrol 3.5)	AKM3630
Range Rover Workshop Manual 1986-89 (petrol 3.5)	SRR660ENWM
Range Rover Workshop Manual 1986-89 (petrol 3.5 & diesel 2.4 - VM)	SRR660ENWM &
	LSM180WS4
Range Rover Workshop Manual 1990-94 (petrol 3.9, 4.2 & diesel 2.5 Tdi, 200 Tdi)	LHAWMENA02
Range Rover Parts Catalogue 1970-85 (petrol 3.5)	RTC9846CH
Range Rover Parts Catalogue 1986-92 (petrol 3.5, 3.9 & diesel 2.4 - VM, 2.5 Tdi)	RTC9908CB
Range Rover Owners' Handbook 1970-80 (petrol 3.5)	606917
Range Rover Owners' Handbook 1981-82 (petrol 3.5)	AKM 8139
Range Rover Owners' Handbook 1983-85 (petrol 3.5)	LSM 0001HB
Range Rover Owners' Handbook 1986-87 (petrol 3.5 & diesel 2.4 - VM)	LSM 129HB
Range Rover Owners' Handbook 1988-89 (petrol 3.5 & diesel 2.4 - VM)	SRR600ENHB

Engine Overhaul Manuals for Land Rover & Range Rover

300 Tdi Engine, R380 Manual Gearbox & LT230T Transfer Gearbox Overhaul Manuals	LRL 003, 070 & 081
Petrol Engine V8 3.5, 3.9, 4.0, 4.2 & 4.6 Overhaul Manuals	LRL 004 & 164
Working in the Wild - Land Rover's Manual for Africa	SMR 684 MI
Land Rover/Range Rover Driving Techniques	LR 369
Winching in Safety	SMR 699MI

Owners' Workhop Manuals
Land Rover 2 / 2A / 3 1959-83 Owners' Workshop Manual
Land Rover 90, 110 & Defender Owners' Workshop Manual

From Land Rover specialists or in case of difficulty, direct from the distributors:
Brooklands Books Ltd., PO Box 146, Cobham, Surrey, KT11 1LG, England.
Telephone: 01932 865051 Fax: 01932 868803
e-mail sales@brooklands-books.com   www.brooklands-books.com
Brooklands Books Ltd., 1/81 Darley St., PO Box 199, Mona Vale, NSW 2103, Australia.
Telephone: 2 9997 8428 Fax: 2 9979 5799
Car Tech, 39966 Grand Avenue, North Branch, MN 55056, USA
Phone: 800 551 4754 & 651 277 1200 Fax: 651 277 1203

Brooklands
Land Rover Titles

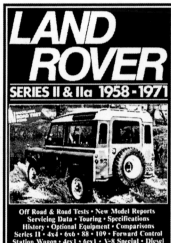
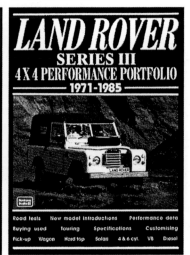
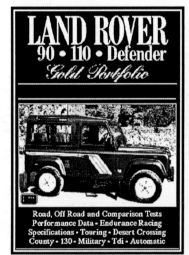
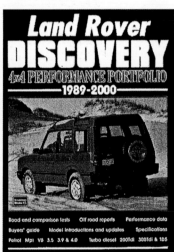

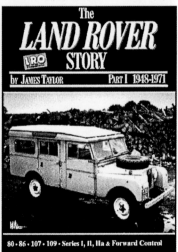